HISTORICAL FIGURES

BEACON LIGHTS OF HISTORY

VOLUME V

THE MIDDLE AGES

HISTORICAL FIGURES

Additional books and e-books in this series can be found on Nova's website under the Series tab.

HISTORICAL FIGURES

BEACON LIGHTS OF HISTORY

VOLUME V

THE MIDDLE AGES

JOHN LORD

Copyright © 2019 by Nova Science Publishers, Inc.

All rights reserved. No part of this book may be reproduced, stored in a retrieval system or transmitted in any form or by any means: electronic, electrostatic, magnetic, tape, mechanical photocopying, recording or otherwise without the written permission of the Publisher.

We have partnered with Copyright Clearance Center to make it easy for you to obtain permissions to reuse content from this publication. Simply navigate to this publication's page on Nova's website and locate the "Get Permission" button below the title description. This button is linked directly to the title's permission page on copyright.com. Alternatively, you can visit copyright.com and search by title, ISBN, or ISSN.

For further questions about using the service on copyright.com, please contact:
Copyright Clearance Center
Phone: +1-(978) 750-8400   Fax: +1-(978) 750-4470   E-mail: info@copyright.com.

NOTICE TO THE READER

The Publisher has taken reasonable care in the preparation of this book, but makes no expressed or implied warranty of any kind and assumes no responsibility for any errors or omissions. No liability is assumed for incidental or consequential damages in connection with or arising out of information contained in this book. The Publisher shall not be liable for any special, consequential, or exemplary damages resulting, in whole or in part, from the readers' use of, or reliance upon, this material. Any parts of this book based on government reports are so indicated and copyright is claimed for those parts to the extent applicable to compilations of such works.

Independent verification should be sought for any data, advice or recommendations contained in this book. In addition, no responsibility is assumed by the Publisher for any injury and/or damage to persons or property arising from any methods, products, instructions, ideas or otherwise contained in this publication.

This publication is designed to provide accurate and authoritative information with regard to the subject matter covered herein. It is sold with the clear understanding that the Publisher is not engaged in rendering legal or any other professional services. If legal or any other expert assistance is required, the services of a competent person should be sought. FROM A DECLARATION OF PARTICIPANTS JOINTLY ADOPTED BY A COMMITTEE OF THE AMERICAN BAR ASSOCIATION AND A COMMITTEE OF PUBLISHERS.

Additional color graphics may be available in the e-book version of this book.

Library of Congress Cataloging-in-Publication Data

ISBN: 978-1-53615-187-9

Published by Nova Science Publishers, Inc. † New York

Contents

List of Illustrations		ix
Preface		xi
Chapter 1	Mohammed: Saracenic Conquests	1
Chapter 2	Charlemagne: Revival of Western Empire	23
Chapter 3	Hildebrand: The Papal Empire	45
Chapter 4	Saint Bernard: Monastic Institutions	69
Chapter 5	Saint Anselm: Mediaeval Theology	91
Chapter 6	Thomas Aquinas: The Scholastic Philosophy	117
Chapter 7	Thomas Becket: Prelatical Power	139
Chapter 8	The Feudal System	161
Chapter 9	The Crusades	183
Chapter 10	William of Wykeham: Gothic Architecture	203
Chapter 11	John Wyclif: Dawn of the Reformation	221
Index		243

Figure 1. Roland Calls for Succor in the Battle of Roncesvalles. *After the painting by Louis Guesnet.*

LIST OF ILLUSTRATIONS

Figure 1. Roland Calls for Succor in the Battle of Roncesvalles.
After the painting by Louis Guesnet. vii

Figure 2. A Reading from the Koran.
After the painting by W. Gentz. 8

Figure 3. Mohammed, Preaching the Unity of God, Enters the City of Mecca.
After the painting by A. Müller. 14

Figure 4. Charlemagne Inflicts the Rite of Baptism on the Saxons.
After the painting by Adolph Maria Mucha. 30

Figure 5. St. Bernard Counselling Conrad III.
After the painting by Adolph Maria Mucha. 85

Figure 6. Canterbury Cathedral.
From a photograph. 105

Figure 7. St. Thomas Aquinas in the School of Albertus Magnus.
After the painting by H. Lerolle. 128

Figure 8. Murder of St. Thomas à Becket.
After the painting by A. Dawant. 157

Figure 9. The Accolade.
After the painting by Sir E. Blair Leighton. 170

Figure 10. Winchester Cathedral.
From a photograph. 213
Figure 11. Facsimile of Page from Wyclif Bible. 234

PREFACE*

Beacon Lights of History is a 14-volume set first published in 1902. This collection of John Lord's lectures spans 6,000 years of European and American history. The first 12 volumes are all Lord's work; the 13th was completed from his notes and the 14th is follow-ups by other authors.

---

* This is an edited, reformatted and augmented version of *Beacon Lights of History. Volume V: The Middle Ages* by John Lord, originally published by New York, J Clarke and Co., dated 1883-1902. The views, opinions, and nomenclature expressed in this book are those of the authors and do not reflect the views of Nova Science Publishers, Inc.

Chapter 1

MOHAMMED[1]: SARACENIC CONQUESTS

A.D. 570-632

The most extraordinary man who arose after the fall of the Roman Empire was doubtless Mohammed; and his posthumous influence has been greater than that of any man since Christianity was declared, if we take into account the number of those who have received his doctrines. Even Christianity never had so rapid a spread. More than a sixth part of the human race are the professed followers of the Arabian prophet.

In regard to Mohammed himself, a great change has taken place in the opinions of critics within fifty years. It was the fashion half a century ago to speak of this man as a hypocrite, an impostor, even as Antichrist. Now he is generally regarded as a reformer; that is, as a man who introduced into Arabia a religion and a morality superior to what previously existed, and he is regarded as an impostor only so far as he was visionary. Few critics doubt his sincerity. He was no hypocrite, since he himself believed in his mission;

---

[1] Spelled also *Mahomet, Mahommed*; but I prefer Mohammed.

and his mission was benevolent, – to turn his countrymen from a gross polytheism to the worship of one God. Although his religion cannot compare with Christianity in purity and loftiness, yet it enforced a higher morality than the old Arabian religions, and assimilated to Christianity in many important respects. The chief fault we have to find in Mohammed was, the propagation of his doctrines by the sword, and the use of wicked means to bring about a good end. The truths he declared have had an immense influence on Asiatic nations, and these have given vitality to his system, if we accept the position that truth alone has vitality.

One remarkable fact stands out for the world to ponder, – that, for more than fourteen hundred years, one hundred and eighty millions (more than a sixth part of the human race) have adopted and cherished the religion of Mohammed; that Christianity never had so astonishing a triumph; and that even the adherents of Christianity, in many countries, have not manifested the zeal of the Mohammedans in most of the countries where it has been acknowledged. Now these startling facts can be explained only on the ground that Mohammedanism has great vital religious and moral truths underlying its system which appeal to the consciousness of mankind, or else that these truths are so blended with dangerous errors which appeal to depraved passions and interests, that the religion spread in consequence of these errors rather than of the truth itself.

The question to be considered, then, is whether Mohammedanism spread in consequence of its truths or in consequence of its errors.

In order to appreciate the influence of the Arabian prophet, we are first led into the inquiry whether his religion was really an improvement on the old systems which previously prevailed in Arabia. If it was, he must be regarded as a benefactor and reformer, even if we admit the glaring evils of his system, when measured by the purer religion of the Cross. And it then simply becomes a question whether it is better to have a prevalent corrupted system of religion containing many important truths, or a system of downright paganism with few truths at all.

In examining the religious systems of Arabia in the age preceding the advent of the Prophet, it would seem that the most prominent of them were the old doctrines of the Magians and Sabaeans, blended with a gross idolatry and a senseless polytheism. Whatever may have been the faith of the ancient Sabaean sages, who noted the aspects of the stars, and supposed they were inhabited by angels placed there by Almighty power to supervise and govern the universe, yet history seems to record that this ancient faith was practically subverted, and that the stars, where were supposed to dwell deities to whom prayers were made, became themselves objects of worship, and even graven images were made in honor of them. Among the Arabs each tribe worshipped a particular star, and set up its particular idol, so that a degrading polytheism was the religion of the land. The object of greatest veneration was the celebrated Black Stone, at Mecca, fabled to have fallen from heaven at the same time with Adam. Over this stone was built the Kaabah, a small oblong stone building, around which has been since built the great mosque. It was ornamented with three hundred and sixty idols. The guardianship of this pagan temple was intrusted to the most ancient and honorable families of Mecca, and to it resorted innumerable pilgrims bringing precious offerings. It was like the shrine of Delphi, as a source of profit to its fortunate guardians.

Thus before Mohammed appeared polytheism was the prevalent religion of Arabia, – a degradation even from the ancient Sabaean faith. It is true there were also other religions. There were many Jews at Medina; and there was also a corrupted form of Christianity in many places, split up into hostile and wrangling sects, with but little of the spirit of the divine Founder, with innumerable errors and superstitions, so that in no part of the world was Christianity so feeble a light. But the great body of the people were pagans. A marked reform was imperatively needed to restore the belief in the unity of God and set up a higher standard of morality.

It is claimed that Mohammed brought such a reform. He was born in the year 570, of the family of Hashem and the tribe of Koreish, to whom was intrusted the keeping of the Black Stone. He therefore belonged to the highest Arabian aristocracy. Early left an orphan and in poverty, he was reared in the family of one of his uncles, under all the influences of idolatry. This uncle was a merchant, and the youth made long journeys with him to distant fairs, especially in Syria, where he probably became acquainted with the Holy Scriptures, especially with the Old Testament. In his twenty-fifth year he entered the service of Cadijeh, a very wealthy widow, who sent to the fairs and towns great caravans, which Mohammed accompanied in some humble capacity, – according to the tradition as camel-driver. But his personal beauty, which was remarkable, and probably also his intelligence and spirit, won the heart of this powerful mistress, and she became his wife.

He was now second to none in the capital of Arabia, and great thoughts began to fill his soul. His wife perceived his greatness, and, like Josephine and the wife of Disraeli, forwarded the fortunes of her husband, for he became rich as well as intellectual and noble, and thus had time and leisure to accomplish more easily his work. From twenty-five to forty he led chiefly a contemplative life, spending months together in a cave, absorbed in his grand reflections, – at intervals issuing from his retreat, visiting the marts of commerce, and gaining knowledge from learned men. It is seldom that very great men lead either a life of perpetual contemplation or of perpetual activity. Without occasional rest, and leisure to mature knowledge, no man can arm himself with the weapons of the gods. To be truly great, a man must blend a life of activity with a life of study, – like Moses, who matured the knowledge he had gained in Egypt amid the deserts of Midian.

With all great men some leading idea rules the ordinary life. The idea which took possession of the mind of Mohammed was the degrading polytheism of his countrymen, the multitude of their idols, the grossness of their worship, and the degrading morals which usually accompany a false theology. He set himself to work to produce a reform, but amid overwhelming obstacles. He talked with his uncles, and they laughed at him. They would not even admit the necessity of a reform. Only Cadijeh listened to him and encouraged him and believed in him. And Mohammed was ever grateful for this mark of confidence, and cherished the memory of his wife in his subsequent apostasy, – if it be true that he fell, like Solomon. Long afterwards, when she was dead, Ayésha, his young and favorite wife, thus addressed him: "Am I not better than Cadijeh? Do you not love me better than you did her? She was a widow, old and ugly." "No, by Allah!" replied the Prophet; "she believed in me when no one else did. In the whole world I had but one friend, and she was that friend." No woman ever retained the affections of a husband superior to herself, unless she had the spirit of

Cadijeh, – unless she proved herself his friend, and believed in him. How miserable the life of Jane Carlyle would have been had she not been proud of her husband! One reason why there is frequent unhappiness in married life is because there is no mutual appreciation. How often have we seen a noble, lofty, earnest man fettered and chained by a frivolous woman who could not be made to see the dignity and importance of the labors which gave to her husband all his real power! Not so with the woman who assisted Mohammed. Without her sympathy and faith he probably would have failed. He told her, and her alone, his dreams, his ecstasies, his visions; how that God at different times had sent prophets and teachers to reveal new truths, by whom religion had been restored; how this one God, who created the heavens and the earth, had never left Himself without witnesses of His truth in the most degenerate times; how that the universal recognition of this sovereign Power and Providence was necessary to the salvation of society. He had learned much from the study of the Talmud and the Jewish Scriptures; he had reflected deeply in his isolated cave; he knew that there was but one supreme God, and that there could be no elevated morality without the sense of personal responsibility to Him; that without the fear of this one God there could be neither wisdom nor virtue.

Hence his soul burned to tell his countrymen his earnest belief in a supreme and personal God, to whom alone prayers should be made, and who alone could rescue by His almighty power. He pondered day and night on this single and simple truth. His perpetual meditations and ascetic habits induced dreams and ecstasies, such as marked primitive monks, and Loyola in his Manresan cave. He became a visionary man, but most intensely earnest, for his convictions were overwhelming. He fancied himself the ambassador of this God, as the ancient Jewish prophets were; that he was even greater than they, his mission being to remove idolatry, – to his mind the greatest evil under the sun, since it was the root of all vices and follies. Idolatry is either a defiance or a forgetfulness of God, – high treason to the majesty of Heaven, entailing the direst calamities.

At last, one day, in his fortieth year, after he had been shut up a whole month in solitude, so that his soul was filled with ecstasy and enthusiasm, he declared to Cadijeh that the night before, while wrapped in his mantle, absorbed in reverie, a form of divine beauty, in a flood of light, appeared to him, and, in the name of the Almighty who created the heavens and the earth, thus spake: "O, Mohammed! of a truth thou art the Prophet of God, and I am his angel Gabriel." "This," says Carlyle, "is the soul of Islam. This is what Mohammed felt and now declared to be of infinite moment, that idols and formulas were nothing; that the jargon of argumentative Greek sects, the vague traditions of Jews, the stupid routine of Arab idolatry were a mockery and a delusion; that there is but one God; that we must let idols alone and look to Him. He alone is reality; He made us and sustains us. Our whole strength lies in submission to Him. The thing He sends us, be it death even, is good, is the best. We resign ourselves to Him."

Such were the truths which Mohammed, with preternatural earnestness, now declared, – doctrines which would revolutionize Arabia. And why not? They are the same substantially which Moses declared to those sensual and degraded slaves whom he led out of Egypt, – yea, the doctrines of David and of Job. "Though He slay me, yet will I trust in Him." What a grand and all-important truth it is to impress upon people sunk in forgetfulness and sensuality and pleasure-seeking and idle schemes of vanity and ambition, that there is a supreme Intelligence who overrules, and whose laws cannot be violated with impunity; from whom no one can escape, even though he "take the wings of the morning and fly to the uttermost parts of the sea." This is the one truth that Moses sought to plant in the minds of the Jews, – a truth always forgotten when there is slavery to epicurean pleasures or a false philosophy.

Now I maintain that Mohammed, in seeking to impress his degenerate countrymen with the idea of the one supreme God, amid a most degrading and almost universal polytheism, was a great reformer. In preaching this he was neither fanatic nor hypocrite; he was a very great man, and thus far a good man. He does not make an original revelation; he reproduces an old truth, – as old as the patriarchs, as old as Job, as old as the primitive religions, – but an exceedingly important one, lost sight of by his countrymen, gradually lost sight of by all peoples when divine grace is withheld; indeed practically by people in Christian lands in times of great degeneracy. "The fool has said in his heart there is no God;" or, Let there be no God, that we may eat and drink before we die. Epicureanism, in its pleasures or in its speculations, is virtually atheism. It was so in Greece. It is so with us.

Mohammed was now at the mature age of forty, in the fullness of his powers, in the prime of his life; and he began to preach everywhere that there is but one God. Few, however, believed in him. Why not acknowledge such a fundamental truth, appealing to the intellect as well as the moral sense? But to confess there is a supreme God, who rewards and punishes, and to whom all are responsible both for words and actions, is to imply a confession of sinfulness and the justice of retribution. Those degraded Arabians would not receive willingly such a truth as this, even as the Israelites ever sought to banish it from their hearts and minds, in spite of their deliverance from slavery. The uncles and friends of Mohammed treated his mission with scorn and derision. Nor do I read that the common people heard him gladly, as they listened to the teachings of Christ. Zealously he labored for three years with all classes; and yet in three years of exalted labor, with all his eloquence and fervor and sincerity, he converted only about thirteen persons, one of whom was his slave. Think of such a man declaring such a truth, and only gaining thirteen followers in three years! How sickened must have been his enthusiastic soul! His worldly relatives urged him to silence. Why attack idols; why quarrel with his own interests; why destroy his popularity? Then exclaimed that great hero: "If the sun stood on my right hand, and the moon on my left, ordering me to hold my peace, I would still declare there is but one God," – a speech rivalled only by Luther at the Diet of Worms. Why urge a great man to be silent on the very thing which makes him great? He cannot be silent. His truth – from which he cannot be separated – is greater than life or death, or principalities or powers.

Buffeted and ridiculed, still Mohammed persevered. He used at first only moral means. He appealed only to the minds and hearts of the people, encouraged by his few believers and sustained by the fancied voice of that angel who appeared to him in his retreat. But his earnest voice was drowned by discordant noises. He was regarded as a lunatic, a demented man, because he professed to believe in a personal God. The angry mob covered his clothes with dust and ashes. They demanded miracles. But at this time he had only truths to declare, – those saving truths which are perpetual miracles. At last hostilities began. He was threatened and he was persecuted. They laid plots to take his life. He sought shelter in the castle of his uncle, Abu Taleh; but he died. Then Mohammed's wife Cadijeh died. The priests of an idolatrous religion became furious. He had laid his hands on their idols. He was regarded as a disorganizer, an innovator, a most dangerous man. His fortunes became darker and darker; he was hated, persecuted, and alone.

Figure 2. A Reading from the Koran. *After the painting by W. Gentz.*

Thus thirteen years passed away in reproach, in persecution, in fear. At last forty picked men swore to assassinate him. Should he remain at Mecca and die, before his mission was accomplished, or should he fly? He concluded to fly to Medina, where there were Jews, and some nominal converts to Christianity, – a new ground. This was in the year 622, and the flight is called the Hegira, – from which the East dates its era, in the fifty-third year of the Prophet's life. In this city he was cordially welcomed, and he soon found himself surrounded with enthusiastic followers. He built a mosque, and openly performed the rites of the new religion.

At this era a new phase appears in the Prophet's life and teachings. Thus far, until his flight, it would seem that he propagated his doctrines by moral force alone, and that these doctrines, in the main, were elevated. He had earnestly declared his great idea of the unity of God. He had pronounced the worship of images to be idolatrous. He held idolatry of all kinds in supreme abhorrence. He enjoined charity, justice, and forbearance. He denounced all falsehood and all deception, especially in trade. He declared that humility, benevolence, and self-abnegation were the greatest virtues. He commanded his disciples to return good for evil, to restrain the passions, to bridle the tongue, to be patient under injuries, to be submissive to God. He enjoined prayer, fastings, and meditation as a means of grace. He laid down the necessity of rest on the seventh day. He copied the precepts of the Bible in many of their essential features, and recognized its greatest teachers as inspired prophets.

It was during these thirteen years at Mecca, amid persecution and ridicule, and with few outward successes, that he probably wrote the Koran, – a book without beginning and without end, *disjecta membra*, regardless of all rules of art, full of repetitions, and yet full of lofty precepts and noble truths of morality evidently borrowed from the Jewish Scriptures, – in which his great ideas stand out with singular eloquence and impressiveness: the unity of God, His divine sovereignty, the necessity of prayer, the soul's immortality, future rewards and punishments. His own private life had been blameless. It was plain and simple. For a whole month he did not light a fire to cook his food. He swept his chamber himself and mended his own clothes. His life was that of an ascetic enthusiast, profoundly impressed with the greatness and dignity of his mission. Thus far his greatest error and fault was in the supposition that he was inspired in the same sense as the ancient Jewish prophets were inspired, – to declare the will and the truth of God. Any man leading such a life of contemplative asceticism and retirement is prone to fall into the belief of special divine illumination. It characterized George Fox, the Anabaptists, Ignatius Loyola, Saint Theresa, and even, to some extent, Oliver Cromwell himself. Mohammed's supreme error was that he was the greatest as well as the last of the prophets. This was fanaticism, but he was probably honest in the belief. His brain was turned by dreams, ecstasies, and ascetic devotions. But with all his visionary ideas of his call, his own morality and his teachings had been lofty, and apparently unsuccessful. Possibly he was discouraged with the small progress he had made, – disgusted, irritated, fierce.

Certainly, soon after he was established at Medina, a great change took place in his mode of propagating his doctrines. His great ideas remained the same, but he adopted a new way to spread them. So that I can almost fancy that some Mephistopheles, some form of Satanic agency, some lying Voice whispered to him in this wise: "O Mohammed! of a truth thou art the Prophet of the living God. Thou hast declared the grandest truths ever uttered in Arabia; but see how powerless they are on the minds and hearts of thy countrymen, with all thy eloquence, sincerity, and fervor. By moral means thou hast effected comparatively nothing. Thou hast preached thirteen years, and only made a few converts. Thy truths are too elevated for a corrupt and wicked generation to accept. Even thine own life is in danger. Thou hast been obliged to fly to these barren rocks and sands. Thou hast failed. Why not pursue a new course, and adapt thy doctrines to men as they are? Thy countrymen are wild, fierce, and warlike: why not incite their martial passions in defence of thy doctrines? They are an earnest people, and, believing in the truths which thou now declarest, they will fight for them and establish them by the sword, not merely in Arabia, but throughout the East. They are a pleasure-loving and imaginative people: why not promise the victors of thy faith a sensual bliss in Paradise? They will not be subverters of your grand truths; they will simply extend them, and jealously, if they have a reward in what their passions crave. In short, use the proper means for a great end. The end justifies the means."

Whether influenced by such specious sophistries, or disheartened by his former method, or corrupted in his own heart, as Solomon was, by his numerous wives, – for Mohammed permitted polygamy and practised it himself, – it is certain that he now was bent on achieving more signal and rapid victories. He resolved to adapt his religion to the depraved hearts of his followers. He would mix up truth with error; he would make truth palatable; he would use the means which secure success. It was success he wanted, and success he thus far had not secured. He was ambitious; he would become a mighty spiritual potentate.

So he allowed polygamy, – the vice of Eastern nations from remote periods; he promised a sensual Paradise to those who should die in defence of his religion; he inflamed the imagination of the Arabians with visions of sensual joys. He painted heaven as a land whose soil was the finest wheaten flour, whose air was fragrant with perfumes, whose streams were of crystal water or milk or wine or honey, flowing over beds of musk and camphor, – a glorious garden of fruits and flowers, whose inhabitants were clothed in garments of gold, sparkling with rubies and diamonds, who reclined in sumptuous palaces and silken pavilions, and on couches of voluptuous ease, and who were served with viands which could be eaten without satiety, and liquors which could be drunk without inebriation; yea, where the blissful warrior for the faith should enjoy an unending youth, and where he would be attended by houris, with black and loving eyes, free from all defects, resplendent in beauty and grace, and rejoicing in perpetual charms.

Such were the views, it is maintained, with which he inflamed the faithful. And, more, he encouraged them to take up arms, and penetrate, as warlike missionaries, to the utmost bounds of the habitable world, in order to convert men to the faith of the one God, whose Prophet he claimed to be. Moreover, he made new and extraordinary "revelations," – that he had ascended into the seventh heaven and held converse with Gabriel; and he now added to his creed that old lie of Eastern theogonies, that base element of all false religions, – that man can propitiate the Deity by works of supererogation; that man can purchase by ascetic labors and sacrifices his future salvation. This falsity enters largely into Mohammedanism. I need not add how discrepant it is with the cheerful teachings of the apostles, especially to the poor, as seen in the deeds of penance, prayers in the corners of the streets, the ablutions, the fasts, and the pilgrimages to which the faithful are exhorted. And moreover he accommodated his fasts and feasts and holidays and pilgrimages to the old customs of the people, thereby teaching lessons of worldly wisdom. Astarte, the old object of Sabaean idolatry, was particularly worshipped on a Friday; and this day was made the Mohammedan Sabbath. Again, the month Rhamadán, from time immemorial, had been set apart for fastings; this month the Prophet adopted, declaring that in it he had received his first revelations. Pilgrimages to the Black Stone were favorite forms of penance; and this was perpetuated in the pilgrimages to Mecca.

Thus it would appear that Mohammed, after his flight, accommodated his doctrines to the customs and tastes of his countrymen, – blending with the sublime truths he declared subtile and pernicious errors. The Jesuit missionaries did the same thing in China and Japan, thinking more of the number of their converts than of the truth itself. Expediency – the accepted Jesuitical principle of the end justifying the means – is seen in almost everything in this world which blazes with success. It is seen in politics, in philanthropy, in ecclesiasticism, and in education. There are political Jesuits and philanthropical Jesuits and Protestant Jesuits, as well as Catholic Jesuits and Mohammedan Jesuits. What do you think of a man, wearing the livery of a gospel minister, devoting all his energies to money-making, versed in the ways of the "heathen Chinee," – "ways that are dark, and tricks that are vain," – all to succeed better in worldly thrift, using all means for that single end, – is not he practically a Jesuit? I do not mean a Catholic Jesuit, belonging to the Society of Jesus, but popularly what we mean by a Jesuit. What would you think of a college which lowered the standard of education in order to draw students, or selected, as the guardians of its higher interests, those men who would contribute the most money to its funds?

This spirit of expediency Mohammed entertained and utilized, in order to gain success. Most of what is false in Mohammedanism is based on expediency. The end was not lost sight of, – the conversion of his countrymen to the belief in the unity and sovereignty of God, but it was sought by means which would make them fanatics or Pharisees. He was not such a miserable creature as one who seeks to make money by trading on the religious capital of the community; but he did adapt his religion to the passions and habits of the people in order that they might more readily be led to accept it. He listened to that same wicked Voice which afterwards appeared in the guise of an angel of light to mediaeval ritualists. And it is thus that Satan has contrived to pervert the best institutions of the world. The moment good men look to outward and superficial triumphs, to the disregard of inward purity, that moment do they accept the Jesuitical lie of all ages, – "The end justifies the means."

But the worst thing which the Prophet did in order to gain his end was to make use of the sword. For thirteen years he appealed to conscience. Now he makes it an inducement for men to fight for his great idea. "Different prophets," said he, in his memorable manifesto, "have been sent by God to illustrate His different attributes: Moses, His providence; Solomon, His wisdom; Christ, His righteousness; but I, the last of the prophets, am sent with the sword. Let those who promulgate my faith enter into no arguments or discussions, but slay all who refuse obedience. Whoever fights for the true faith, whether he fall or conquer, will assuredly receive a glorious reward, for the sword is the key of heaven. All who draw it in defence of the faith shall receive temporal and future blessings. Every drop of their blood, every peril and hardship, will be registered on high as more meritorious than fasting or prayer. If they fall in battle their sins will be washed away, and they shall be transported into Paradise, to revel in eternal pleasures, and in the arms of black-eyed houris." Thus did he stimulate the martial fanaticism of a warlike and heroic people with the promise of future happiness. What a monstrous expediency, – worse than all the combined usurpations of the popes!

And what was the result? I need not point to the successive conquests of the Saracens with such a mighty stimulus. They were loyal to the truth for which they fought. They never afterwards became idolaters; but their religion was built up on the miseries of nations. To propagate the faith of

Mohammed they overran the world. Never were conquests more rapid and more terrible.

Figure 3. Mohammed, Preaching the Unity of God, Enters the City of Mecca. *After the painting by A. Müller.*

At first Mohammed's followers in Medina sallied out and attacked the caravans of Arabia, and especially all belonging to Mecca (the city which had rejected him), until all the various tribes acknowledged the religion of the Prophet, for they were easily converted to a faith which flattered their predatory inclinations and promised them future immunities. The first cavalcade which entered Medina with spoils made Mussulmans of all the inhabitants, and gave Mohammed the control of the city. The battle of Moat gave him a triumphal entrance into Mecca. He soon found himself the sovereign of all Arabia; and when he died, at the age of 63, in the eleventh year after his Hegira, or flight from Mecca, he was the most successful founder of a religion the world has known, next to Buddha. A religion appealing to truth alone had made only a few converts in thirteen years; a religion which appealed to the sword had made converts of a great nation in eleven years.

It is difficult to ascertain what the private life of the Prophet was in these years of dazzling success. The authorities differ. Some represent him as sunk in a miserable sensuality which shortened his days. But I think this statement may be doubted. He never lost the veneration of his countrymen, – and no veneration can last for a man steeped in sensuality. Even Solomon lost his prestige and popularity when he became vain and sensual. Those who were nearest to the Prophet reverenced him most profoundly. With his wife Ayésha he lived with great frugality. He was kindly, firm in friendship, faithful and tender in his family, ready to forgive enemies, just in decision. The caliphs who succeeded him, for some time, were men of great simplicity, and sought to imitate his virtues. He was doubtless warlike and fanatical, but conquests such as he and his successors made are incompatible with luxury and effeminacy. He stands arraigned at the bar of eternal justice for perverting truth, for blending it with error, for making use of wicked means to accomplish what he deemed a great end.

I have no patience with Mr. Carlyle, great and venerable as is his authority, for seeming to justify Mohammed in assuming the sword. "I care little for the sword," says this sophistical writer. "I will allow a thing to struggle for itself in this world, with any sword or tongue or implement it has or can lay hold on. What is better than itself it cannot put away, but only what is worse. In this great life-duel Nature herself is umpire, and can do no wrong," That is, might makes right; only evil perishes in the conflict of principles; whatever prevails is just. In other words, if Mohammed-anism, by any means it may choose to use, proves itself more formidable than other religions, then it ought to prevail. Suppose that the victories of the Saracens had extended over Europe, as well as Asia and Africa, – had not been arrested by Charles Martel, – would Carlyle then have preferred Mohammedanism to the Christianity of degenerate nations? Was Mohammedanism a better religion than the Christianity which existed in Asia Minor and in various parts of the Greek empire in the sixth and seventh centuries? Was it a good thing to convert the church of Saint Sophia into a Saracenic mosque, and the city of the later Christian emperors into the capital of the Turks? Is a united Saracenic empire better than a divided, wrangling Christian empire?

But I will not enter upon that discussion. I confine myself to facts. It is certain that Mohammedanism, by means of the sword, spread with marvelous and unprecedented rapidity. The successors of the Prophet carried their conquests even to India. Neither the Syrians nor the Egyptians could cope with men who felt that the sacrifice of life in battle would secure an eternity of bliss. The armies of the Greek emperor melted away before the generals of the caliph. The Cross waned before the Crescent. The banners of the Moslems floated over the proudest battlements of ancient Roman grandeur.

In the fifth year of the caliph Omar, only seventeen years from the Prophet's flight from Mecca, the conquest of Syria was completed. The Christians were forbidden to build churches, or speak openly of their religion, or sit in the presence of a Mohammedan, or to sell wine, or bear arms, or use the saddle in riding, or have a domestic who had been in the Mohammedan service. The utter prostration of all civil and religious liberty took place in the old scenes of Christian triumph. This was an instance in which persecution proved successful; and because it was successful it is a proof, in the eyes of Carlyle, that the persecuting religion was the better, because it was outwardly the stronger.

The conquest of Egypt rapidly followed that of Syria; and with the fall of Alexandria perished the largest library of the world, the thesaurus of all the intellectual treasures of antiquity.

Then followed the conquest of Persia. A single battle, as in the time of Alexander, decided its fate. The marvel is that the people should have changed their religion; but then, it was Mohammedanism or death. And a still greater marvel it is, – an utter mystery to me, – why that Oriental country should have continued faithful to the new religion. It must have had some elements of vitality almost worth fighting for, and which we do not comprehend.

Nor did Saracenic conquests end until the Arabs of the desert had penetrated southward into India farther than had Alexander the Great, and westward until they had subdued the northern kingdoms of Africa, and carried their arms to the Pillars of Hercules; yea, to the cities of the Goths in Spain, and were only finally arrested in Europe by the heroism of Charles Martel.

Such were the rapid conquests of the Saracens – and permanent conquests also – in Asia and Africa, under the stimulus of religious fanaticism, until they had reduced thirty-six thousand cities, towns, and castles, and built fourteen thousand mosques.

Now what are the deductions to be logically drawn from these stupendous victories and the consolidation of the various religions of the conquered into the creed of Mohammed, – not repudiated when the pressure was removed, but apparently cherished by one hundred and eighty millions of people for more than a thousand years?

We must take the ground that the religion of Mohammed has marvelous and powerful truths, which we have overlooked and do not understand, which appeal to the heart and conscience, and excite a great enthusiasm, – so great as to stimulate successive generations with an almost unexampled ardor, and to defend which they were ready to die; a religion which has bound diverse nations together for nearly fourteen hundred years. If so, it cannot be abused, or ridiculed, or sneered at, any more than can the dominion of the popes in the Middle Ages, but remains august in impressive mystery to us, and even to future ages.

But if, in comparison with Christianity, it is a corrupt and false religion, as many assume, then what deductions must we draw from its amazing triumphs? For the fact stares us in the face that it is rooted deeply in a large part of the Eastern world, or, at least, has prevailed victorious for more than a thousand years.

First, we must conclude that the external triumph of a religion, especially among ignorant or wicked people, is not so much owing to the purity and loftiness of its truths, as to its harmony with prevailing errors and corruptions. When Mohammed preached his sublimest doctrines, and appealed to reason and conscience, he converted about a score of people in thirteen years. When he invoked demoralizing passions, he converted all Arabia in eleven years. And does not this startling conclusion seem to be confirmed by the whole history of mankind? How slow the progress of Christianity for two hundred years, except when assisted by direct supernatural influences! How rapid its triumphs when it became adapted to the rude barbaric mind, or to the degenerate people of the Empire! How popular and prevalent and widespread are those religions which we are accustomed to regard as most corrupt! Buddhism and Brahmanism have had more adherents than even Mohammedanism. How difficult it was for Moses and the prophets to keep the Jews from idolatry! What caused the rapid eclipse of faith in the antediluvian world? Why could not Noah establish and perpetuate his doctrines among his own descendants before he was dead? Why was the Socratic philosophy unpopular? Why were the Epicureans so fashionable? Why was Christianity itself most eagerly embraced when its light was obscured by fables and superstitions? Why did the Roman Empire perish, with all the aid of a magnificent civilization; why did this civilization itself retrograde; why did its art and literature decline? Why did the grand triumphs of Protestantism stop in half a century after Luther delivered his message? What made the mediaeval popes so powerful? What gave such ascendency to the Jesuits? Why is the simple faith of the primitive Christians so obnoxious to the wise, the mighty, and the noble? What makes the most insidious heresies so acceptable to the learned? Why is modern literature, when fashionable and popular, so antichristian in its tone and spirit? Why have not the doctrines of Luther held their own in Germany, and those of

Calvin in Geneva, and those of Cranmer in England, and those of the Pilgrim Fathers in New England? Is it because, as men become advanced in learning and culture, they are theologically wiser than Moses and Abraham and Isaiah?

I do not cite the rapid decline of modern civilized society, in a political or social view, in the most favored sections of Christendom; I do not sing dirges over republican institutions; I would not croak Jeremiads over the changes and developments of mankind. I simply speak of the marvelous similarity which the spread and triumph of Mohammedanism seem to bear to the spread and triumph of what is corrupt and wicked in all institutions and religions since the fall of man. Everywhere it is the frivolous, the corrupt, the false, which seem to be most prevalent and most popular. Do men love truth, or readily accept it, when it conflicts with passions and interests? Is any truth popular which is arrayed against the pride of reason? When has pure moral truth ever been fashionable? When have its advocates not been reviled, slandered, misrepresented, and persecuted, if it has interfered with the domination of prevailing interests? The lower the scale of pleasures the more eagerly are they sought by the great mass of the people, even in Christian communities. You can best make colleges thrive by turning them into schools of technology, with a view of advancing utilitarian and material interests. You cannot make a newspaper flourish unless you fill it with pictures and scandals, or make it a vehicle of advertisements, – which are not frivolous or corrupt, it is true, but which have to do with merely material interests. Your libraries would never be visited, if you took away their trash. Your Sabbath-school books would not be read, unless you made them an insult to the human understanding. Your salons would be deserted, if you entertained your guests with instructive conversation. There would be no fashionable gatherings, if it were not to display dresses and diamonds. Your pulpits would be unoccupied, if you sought the profoundest men to fill them.

Everything, even in Christian communities, shows that vanities and follies and falsehoods are the most sought, and that nothing is more discouraging than appeals to high intelligence or virtue, even in art. This is the uniform history of the race, everywhere and in all ages. Is it darkness or light which the world loves? I never read, and I never heard, of a great man with a great message to deliver, who would not have sunk under disappointment or chagrin but for his faith. Everywhere do you see the fascination of error, so that it almost seems to be as vital as truth itself. When and where have not lies and sophistries and hypocrisies reigned? I appeal to history. I appeal to the observation and experience of every thoughtful and candid mind. You cannot get around this truth. It blazes and it burns like the fires of Sinai. Men left to themselves will more and more retrograde in virtue.

What, then, is the hope of the world? We are driven to this deduction, – that if truth in itself is not all-conquering, the divine assistance, given at times to truth itself, as in the early Church, is the only reason why truth conquers. This divine grace, promised in the Bible, has wrought wonders whenever it has pleased the Almighty to bestow it, and only then. History teaches this as impressively as revelation. Christianity itself, unaided, would probably die out in this world. And hence the grand conclusion is, that it is the mysterious, or, as some call it, the supernatural, spirit of Almighty power which is, after all, the highest hope of this world. This is not discrepant with the oldest traditions and theogonies of the East, – the hidden wisdom of ancient Indian and Persian and Egyptian sages, concealed from the vulgar, but really embraced by the profoundest men, before corruptions perverted even their wisdom. This certainly is the earliest revelation of the Bible. This is the power which Moses recognized, and all the prophets who succeeded him. This is the power which even Mohammed, in the loftiness of his contemplations, more dimly saw, and imperfectly taught to the idolaters around him, and which gives to his system all that was really valuable. Ask not when and where this power shall be most truly felt. It is around us, and above us, and beneath us. It is the mystery and grandeur of the ages. "It is not by might nor by power, but by my spirit," saith the Lord. Man is nothing, his aspirations are nothing, the universe itself is nothing, without the living, permeating force which comes from this supernal Deity we adore, to interfere and save. Without His special agency, giving to His truths vitality, this world would soon become a hopeless and perpetual pandemonium. Take away the necessity of this divine assistance as the one great condition of all progress, as well as the highest boon which mortals seek, – then prayer itself, recognized even by Mohammedans as the loftiest aspiration and expression of a dependent soul, and regarded by prophets and apostles and martyrs as their noblest privilege, becomes a superstition, a puerility, a mockery, and a hopeless dream.

AUTHORITIES

The Koran
Dean Prideaux's *Life of Mohammed*
Vie de Mahomet, by the Comte de Boulainvilliers
Gagnier's *Life of Mohammed*
Ockley's *History of the Saracens*
Gibbon, fiftieth chapter
Hallam's *Middle Ages*
Milman's *Latin Christianity*
Dr. Weil's *Mohammed der Prophet, sein Leben und seine Lehre*
Renan, *Revue des Deux Mondes*, 1851
Bustner's *Pilgrimage to El Medina and Mecca*
Life of Mahomet, by Washington Irving
Essai sur l'Histoire des Arabes, par A.P. Caussin de Perceval
Carlyle's *Lectures on Heroes and Hero Worship*
E.A. Freeman's *Lectures on the History of the Saracens*
Forster's *Mahometanism Unveiled*
Maurice on the *Religions of the World*
Life and Religion of Mohammed, translated from the Persian, by Rev. I.L. Merrick.

Chapter 2

CHARLEMAGNE:
REVIVAL OF WESTERN EMPIRE

A.D. 742-814

The most illustrious monarch of the Middle Ages was doubtless Charlemagne. Certainly he was the first great statesman, hero, and organizer that looms up to view after the dissolution of the Roman Empire. Therefore I present him as one with whom is associated an epoch in civilization. To him we date the first memorable step which Europe took out of the anarchies of the Merovingian age. His dream was to revive the Empire that had fallen. He was the first to labor, with giant strength, to restore what vice and violence had destroyed. He did not succeed in realizing the great ends to which he aspired, but his aspirations were lofty. It was not in the power of any man to civilize semi-barbarians in a single reign; but if he attempted impossibilities he did not live in vain, since he bequeathed some permanent conquests and some great traditions. He left a great legacy to civilization. His life has not dramatic interest like that of Hildebrand, nor poetic interest like the lives of the leaders of the Crusades; but it is very instructive. He was the pride of his own generation, and the boast of succeeding ages, "claimed," says Sismondi, "by the Church as a saint, by the French as the greatest of their kings, by the Germans as their countryman, and by the Italians as their emperor."

His remote ancestors, it is said, were ecclesiastical magnates. His grandfather was Charles Martel, who gained such signal victories over the Mohammedan Saracens; his father was Pepin, who was a renowned conqueror, and who subdued the southern part of France, or Gaul. He did not rise, like Clovis, from the condition of a chieftain of a tribe of barbarians; nor, like the founder of his family, from a mayor of the palace, or minister of the Merovingian kings. His early life was spent amid the turmoils and dangers of camps, and as a young man he was distinguished for precocity of talent, manly beauty, and gigantic physical strength. He was a type of chivalry, before chivalry arose. He was born to greatness, and early succeeded to a great inheritance. At the age of twenty-six, in the year 768, he became the monarch of the greater part of modern France, and of those provinces which border on the Rhine. By unwearied activities this inheritance, greater than that of any of the Merovingian kings, was not only kept together and preserved, but was increased by successive conquests, until no so great an empire has ever been ruled by any one man in Europe, since the fall of the Roman Empire, from his day to ours. Yet greater than the conquests of Charlemagne was the greatness of his character. He preserved simplicity and gentleness amid all the distractions attending his government.

His reign affords a striking contrast to that of all his predecessors of the Merovingian dynasty, – which reigned from the immediate destruction of the Roman Empire. The Merovingian princes, with the exception of Clovis and a few others, were mere barbarians, although converted to a nominal Christianity. Some of them were monsters, and others were idiots. Clotaire burned to death his own son and wife and daughters. Frédegunde armed her assassins with poisoned daggers. "Thirteen sovereigns reigned over the Franks in one hundred and fourteen years, only two of whom attained to man's estate, and not one to the full development of intellectual powers. There was scarcely one who did not live in a state of perpetual intoxication, or who did not rival Sardanapalus in effeminacy, and Commodus in cruelty." As these sovereigns were ruled by priests, their iniquities were glossed over by Gregory of Tours. In *his* annals they may pass for saints, but history consigns them to an infamous immortality.

It is difficult to conceive a more dreary and dismal state of society than existed in France, and in fact over all Europe, when Charlemagne began to reign. The Roman Empire was in ruins, except in the East, where the Greek emperors reigned at Constantinople. The western provinces were ruled by independent barbaric kings. There was no central authority, although there was an attempt of the popes to revive it, – a spiritual rather than a temporal power; a theocracy whose foundation had been laid by Leo the Great when he established the *jus divinum* principle, – that he was the successor of Peter, to whom were given the keys of heaven and hell. If there was an interesting feature in the times it was this spiritual authority exercised by the bishops of Rome: the most useful and beneficent considering the evils which prevailed, – the reign of brute force. The barbaric chieftains yielded a partial homage to this spiritual power, and it was some check on their rapacity of violence. It is mournful to think that so little of the ancient civilization remained in the eighth century. Its eclipse was total. The shadows of a dark and long night of superstition and ignorance spread over Europe. Law was silenced by the sword. Justinian's glorious legacy was already forgotten. The old mechanism which had kept society together in the fifth century was worn out, broken, rejected. There was no literature, no philosophy, no poetry, no history, and no art. Even the clergy had become ignorant, superstitious, and idle. Forms had taken the place of faith. No great theologians had arisen since Saint Augustine. The piety of the age hid itself in monasteries; and these monasteries were as funereal as society itself. Men despaired of the world, and retreated from it to sing mournful songs. The architecture of the age expressed the sentiments of the age, and was heavy, gloomy, and monotonous. "The barbarians ruthlessly marched over the ruins of cities and palaces, having no regard for the treasures of the classic world, and unmoved by the lessons of its past experience." Rome itself, repeatedly sacked, was a heap of ruins. No reconstruction had taken place. Gardens and villas were as desolate as the ruined palaces, which were the abodes of owls and spiders. The immortal creations of the chisel were used to prop up old crumbling walls. The costly monuments of senatorial pride were broken to pieces in sport or in caprice, and those structures which had excited the admiration of ages were pulled down that their material might be used in erecting tasteless edifices. Literature shared the general desolation. The valued manuscripts of classical ages were mutilated, erased, or burned. The monks finished the destruction which the barbarians began. Ignorance as well as anarchy veiled Europe in darkness. The rust of barbarism became harder and thicker. The last hope of man had fled, and glory was succeeded by shame. Even slavery, the curse of the Roman Empire, was continued by the barbarians; only, brute force was not made subservient to intellect, but intellect to brute force. The descendants of ancient patrician families were in bondage to barbarians. The age was the jubilee of monsters. Assassination was common, and was unavenged by law. Every man was his own avenger of crime, and his bloody weapons were his only law.

Nor were there seen among the barbaric chieftains the virtues of ancient Pagan Rome and Greece, for Christianity was nominal. War was universal; for the barbarians, having no longer the Romans to fight, fought among themselves. There were incessant irruptions of different tribes passing from one country to another, in search of plunder and pillage. There was no security of life or property, and therefore no ambition for acquisition. Men hid themselves in morasses, in forests, on the tops of inaccessible hills, and amid the recesses of valleys, for violence was the rule and not the exception. Even feudalism was not then born, and still less chivalry. We find no elevated sentiments. The only refuge for the miserable was in the Church, and the Church was governed by narrow and ignorant priests. A cry of despair went up to heaven among the descendants of the old population. There was no commerce, no travel, no industries, no money, no peace. The chastisement of Almighty Power seems to have been sent on the old races and the new alike. It was a desolation greater than that predicted by Jeremy the prophet. The very end of the world seemed to be at hand. Never in the old seats of civilization was there such a disintegration; never such a combination of evils and miseries. And there appeared to be no remedy: nothing but a long night of horrors and sufferings could be predicted. Gaul, or France, was the scene of turbulence, invasions, and anarchies; of murders, of conflagrations, and of pillage by rival chieftains, who sought to divide its territories among themselves. The people were utterly trodden down. England was the battle-field of Danes, Saxons, and Celts, invaded perpetually, and split up into petty Saxon kingdoms. The roads were infested with robbers, and agriculture was rude. The people lived in cabins, dressed themselves in skins, and fed on the coarsest food. Spain was invaded by Saracens, and the Gothic kingdoms succumbed to these fierce invaders. Italy was portioned out among different tribes, Gothic and Slavonic. But the prevailing races in Europe were Germanic (who had conquered both the Celts and the Romans), the Goths in Spain, the Franks and Burgundians in France, the Lombards in Italy, the Saxons in England.

What a commentary on the imperial government of the Caesars! – that government which, with all its mechanisms and traditions, lasted scarcely four hundred years. Was there ever, in the whole history of the world, so sudden and mournful a change from civilization to barbarism, – and this in spite of art, science, law, and Christianity itself? Were there no conservative forces in that imposing Empire? Why did society constantly decline for four hundred years, with that civilization which was its boast and hope? Oh, ye optimists, who talk so glibly about the natural and necessary progress of humanity, why was the Roman Empire swept away, with all its material glories, to give place to such a state of society as I have just briefly described?

And yet men should arise in due time, after the punishment of five centuries of crime and violence, wretchedness and despair, to reconstruct, not from the old Pagan materials of Greece and Rome, but with the fresh energies of new races, aided and inspired by the truths of the everlasting gospel. The infancy of the new races, sprung however from the same old Aryan stock, passed into vigorous youth when Charlemagne appeared. From him we date the first decided impulse given to the Gothic civilization. He was the morning star of European hopes and aspirations.

Let us now turn to his glorious deeds. What were the services he rendered to Europe and Christian civilization?

It was necessary that a truly great man should arise in the eighth century, if the new forces of civilization were to be organized. To show what he did for the new races, and how he did it, is the historian's duty and task in describing the reign of Charlemagne, – sent, I think, as Moses was, for a providential mission, in the fullness of time, after the slaveries of three hundred years, which prepared the people for labor and industry. Better was it that they should till the lands of allodial proprietors in misery and sorrow, attacked and pillaged, than to wander like savages in forests and morasses in quest of a precarious support, or in great predatory bands, as they did in the fourth and fifth centuries, when they ravaged the provinces of the falling Empire. Nothing was wanted but their consolidation under central rule in order to repel aggressors. And that is what Charlemagne attempted to do.

He soon perceived the greatness of the struggle to which he was destined, and he did not flinch from the contest which has given him immortality. He comprehended the difficulties which surrounded him and the dangers which menaced him.

The great perils which threatened Europe were from unsubdued barbarians, who sought to replunge it into the miseries which the great irruptions had inflicted three hundred years before. He therefore bent all the energies of his mind and all the resources of his kingdom to arrest these fresh waves of inundation. And so long was his contest with Saxons, Avares, Lombards, and other tribes and races that he is chiefly to be contemplated as a man who struggled against barbarism. And he fought them, not for excitement, not for the love of fighting, not for useless conquests, not for military fame, not for aggrandizement, but because a stern necessity was laid upon him to protect his own territories and the institutions he wished to conserve.

Of these barbarians there was one nation peculiarly warlike and ferocious, and which cherished an inextinguishable hatred not merely of the Franks, but of civilization itself. They were obstinately attached to their old superstitions, and had a great repugnance to Christianity. They were barbarians, like the old North American Indians, because they determined to be so; because they loved their forests and the chase, indulged in amusements which were uncertain and dangerous, and sought for nothing beyond their immediate inclinations. They had no territorial divisions, and abhorred cities as prisons of despotism. But, like all the Germanic barbarians, they had interesting traits. They respected women; they were brave and daring; they had a dogged perseverance, and a noble passion for personal independence. But they were nevertheless the enemies of civilization, of a regular and industrious life, and sought plunder and revenge. The Franks and Goths were once like them, before the time of Clovis; but they had made settlements, they tilled the land, and built villages and cities: they were partially civilized, and were converted to Christianity. But these new barbarians could not be won by arts or the ministers of religion. These people were the Saxons, and inhabited those parts of Germany which were bounded by the Rhine, the Oder, the North Sea, and the Thuringian forests. They were fond of the sea, and of daring expeditions for plunder. They were a kindred race to those Saxons who had conquered England, and had the same elements of character. They were poor, and sought to live by piracy and robbery. They were very dangerous enemies, but if brought under subjection to law, and converted to Christianity, might be turned into useful allies, for they had the materials of a noble race.

With such a people on his borders, and every day becoming more formidable, what was Charlemagne's policy? What was he to do? The only thing to the eye of that enlightened statesman was to conquer them, if possible, and add their territories to the Frankish Empire. If left to themselves, they might have conquered the Franks. It was either anvil or hammer. There could be no lasting peace in Europe while these barbarians were left to pursue their depredations. A vigorous warfare was imperative, for, unless subdued, a disadvantageous war would be carried on near the frontiers, until some warrior would arise among them, unite the various chieftains, and lead his followers to successful invasion. Charlemagne knew that the difficult and unpleasant work of subjugation must be done by somebody, and he was unwilling to leave the work to enervated successors. The work was not child's play. It took him the best part of his life to accomplish it, and amid great discouragements. Of his fifty-three expeditions, eighteen were against the Saxons. As soon as he had cut off one head of the monster, another head appeared. How allegorical of human labor is that old fable of the Hydra! Where do man's labors cease? Charlemagne fought not only amid great difficulties, but perpetual irritations. The Saxons cheated him; they broke their promises and their oaths. When beaten, they sued for peace; but the moment his back was turned, they broke out in new insurrections. The fame of Caesar chiefly rests on his eight campaigns in Gaul. But Caesar had the disciplined Legions of Rome to fight with. Charlemagne had no such disciplined troops. Yet he had as many difficulties to surmount as Caesar, – rugged forests to penetrate, rapid rivers to cross, morasses to avoid, and mountains to climb. It is a very difficult thing to subdue even savages who are desperate, determined, and united.

Figure 4. Charlemagne Inflicts the Rite of Baptism on the Saxons. *After the painting by Adolph Maria Mucha.*

Charlemagne fought the Saxons for thirty-three years. Though he never lost a battle, they still held out. At first he was generous and forgiving, for he was more magnanimous than Caesar; but they could not be won by kindness. He was obliged to change his course, and at last was as summary as Oliver Cromwell in Ireland. He is even accused of cruelties. But war in the hands of masters has no quarter to give, and no tears to shed. It was necessary to conquer the Saxons, and Charlemagne used the requisite means. Sometimes the harshest measures will most speedily effect the end. Did our fathers ever dream of compromise with treacherous and hostile Indians? War has a horrid maxim, – that "nothing is so successful as success." Charlemagne, at last, was successful. The Saxons were so completely subdued at the end of thirty-three years, that they never molested civilized Europe again. They became civilized, like the once invading Celts and Goths; and they even embraced the religion of the conquerors. They became ultimately the best people in Europe, – earnest, honest, and brave. They formed great kingdoms and states, and became new barriers against fresh inundations from the North and East. The Saxons formed the nucleus of the great German Empire (or were incorporated with it) which arose in the Middle Ages, and which to-day is the most powerful in Europe, and the least corrupted by the vices of a luxurious life. The descendants of those Saxons are among the most industrious and useful settlers in the New World.

There was one mistake which Charlemagne made in reference to them. He forced their conversion to a nominal Christianity. He immersed them in the rivers of Saxony, whether they would or no. He would make them Christians in his way. But then, who does not seek to make converts in his way, whether enlightened or not? When have the principles of religious toleration been understood? Did the Puritans understand them, with all their professions? Do we tolerate, in our hearts, those who differ from us? Do not men look daggers, though they dare not use them? If we had the power, would we not seek to produce conformity with our notions, like Queen Elizabeth, or Oliver Cromwell, or Archbishop Laud? There is not perhaps a village in America where a true Catholicism reigns. There is not a spot upon the globe where there is not some form of religious persecution. Nor is there anything more sincere than religious bigotry. And when people have not fundamental principles to fight about, they will fight about technicalities and matters of no account, and all the more bitterly sometimes when the objects of contention are not worth fighting about at all, – as in forms of worship, or baptism. Such is the weakness of human nature. Charlemagne was no exception to the race. But if he wished to make Christians in his way, he was, on the whole, enlightened. He caused the young Saxons, whom he baptized and marked with the sign of the Cross, to be educated. He built monasteries and churches in the conquered territories. He recognized this, – that Christianity, whatever it be, is the mightiest power of the world; and he bore his testimony in behalf of the intellectual dignity of the clergy in comparison with other classes. He encouraged missions as well as schools.

There was another Germanic tribe at that time which he held in great alarm, but which he did not attack, since they were not immediately dangerous. This tribe or race was the Norman, just then beginning their ravages, – pirates in open boats. They had dared to enter a port in Narbonensis Gaul for purposes of plunder. Some took them for Africans, and others for British merchants. Nay, said Charlemagne, they are not merchants, but cruel enemies; and he covered his face with his iron hands and wept like a child. He did not fear these barbarians, but he wept when he foresaw the evil they would do when he was dead. "I weep," said he, "that they should dare almost to land on my shores, in my lifetime." These Normans escaped him. They conquered and they founded kingdoms. But they did not replunge Europe in darkness. A barrier had been made against their inundation. The Saxon conquest was that barrier. Moreover, the Normans were the noblest race of barbarians which then roamed through the forests of Germany, or skirted the shores of Scandinavia. They had grand natural traits of character. They were poetic, brave, and adventurous. They were superior to the Saxons and the Franks. When converted, they were the great allies of the Pope, and early became civilized. To them we trace the noblest development of Gothic architecture. They became great scholars and statesmen. They were more refined by nature than the Saxons, and avoided their gluttonous habits. In after times they composed the flower of European chivalry. It was providential that they were not subdued, – that they became the leading race in Northern Europe. To them we trace the mercantile greatness of England, for they were born sailors. They never lost their natural heroism, or love of power.

The next important conquest of Charlemagne was that of the Avares, – a tribe of the Huns, of Slavonic origin. They are represented as very hideous barbarians, and only thought of plunder. They never sought to reconstruct. There seemed to be no end of their invasions from the time of Attila. They were more formidable for their numbers and destructive ravages than for their military skill. There was a time, however, when they threatened the combined forces of Germany and Rome; but Europe was delivered by the battle of Poictiers, – the bloodiest battle on record, – when they seemed to be annihilated. But they sprang up again, in new invasions, in the ninth century. Had they conquered, civilization would have been crushed out. But Charlemagne was successful against them, and from that time to this they were shut out from western Europe. They would be formidable now, for the Russians are the descendants of these people, were it not for the barrier raised against them by the Germans. The necessities of Europe still require the vast military strength and organization of Germany, not to fight France, but to awe Russia. Napoleon predicted that Europe would become either French or Cossack; but there is little probability of Russian aggressions in Europe, so long as Russia is held in check by Germany.

Charlemagne had now delivered France and Germany from external enemies. He then turned his arms against the Saracens of Spain. This was the great mistake of his life. Yet everyone makes mistakes, however great his genius. Alexander made the mistake of pushing his arms into India; and Napoleon made a great blunder in invading Russia. Even Caesar died at the right time for his military fame, for he was on the point of attempting the conquest of Parthia, where, like Crassus, he would probably have perished, or have lost his army. Needless conquests seem to be impossible in the moral government of God, who rules the fate of war. Conquests are only possible when civilization seems to require them. In seeking to invade Spain, Charlemagne warred against a race from whom Europe had nothing more to fear. His grandfather, Charles Martel, had arrested the conquests of the Saracens; and they were quiet in their settlements in Spain, and had made considerable attainments in science and literature. Their schools of medicine and their arts were in advance of the rest of Europe. They were the translators of Aristotle, who reigned in the rising universities during the Middle Ages.

As this war was unnecessary, Providence seemed to rebuke Charlemagne. His defeat at Roncesvalles was one of the most memorable events in his military history. Prodigies of valor were wrought by him and his gallant Paladins. The early heroic poetry of the Middle Ages has commemorated his exploits, as well as those of his nephew Roland, to whom some writers have ascribed the origin of Chivalry. But the Frankish forces were signally defeated amid the passes of the Pyrenees; and it was not until after several centuries that the Gothic princes of Spain shook off the yoke of their Saracenic conquerors, and drove them from Europe.

The Lombard wars of Charlemagne are the last to which I allude. These were undertaken in defence of the Church, to rescue his ally the Pope. The Lombards belonged to the great Germanic family, but they were unfriendly to the Pope and to the Church. They stood out against the Empire, which was then the chief hope of Europe and of civilization. They would have reduced the Pope to insignificance and seized his territories, without uniting Italy. So Charlemagne, like his father Pepin, lent his powerful aid to the Roman bishop, and the Lombards were easily subdued. This conquest, although the easiest which he ever made, most flattered his pride. Lombardy was not only joined to his Empire, but he received unparalleled honors from the Pope, being crowned by him Emperor of the West.

It was a proud day when, in the ancient metropolis of the world, and in the fulness of his fame, Pope Leo III placed the crown of Augustus upon Charlemagne's brow, and gave to him, amid the festivities of Christmas, his apostolic benediction. His dominions now extended from Catalonia to the Bohemian forests, embracing Germany, France, the Netherlands, Italy, and the Spanish main, – the largest empire which any one man has possessed since the fall of the Roman Empire. What more natural than for Charlemagne to feel that he had restored the Western Empire? What more natural than that he should have taken the title, still claimed by the Austrian emperor, in one sense his legitimate successor, – Kaiser, or Caesar? In the possession of such enormous power, he naturally dreamed of establishing a new universal military monarchy like that of the Romans, – as Charles V. dreamed, and Napoleon after him. But this is a dream that Providence has rebuked among all successive conquerors. There may have been need of the universal monarchy of the Caesars, that Christianity might spread in peace, and be protected by a reign of law and order. This at least is one of the platitudes of historians. Froude himself harps on it in his life of Caesar. Historians are fond of exalting the glories of imperialism, and everybody is dazzled by the splendor and power of ancient Roman emperors. They do not, I think, sufficiently consider the blasting influence of imperialism on the life of nations, – how it dries up the sources of renovation, how it necessarily withers literature and philosophy, how nothing can thrive under it but pomp and material glories, how it paralyzes all virtuous impulses, how it kills all enthusiasm, how it crushes out all hope and lofty aspirations, how it makes slaves of its best subjects, how it fills the earth with fear, how it drains national resources to support standing armies, how it mocks all enterprises which do not receive imperial approbation, how everything is concentrated to reflect the glory of one man or family; how impossible, under its withering shade, is manly independence, or the free expression of opinions or healthy growth; how it buries up, under its armies, discontents and aspirations alike, and creates nothing but machinery which must ultimately wear out and leave a world in ruins, with nothing stable to take its place. Law and order are good things, the preservation of property is desirable, the punishment of crime is necessary; but there are other things which are valuable also. Nothing is so valuable as the preservation of national life; nothing is so healthy as scope for energies; nothing is so contemptible and degrading as universal sycophancy to official rule. There are no tyrants more oppressive than the tools of absolute power. See in what a state imperialism left the Roman Empire when it fell. There were no rallying forces; there was no resurrection of heroes. Vitality had fled. Where would Turkey be to-day without the European powers, if the Sultan's authority were to fall? It would be in the state of ancient Babylon or Persia when those empires fell.

There is another side to imperialism besides dreaded anarchies. Moreover, the whole progress of civilization has been counter to it. The fiats of eternal justice have pronounced against it, because it is antagonistic to the dignity of man and the triumphs of reason. I would not fall in with the cant of the dignity of man, because there is no dignity to man without aid from God Almighty through His spirit and the message he has sent in Christianity.

But there is dignity in man with the aid of a regenerating gospel. Some people talk of the triumphs of Christianity under the Roman emperors; but see how rapidly it was corrupted by them when they sought the aid of its institutions to bolster up their power. The power of Christianity is in its truths; in its religion, and not in its forms and institutions, in its inventions to uphold the arms of despotism and the tools of despotism. It is, and it was, and it will be through all the ages the great power of the world, against which it is vain to rebel. And that government is really the best which unfetters its spiritual influence, and encourages it; and not that government which seeks to perpetuate its corrupt and worldly institutions. The Roman emperors made Christianity an institution, and obscured its truths. And perhaps that is one reason why Providence permitted their despotism to pass away, – preferring the rude anarchy of the Germanic nations to the dead mechanism of a lifeless Church and imperial rottenness. Imperialism must ever end in rottenness. And that is one reason why the heart of Christendom – I mean the people of Europe, in its enlightened and virtuous sections – has ever opposed imperialism. The progress has been slow, but marked, towards representative governments, – not the reign of the people directly, but of those whom they select to represent them. The victory has been nearly gained in England. In France the progress has been uniform since the Revolution. Napoleon revived, or sought to revive, the imperialism of Rome. He failed. There is nothing which the French now so cordially detest, since their eyes have been opened to the character and ends of that usurper, as his imperialism. It cannot be revived any more easily than the oracles of Dodona. Even in Germany there are dreadful discontents in view of the imperialism which Bismarck, by the force of successful wars, has seemingly revived. The awful standing armies are a menace to all liberty and progress and national development. In Italy itself there is the commencement of constitutional authority, although it is united under a king. The great standing warfare of modern times is constitutional authority against the absolute power of kings and emperors. And the progress has been on the side of liberty everywhere, with occasional drawbacks, such as when Louis Napoleon revived the accursed despotism of his uncle, and by the same means, – a standing army and promises of military glory.

Hence, in the order of Providence, the dream of Charlemagne as to unbounded military aggrandizement could not be realized. He could not revive the imperialism of Rome or Persia. No man will ever arise in Europe who can re-establish it, except for a brief period. It will be rebuked by the superintending Power, because it is fatal to the highest development of nations, because all its glories are delusory, because it sows the seeds of ruin. It produces that very egotism, materialism, and sensuality, that inglorious rest and pleasure, which, as everybody concedes, prepared the way for violence.

And hence Charlemagne's empire went to pieces as soon as he was dead. There was nothing permanent in his conquests, except those made against barbarism. He was raised up to erect barriers against fresh inroads of barbarians. His whole empire was finally split up into petty sovereignties. In one sense he founded States, "since he founded the States which sprang up from the dismemberment of his empire. The kingdoms of Germany, Italy, France, Burgundy, Lorraine, Navarre, all date to his memorable reign." But these mediaeval kingdoms were feudal; the power of the kings was nominal. Government passed from imperialism into the hands of nobles. The government of Europe in the Middle Ages was a military aristocracy, only powerful as the interests of the people were considered. Kings and princes did not make much show, except in the trappings of royalty, – in gorgeous dresses of purple and gold, to suit a barbaric taste, – in the insignia of power without its reality. The power was among the aristocracy, who, it must be confessed, ground down the people by a hard feudal rule, but who did not grind the souls out of them, like the imperialism of absolute monarchies, with their standing armies. Under them the feudal nobles of Europe at length recuperated. Virtues were born everywhere, – in England, in France, in Germany, in Holland, – which were a savor of life unto life: loyalty, self-respect, fidelity to covenants, chivalry, sympathy with human misery, love of home, rural sports, a glorious rural life, which gave stamina to character, – a material which Christianity could work upon, and kindle the latent fires of freedom, and the impulses of a generous enthusiasm. It was under the fostering influences of small, independent chieftains that manly strength and organized social institutions arose once more, – the reserved power of unconquerable nations. Nobody hates feudalism – in its corruptions, in its oppressions – more than I do. But it was the transition stage from the anarchy which the collapse of imperialism produced to the constitutional governments of our times, if we could forget the absolute monarchies which flourished on the breaking up of feudalism, when it became a tyranny and a mockery, but which absolute monarchies flourished only one or two hundred years, – a sort of necessity in the development of nations to check the insolence and overgrown power of nobles, but after all essentially different from the imperialism of Caesar or Napoleon, since they relied on the support of nobles and municipalities more than on a standing army; yea, on votes and grants from parliaments to raise money to support the army, – certainly in England, as in the time of Elizabeth. The Bourbons, indeed, reigned without grants from the people or the nobility, and what was the logical result? – a French Revolution! Would a French Revolution have been possible under the Roman Caesars?

But I will not pursue this gradual development of constitutional government from the anarchies which arose out of the fall of the Roman Empire, – just the reverse of what happened in the history of Rome; I say no more of the imperialism which Charlemagne sought to restore, but was not permitted by Providence, and which, after all, was the dream of his latter days, when, like Napoleon, he was intoxicated by power and brilliant conquests; and I turn to consider briefly his direct effects in civilization, which showed his great and enlightened mind, and on which his fame in no small degree rests.

Charlemagne was no insignificant legislator. His Capitularies may not be equal to the laws of Justinian in natural justice, but were adapted to his times and circumstances. He collected the scattered codes, so far as laws were codified, of the various Germanic nations, and modified them. He introduced a great Christian element into his jurisprudence. He made use of the canons of the Church. His code is more ecclesiastical than that of Theodosius even, the last great Christian emperor. But in his day the clergy wielded great power, and their ordinances and decisions were directed to society as it was. The clergy were the great jurists of their day. The spiritual courts decided matters of great importance, and took cognizance of cases which were out of the jurisdiction of temporal courts. Charlemagne recognized the value of these spiritual courts, and aided them. He had no quarrels with ecclesiastics, nor was he jealous of their power. He allied himself with it. He was a friend of the clergy. One of the peculiarities of all the Germanic laws, seen especially in those of Ina and Alfred, was pecuniary compensation for crime: fifty shillings, in England, would pay for the loss of a foot, and twenty for a nose and four for a tooth; thus recognizing a principle seen in our times in railroad accidents, though not recognized in our civil laws in reference to crimes. This system of compensation Charlemagne retained, which perhaps answered for his day.

He was also a great administrator. Nothing escaped his vigilance. I do not read that he made many roads, or effected important internal improvements. The age was too barbarous for the development of national industries, – one of the main things which occupy modern statesmen and governments. But whatever he did was wise and enlightened. He rewarded merit; he made an alliance with learned men; he sought out the right men for important posts; he made the learned Alcuin his teacher and counsellor; he established libraries and schools; he built convents and monasteries; he gave encouragement to men of great attainments; he loved to surround himself with learned men; the scholars of all countries sought his protection and patronage, and found him a friend. Alcuin became one of the richest men in his dominions, and Englebert received one of his daughters in marriage. Napoleon professed a great admiration for Charlemagne, although Frederic II was his model sovereign. But how differently Napoleon acted in this respect! Napoleon was jealous of literary genius. He hated literary men. He rarely invited them to his table, and was constrained in their presence. He drove them out of the kingdom even. He wanted nothing but homage, – and literary genius has no sympathy with brute force, or machinery, or military exploits. But Charlemagne, like Peter the Great, delighted in the society of all who could teach him anything. He was a tolerably learned man himself, considering his life of activity. He spoke Latin as fluently as his native German, and it is said that he understood Greek. He liked to visit schools, and witness the performances of the boys; and, provided they made proficiency in their studies, he cared little for their noble birth. He was no respecter of persons. With wrath he reproved the idle. He promised rewards to merit and industry.

The most marked feature of his reign, outside his wars, was his sympathy with the clergy. Here, too, he differed from Napoleon and Frederic II. Mr. Hallam considers his alliance with the Church the great error of his reign; but I believe it built up his throne. In his time the clergy were the most influential people of the Empire and the most enlightened; but at that time the great contest of the Middle Ages between spiritual and temporal authority had not begun. Ambrose, indeed, had rebuked Theodosius, and set in defiance the empress when she interfered with his spiritual functions; and Leo had laid the corner-stone of the Papacy by instituting a divine right to his decrees. But a Hildebrand and a Becket had not arisen to usurp the prerogatives of their monarchs. Least of all did popes then dream of subjecting the temporal powers and raising the spiritual over them, so as to lead to issues with kings. That was a later development in the history of the papacy. The popes of the eighth and ninth centuries sought to heal disorder, to punish turbulent chieftains, to sustain law and order, to establish a tribunal of justice to which the discontented might appeal. They sought to conserve the peace of the world. They sought to rule the Church, rather than the world. They aimed at a theocratic ministry, – to be the ambassadors of God Almighty, – to allay strife and division.

The clergy were the friends of order and law, and they were the natural guardians of learning. They were kind masters to the slaves, – for slavery still prevailed. That was an evil with which the clergy did not grapple; they would ameliorate it, but did not seek to remove it. Yet they shielded the unfortunate and the persecuted and the poor; they gave the only consolation which an iron age afforded. The Church was gloomy, ascetic, austere, like the cathedrals of that time. Monks buried themselves in crypts; they sang mournful songs; they saw nothing but poverty and misery, and they came to the relief in a funereal way. But they were not cold and hard and cruel, like baronial lords. Secular lords were rapacious, and ground down the people, and mocked and trampled upon them; but the clergy were hospitable, gentle, and affectionate. They sympathized with the people, from whom they chiefly sprang. They had their vices, but those vices were not half so revolting as those of barons and knights. Intellectually, the clergy were at all times the superiors of these secular lords. They loved the peaceful virtues which were generated in the consecrated convent. The passions of nobles urged them on to perpetual pillage, injustice, and cruelty. The clergy only quarreled among themselves. Their vices were those of envy, and perhaps of gluttony; but they were not public robbers. They were the best farmers of their times; they cultivated lands, and made them attractive by fruits and flowers. They were generally industrious; every convent was a beehive, in which various kinds of manufactures were produced. The monks aspired even to be artists. They illuminated manuscripts, as well as copied them; they made tapestries and beautiful vestments. They were a peaceful and useful set of men, at this period outside their spiritual functions; they built grand churches; they had fruitful gardens; they were exceedingly hospitable. Every monastery was an inn, as well as a beehive, to which all travelers resorted, and where no pay was exacted. It was a retreat for the unfortunate, which no one dared assail. And it was vocal with songs and anthems.

The clergy were not only thus general benefactors in an age of turbulence and crime, in spite of all their narrowness and spiritual pride and ghostly arts and ambition for power, but they lent a helping hand to the peasantry. The Church was democratic, and enabled the poor to rise according to their merits, while nobles combined to crush them or keep them in an ignoble sphere. In the Church, the son of a murdered peasant could rise according to his deserts; but if he followed a warrior to the battle-field, no virtues, no talents, no bravery could elevate him, – he was still a peasant, a low-born menial. If he entered a monastery, he might pass from office to office until as a mitred abbot he would become the master of ten thousand acres, the counsellor of kings, the equal of that proud baron in whose service his father spent his abject life. The great Hildebrand was the son of a carpenter. The Church ever recognized, what feudality did not, – the claims of man as man; and enabled peasants' sons, if they had abilities and virtues, to rise to proud positions, – to be the patrons of the learned, the companions of princes, the ministers of kings.

And that is the reason why Charlemagne befriended the Church and elevated it, because its influence was civilizing. He sought to establish among the clergy a counterbalancing power to that of nobles. Who can doubt that the influence of the Church was better than that of nobles in the Middle Ages? If it ground down society by a spiritual yoke, that yoke was necessary, for the rude Middle Ages could be ruled only by fear. What fear more potent than the destruction of the soul in a future life! It was by this weapon – excommunication – that Europe was governed. We may abhor it, but it was the great idea of Mediaeval Europe, which no one could resist, and which kept society from dissolution. Charlemagne may have erred in thus giving power and consideration to the clergy, in view of the subsequent encroachments of the popes. But he never anticipated the future quarrels between his successors and the popes, for the popes were not then formidable as the antagonists of kings. I believe his policy was the best for Europe, on the whole. The infancy of the Gothic races was long, dark, dreary, and unfortunate, but it prepared them for the civilization which they scorned.

Such were the services which this great sovereign rendered to his times and to Europe. He probably saved it from renewed barbarism. He was the great legislator of the Middle Ages, and the greatest friend – after Constantine and Theodosius – of which the Church can boast. With him dawned the new civilization. He brought back souvenirs of Rome and the Empire. Not for himself did he live, but for the welfare of the nations he governed. It was his example which Alfred sought to imitate. Though a warrior, he saw something greater than the warrior's excellence. It is said he was eloquent, like Julius Caesar. He loved music and all the arts. In his palace at Aix-la-Chapelle were sung the songs of the earliest poets of Germany. He took great pains to introduce the Gregorian chant. He was simple in dress, and only on rare occasions did he indulge in parade. He was temperate in eating and drinking, as all the famous warriors have been. He absolutely abhorred drunkenness, the great vice of the Northern nations. During meals he listened to the lays of minstrels or the readings of his secretaries. He took unwearied pains with the education of his daughters, and he was so fond of them that they even accompanied him in his military expeditions. He was not one of those men that Gibbon appreciated; but his fame is steadily growing, after a lapse of a thousand years. His whole appearance was manly, cheerful, and dignified. His countenance reflected a child-like serenity. He was one of the few men, like David, who was not spoiled by war and flatteries. Though gentle, he was subject to fits of anger, like Theodosius; but he did not affect anger, like Napoleon, for theatrical effect. His greatness and his simplicity, his humanity and his religious faith, are typical of the Germanic race. He died A.D. 814, after a reign of half a century, lamented by his own subjects and to be admired by succeeding generations. Hallam, though not eloquent generally, has pronounced his most beautiful eulogy, "written in the disgraces and miseries of succeeding times. He stands alone like a rock in the ocean, like a beacon on a waste. His sceptre was the bow of Ulysses, not to be bent by a weaker hand. In the dark ages of European history, his reign affords a solitary resting-place between two dark periods of turbulence and ignominy, deriving the advantage of contrast both from that of the preceding dynasty and of a posterity for whom he had founded an empire which they were unworthy and unequal to maintain."

To such a tribute I can add nothing. His greatness consists in this, that, born amidst barbarism, he was yet the friend of civilization, and understood its elemental principles, and struggled forty-seven years to establish them, – failing only because his successors and subjects were not prepared for them, and could not learn them until the severe experience of ten centuries, amidst disasters and storms, should prove the value of the "old basal walls and pillars" which remained unburied amid the despised ruins of antiquity, and show that no structure could adequately shelter the European nations which was not established by the beautiful union of German vigor with Christian art, – by the combined richness of native genius with those immortal treasures which had escaped the wreck of the classic world.

AUTHORITIES

Eginhard's *Vita Caroli Magni*
Le Clerc's *De la Bruyère, Histoire du Règne de Charlemagne*
Haureau's *Charlemagne et son Cour*
Gaillard's *Histoire de Charlemagne*
Lorenz's *Karls des Grossen.*
There is a tolerably popular history of Charlemagne by James Bulfinch, entitled "*Legends of Charlemagne*;" also a *Life* by James the novelist. Henri Martin, Sismondi, and Michelet may be consulted also Hallam's *Middle Ages*, Milman's *Latin Christianity*, Gibbon's *Decline and Fall of the Roman Empire*, *Biographic Universelle*, and the *Encyclopaedias*.

Chapter 3

HILDEBRAND: THE PAPAL EMPIRE

A.D. 1020-1085

We associate with Hildebrand the great contest of the Middle Ages between spiritual and temporal authority, the triumph of the former, and its supremacy in Europe until the Reformation. What great ideas and events are interwoven with that majestic domination, – not in one age, but for fifteen centuries; not religious merely, but political, embracing as it were the whole progress of European society, from the fall of the Roman Empire to the Protestant Reformation; yea, intimately connected with the condition of Europe to the present day, and not of Europe only, but America itself! What an august power is this Catholic empire, equally great as an institution and as a religion! What lessons of human experience, what great truths of government, what subtile influences, reaching alike the palaces of kings and the hovels of peasants, are indissolubly linked with its marvelous domination, so that whether in its growth or decay it is more suggestive than the rise and fall of any temporal empire. It has produced, probably, more illustrious men than any political State in Europe. It has aimed to accomplish far grander ends. It is invested with more poetic interest. Its policy, its heroes, its saints, its doctors, its dignitaries, its missions, its persecutions, all rise up before us with varied but never-ending interest, when seriously contemplated. It has proved to be the most wonderful fabric of what we call worldly wisdom that our world has seen, – controlling kings, dictating laws to ancient monarchies, and binding the souls of millions with a more perfect despotism than Oriental emperors ever sought or dreamed. And what a marvelous vitality it seems to have! It has survived the attacks of its countless enemies; it has recovered from the shock of the Reformation; it still remains majestic and powerful, extending its arms of paternal love or Briarean terror over half of Christendom. As a temporal government, rivalling kings in the pomps of war and the pride of armies, it may be passing away; but as an organization to diffuse and conserve religious truths, – yea, even to bring a moral pressure on the minds of princes and governors, and reinforce its ranks with the mighty and the noble, – it seems to be as potent as ever. It is still sending its missionaries, its prelates, and its cardinals into the heart of Protestant countries, who anticipate and boast of new victories. It derides the dissensions and the rationalistic speculations of the Protestants, and predicts that they will either become open Pagans or re-enter the fold of Saint Peter. No longer do angry partisans call it the "Beast" or the "Scarlet Mother" or the "predicted Antichrist," since its religious creeds in their vital points are more in harmony with the theology of venerated Fathers than those of some of the progressive and proudest parties which call themselves Protestant. In Germany, in France, – shall I add, in England and America? – it is more in earnest, and more laborious and self-denying than many sects among the Protestants. In Germany – in those very seats of learning and power and fashion which once were kindled into lofty enthusiasm by the voice of Luther – who is it that desert the churches and disregard the sacraments, the Catholics or the Protestants?

Surely such a power, whether we view it as an institution or as a religion, cannot be despised, even by the narrowest and most fanatical Protestant. It is too grand and venerable for sarcasm, ridicule, or mockery. It is too potent and respectable to be sneered at or lied about. No cause can be advanced permanently except by adherence to the truth, whether it be agreeable or not. If the Papacy were a mere despotism, having nothing else in view than the inthralment of mankind, – of which it has been accused, – then mankind long ago, in lofty indignation, would have hurled it from its venerable throne. But despotic as its yoke is in the eyes of Protestants, and always has been and always may be, it is something more than that, having at heart the welfare of the very millions whom it rules by working on their fears. In spite of dogmas which are deductions from questionable premises, or which are at war with reason, and ritualism borrowed from other religions, and "pious frauds," and Jesuitical means to compass desirable ends, – which Protestants indignantly discard, and which they maintain are antagonistic to the spirit of primitive Christianity, – still it is also the defender and advocate of vital Christian truths, to which we trace the hopes and consolations of mankind. As the conservator of doctrines common to all Christian sects it cannot be swept away by the hand of man; nor as a government, confining its officers and rules to the spiritual necessities of its members. Its empire is spiritual rather than temporal. Temporal monarchs are hurled from their thrones. The long line of the Bourbons vanishes before the tempests of revolution, and they who were borne into power by these tempests are in turn hurled into ignominious banishment; but the Pope – he still sits secure on the throne of the Gregories and the Clements, ready to pronounce benedictions or hurl anathemas, to which half of Europe bows in fear or love.

Whence this strange vitality? What are the elements of a power so enduring and so irresistible? What has given to it its greatness and its dignity? I confess I gaze upon it as a peasant surveys a king, as a boy contemplates a queen of beauty, – as something which may be talked about, yet removed beyond our influence, and no more affected by our praise or censure than is a procession of cardinals by the gaze of admiring spectators in Saint Peter's Church. Who can measure it, or analyze it, or comprehend it? The weapons of reason appear to fall impotent before its haughty dogmatism. Genius cannot reconcile its inconsistencies. Serenely it sits, unmoved amid all the aggressions of human thought and all the triumphs of modern science. It is both lofty and degraded; simple, yet worldly wise; humble, yet scornful and proud; washing beggars' feet, yet imposing commands on the potentates of earth; benignant, yet severe on all who rebel; here clothed in rags, and there reveling in palaces; supported by charities, yet feasting the princes of the earth; assuming the title of "servant of the servants of God," yet arrogating the highest seat among worldly dignitaries.

Was there ever such a contradiction? – "glory in debasement, and debasement in glory," – type of the misery and greatness of man? Was there ever such a mystery, so occult are its arts, so subtile its policy, so plausible its pretensions, so certain its shafts? How imposing the words of paternal benediction! How grand the liturgy brought down from ages of faith! How absorbed with beatific devotion appears to be the worshipper at its consecrated altars! How ravishing the music and the chants of grand ceremonials! How typical the churches and consecrated monuments of the passion of Christ! Everywhere you see the great emblem of our redemption, – on the loftiest pinnacle of the Mediaeval cathedral, on the dresses of the priests, over the gorgeous altars, in the ceremony of the Mass, in the baptismal rite, in the paintings of the side chapels; everywhere are rites and emblems betokening maceration, grief, sacrifice, penitence, the humiliation of humanity before the awful power of divine Omnipotence, whose personality and moral government no Catholic dares openly to deny.

And yet, of what crimes and abominations has not this government been, accused? If we go back to darker ages, and accept what history records, what wars has not this Church encouraged, what discords has she not incited, what superstitions has she not indorsed, what pride has she not arrogated, what cruelties has she not inflicted, what countries has she not robbed, what hardships has she not imposed, what deceptions has she not used, what avenues of thought has she not guarded with a flaming sword, what truth has she not perverted, what goodness has she not mocked and persecuted? Ah, interrogate the Albigenses, the Waldenses, the shades of Jerome of Prague, of Huss, of Savonarola, of Cranmer, of Coligny, of Galileo; interrogate the martyrs of the Thirty Years' War, and those who were slain by the dragonnades of Louis XIV, those who fell by the hand of Alva and Charles IX; go to Smithfield, and Paris on Saint Bartholomew; think of gunpowder plots and inquisitions, and Jesuit intrigues and Dominican tortures, of which history accuses the Papal Church, – barbarities worse than those of savages, inflicted at the command of the ministers of a gospel of love!

I am compelled to allude to these things; I do not dwell on them, since they were the result of the intolerance of human nature as much as the bigotry of the Church, – faults of an age, more than of a religion; although, whether exaggerated or not, more disgraceful than the persecutions of Christians by Roman emperors.

As for the supreme rulers of this contradictory Church, so benevolent and yet so cruel, so enlightened and yet so fanatical, so humble and yet so proud, – this institution of blended piety and fraud, equally renowned for saints, theologians, statesmen, drivellers, and fanatics; the joy and the reproach, the glory and the shame of earth, – there never were greater geniuses or greater fools: saints of almost preternatural sanctity, like the first Leo and Gregory, or hounds like Boniface VIII or Alexander VI; an array of scholars and dunces, ascetics and gluttons, men who adorned and men who scandalized their lofty position; and yet, on the whole, we are forced to admit, the most remarkable body of rulers any empire has known, since they were elevated by their peers, and generally for talents or services, at a period of life when character is formed and experience is matured. They were not greater than their Church or their age, like the Charlemagnes and Peters of secular history, but they were the picked men, the best representatives of their Church; ambitious, doubtless, and worldly, as great potentates generally are, but made so by the circumstances which controlled them. Who can wield irresponsible power and not become arrogant, and perhaps self-indulgent? It requires the almost superhuman virtue of a Marcus Aurelius or a Saint Louis to crucify the pride of rank and power. If the president of a college or of a railroad or of a bank becomes a different man to the eye of an early friend, what can be expected of those who are raised above public opinion, and have no fetters on their wills, – men who are regarded as infallible and feel themselves supreme!

But of all these three hundred or four hundred men who have swayed the destinies of Europe, – an uninterrupted line of pontiffs for fifteen hundred years or more, – no one is so famous as Gregory VII for the grandeur of his character, the heroism of his struggles, and the posthumous influence of his deeds. He was too great a man to be called by his papal title. He is best known by his baptismal name, Hildebrand, the greatest hero of the Roman Church. There are some men whose titles add nothing to their august names, – David, Julius, Constantine, Augustine. When a man has become very eminent we drop titles altogether, except in military life. We say Daniel Webster, Edward Everett, Jonathan Edwards, Thomas Jefferson, Benjamin Franklin, William Pitt. Hildebrand is a greater name than Gregory VII., and with him is identified the greatest struggle of the Papacy against the temporal powers. I do not aim to dissect his character so much as to present his services to the Church. I wish to show why and how he is identified with movements of supreme historical importance. It would be easy to make him out a saint and martyr, and equally so to paint him as a tyrant and usurper. It is of little consequence to us whether he was ascetic or ambitious or unscrupulous; but it *is* of consequence to show the majestic power of those ideas by which he ruled the Middle Ages, and which will never pass away as sublime agencies so long as men are ignorant and superstitious. As a man he no longer lives, but his thunderbolts are perpetual powers, since they still alarm the fears of men.

Still, his personal history is not uninteresting. Born of humble parents in Italy in the year 1020, the son of a carpenter, he rose by genius and virtue to the highest offices and dignities. But his greatness was in force of character rather than original ideas, – like that of Washington, or William III, or the Duke of Wellington. He had not the comprehensive intellect of Charlemagne, nor the creative genius of Peter of Russia, but he had the sagacity of Richelieu and the iron will of Napoleon. He was statesman as well as priest, – marvellous for his activity, insight into human nature, vast executive abilities, and dauntless heroism. He comprehended the only way whereby Christendom could be governed, and unscrupulously used the means of success. He was not a great scholar, or theologian, or philosopher, but a man of action, embracing opportunities and striking decisive blows. From first to last he was devoted to his cause, which was greater than himself, – even the spiritual supremacy of the Papacy. I do not read of great intellectual precocity, like that of Cicero and William Pitt, nor of great attainments, like those of Abélard and Thomas Aquinas, nor even an insight, like that of Bacon, into what constitutes the dignity of man and the true glory of civilization; but, like Ambrose and the first Leo, he was early selected for important missions and responsible trusts, all of which he discharged with great fidelity and ability. His education was directed by the monks of Cluny, – that princely abbey in Burgundy where "monks were sovereigns and sovereigns were monks." Like all earnest monks, he was ascetic, devotional, and self-sacrificing. Like all men ambitious to rule, "he learned how to obey." He pondered on the Holy Scriptures as well as on the canons of the Church. So marked a man was he that he was early chosen as prior of his convent; and so great were his personal magnetism, eloquence, and influence that "he induced Bruno, the Bishop of Toul, when elected pope by the Emperor of Germany, to lay aside the badges and vestments of the pontifical office, and refuse his title, until he should be elected by the clergy and people of Rome," – thus showing that at the age of twenty-nine he comprehended the issues of the day, and meditated on the gigantic changes it was necessary to make before the pope could be the supreme ruler of Christendom.

The autocratic idea of Leo I, and the great Gregory who sent his missionaries to England, was that to which Hildebrand's ardent soul clung with preternatural earnestness, as the only government fit for turbulent and superstitious ages. He did not originate this idea, but he defended and enforced it as had never been done before, so that to many minds he was the great architect of the papal structure. It was a rare spectacle to see a sovereign pontiff lay aside the insignia of his grandeur at the bidding of this monk of Cluny; it was grander to see this monk laying the foundation of an irresistible despotism, which was to last beyond the time of Luther. Not merely was Leo IX his tool, but three successive popes were chosen at his dictation. And when he became cardinal and archdeacon he seems to have been the inspiring genius of the papal government, undertaking the most important missions, curbing the turbulent spirit of the Roman princes, and assisting in all ecclesiastical councils. It was by his suggestion that abbots were deposed, and bishops punished, and monarchs reprimanded. He was the prime minister of four popes before he accepted that high office to which he doubtless had aspired while meditating as a monk amid the sunny slopes of Cluny, since he knew that the exigences of the Church required a bold and able ruler, – and who in Christendom was bolder and more far-reaching than he? He might have been elevated to the chair of Saint Peter at an earlier period, but he was contented with power rather than glory, knowing that his day would come, and at a time when his extraordinary abilities would be most needed. He could afford to wait; and no man is truly great who cannot bide his time.

At last Hildebrand received the reward of his great services, – "a reward," says Stephen, "which he had long contemplated, but which, with self-controlling policy, he had so long declined." In the year 1073 Hildebrand became Gregory VII, and his memorable pontificate began as a reformer of the abuses of his age, and the intrepid defender of that unlimited and absolute despotism which inthralled not merely the princes of Europe, but the mind of Christendom itself. It was he who not only proclaimed the liberties of the people against nobles, and made the Church an asylum for misery and oppression, but who realized the idea that the Church was the mother of spiritual principles, and that the spiritual authority should be raised over all temporal power.

In the great crises of States and Empires deliverers seem to be raised up by Divine Providence to restore peace and order, and maintain the first condition of society, or extricate nations from overwhelming calamities. Thus Charlemagne appeared at the right time to prevent the overthrow of Europe by new waves of barbaric invasion. Thus William the Silent preserved the nationality of Holland, and Gustavus Adolphus gave religious liberty to Germany when persecution was apparently successful. Thus Richelieu undermined feudalism in France, and established absolutism as one of the needed forces of his turbulent age, even as Napoleon gave law and order to France when distracted by the anarchism of a revolution which did not comprehend the liberty which was invoked. So Hildebrand was raised up to establish the only government which could rescue Europe from the rapacities of feudal nobles, and establish law and order in the hands of the most enlightened class; so that, like Peter the Great, he looms up as a reformer as well as a despot. He appears in a double light.

Now you ask: "What were his reforms, and what were his schemes of aggrandizement, for which we honor him while we denounce him?" We cannot see the reforms he attempted without glancing at the enormous evils which stared him in the face.

Society in Europe, in the eleventh century, was nearly as dark and degraded as it was on the fall of the Merovingian dynasty. In some respects it had reached the lowest depth of wretchedness which the Middle Ages ever saw. Never had the clergy been more ignorant, more sensual, and more worldly. They had not the piety of the fourth century, nor the intelligence of the sixteenth century; they were powerful and wealthy, but exceedingly corrupt. Monastic institutions covered the face of Europe, but the monks had sadly departed from the virtues which partially redeemed the miseries that succeeded the fall of the Roman Empire. The lives of the clergy, regular and secular, still compared favorably with the lives of the feudal nobility, who had, in addition to priestly vices, the vices of robbers and bandits. But still the clergy were notoriously ignorant, superstitious, and sensual. Monasteries sought to be independent of all foreign control and of episcopal jurisdiction. They had been enormously enriched by princes and barons, and they owned, with the other clergy, half the lands of Europe, and more than half its silver and gold. The monks fattened on all the luxuries which then were known; they neglected the rules of their order and lived in idleness, – spending their time in the chase, or in taverns and brothels. Hardly a great scholar or theologian had arisen among them since the Patristic age, with the exception of a few schoolmen like Anselm and Peter Lombard. Saint Bernard had not yet appeared to reform the Benedictines, nor Dominic and Saint Francis to found new orders. Gluttony and idleness were perhaps the characteristic vices of the great body of the monks, who numbered over one hundred thousand. Hunting and hawking were the most innocent of their amusements. They have been accused of drinking toasts in honor of the Devil, and celebrating Mass in a state of intoxication. "Not one in a thousand," says Hallam, "could address to one another a common letter of salutation." They were a walking libel on everything sacred. Read the account of their banquets in the annals which have come down to us of the tenth and eleventh centuries, when convents were so numerous and rich. If Dugdale is to be credited, their gluttony exceeded that of any previous or succeeding age. Their cupidity, their drunken revels, their infamous haunts, their disgusting coarseness, their hypocrisy, ignorance, selfishness, and superstition were notorious. Yet the monks were not worse than the secular clergy, high and low. Bishoprics and all benefices were bought and sold; "canons were trodden under foot; ancient traditions were turned out of doors;

old customs were laid aside;" boys were made archbishops; ludicrous stories were recited in the churches; the most disgraceful crimes were pardoned for money. Desolation, according to Cardinal Baronius, was seen in the temples of the Lord. As Petrarch said of Avignon in a better age, "There is no pity, no charity, no faith, no fear of God. The air, the streets, the houses, the markets, the beds, the hotels, the churches, even the altars consecrated to God, are all peopled with knaves and liars;" or, to use the still stronger language of a great reviewer, "The gates of hell appeared to roll back on their infernal hinges, that there might go forth malignant spirits to empty the vials of wrath on the patrimony even of the great chief of the apostles."

These vices, it is true, were not confined to the clergy. All classes were alike forlorn, miserable, and corrupt. It was a gloomy period. The Church, whenever religious, was sad and despairing. The contemplative hid themselves in noisome and sepulchral crypts. The inspiring chants of Ambrose gave place to gloomy and monotonous antiphonal singing, – that is, when the monks confined themselves to their dismal vocation. What was especially needed was a reform among the clergy themselves. They indeed owned their allegiance to the Pope, as the supreme head of the Church, but their fealty was becoming a mockery. They could not support the throne of absolutism if they were not respected by the laity. Baronial and feudal power was rapidly gaining over spiritual, and this was a poor exchange for the power of the clergy, if it led to violence and rapine. It is to maintain law and order, justice and safety, that all governments are established.

Hildebrand saw and lamented the countless evils of the day, especially those which were loosening the bands of clerical obedience, and undermining the absolutism which had become the great necessity of his age. He made up his mind to reform these evils. No pope before him had seriously undertaken this gigantic task. The popes who for two hundred years had preceded him were a scandal and a reproach to their exalted position. These heirs of Saint Peter wasted their patrimony in pleasures and pomps. At no period of the papal history was the papal chair filled with such bad or incompetent men. Of these popes two were murdered, five were driven into exile, and four were deposed. Some were raised to prominence by arms, and others by money. John X. commanded an army in person; John

XI died in a fit of debauchery; and John XII was murdered by one of the infamous women whom he patronized. Benedict IX was driven from the throne by robbery and murder, while Gregory VI purchased the papal dignity. For two hundred years no commanding character had worn the tiara.

Hildebrand, however, set a new example, and became a watchful shepherd of his fold. His private life was without reproach; he was absorbed in his duties; he sympathized with learning and learned men. He was the friend of Lanfranc, and it was by his influence that this great prelate was appointed to the See of Canterbury, and a closer union was formed with England. He infused by his example a quiet but noble courage into the soul of Anselm. He had great faults, of course, – faults of his own and faults of his age. I wonder why so *strong* a man has escaped the admiring eulogium of Carlyle. Guizot compares him with the Russian Peter. In some respects he reminds me of Oliver Cromwell; since both equally deplored the evils of the day, and both invoked the aid of God Almighty. Both were ambitious, and unscrupulous in the use of tools. Neither of them was stained by vulgar vices, nor seduced from his course by love of ease or pleasure. Both are to be contemplated in the double light of reformer and usurper. Both were honest, and both were unscrupulous; honest in seeking to promote public morality and the welfare of society, and unscrupulous in the arts by which their power was gained.

That which filled the soul of Hildebrand with especial grief was the alienation of the clergy from their highest duties, their worldly lives, and their frail support in his efforts to elevate the spiritual power. Therefore he determined to make a reform of the clergy themselves, having in view all the time their assistance in establishing the papal supremacy. He attacked the clergy where they were weakest. They – the secular ones, the parish priests – were getting married, especially in Germany and France. They were setting at defiance the laws of celibacy; they not only sought wives, but they lived in concubinage.

Now celibacy had been regarded as the supernal virtue from the time of Saint Jerome. It was supposed to be a state most favorable to Christian perfection; it animated the existence of the most noted saints. Says Jerome, "Take axe in hand and hew down the sterile tree of marriage." This notion of the superior virtue of virginity was one of the fruits of those Eastern theogonies which were engrafted on the early Church, growing out of the Oriental idea of the inalienable evil of matter. It was one of the fundamental principles of monasticism; and monasticism, wherever born – whether in India or the Syrian deserts – was one of the established institutions of the Church. It was indorsed by Benedict as well as by Basil; it had taken possession of the minds of the Gothic nations more firmly even than of the Eastern. The East never saw such monasteries as those which covered Italy, France, Germany, and England; they were more needed among the feudal robbers of Europe than in the effeminate monarchies of Asia. Moreover it was in monasteries that the popes had ever found their strongest adherents, their most zealous supporters. Without the aid of convents the papal empire might have crumbled. Monasticism and the papacy were strongly allied; one supported the other. So efficient were monastic institutions in advocating the idea of a theocracy, as upheld by the popes, that they were exempted from episcopal authority. An abbot was as powerful and independent as a bishop. But to make the Papacy supreme it was necessary to call in the aid of the secular priests likewise. Unmarried priests, being more like monks, were more efficient supporters of the papal throne. To maintain celibacy, therefore, was always in accordance with papal policy.

But Nature had gradually asserted its claims over tradition and authority. The clergy, especially in France and Germany, were setting at defiance the edicts of popes and councils. The glory of celibacy was in an eclipse.

No one comprehended the necessity of celibacy, among the clergy, more clearly than Hildebrand, – himself a monk by education and sympathy. He looked upon married life, with all its hallowed beauty, as a profanation for a priest. In his eyes the clergy were married only to the Church. "Domestic affections suited ill with the duties of a theocratic ministry." Anything which diverted the labors of the clergy from the Church seemed to him an outrage and a degeneracy. How could they reach the state of beatific existence if they were to listen to the prattle of children, or be engrossed with the joys of conjugal or parental love? So he assembled a council, and caused it to pass canons to the effect that married priests should not perform any clerical office; that the people should not even be present at Mass celebrated by them; that all who had wives – or concubines, as he called them – should put them away; and that no one should be ordained who did not promise to remain unmarried during his whole life.

Of course there was a violent opposition. A great outcry was raised, especially in Germany. The whole body of the secular priests exclaimed against the proceeding. At Mentz they threatened the life of the archbishop, who attempted to enforce the decree. At Paris a numerous synod was assembled, in which it was voted that Gregory ought not here to be obeyed. But Gregory was stronger than his rebellious clergy, – stronger than the instincts of human nature, stronger than the united voice of reason and Scripture. He fell back on the majestic power of prevailing ideas, on the ascetic element of the early Church, on the traditions of monastic life. He was supported by more than a hundred thousand monks, by the superstitions of primitive ages, by the example of saints and martyrs, by his own elevated rank, by the allegiance due to him as head of the Church. Excommunications were hurled, like thunderbolts, into remotest hamlets, and the murmurs of indignant Christendom were silenced by the awful denunciations of God's supposed vicegerent. The clergy succumbed before such a terrible spiritual force, the fear of hell – the great idea by which the priests themselves controlled their flocks – was more potent than any temporal good. What priest in that age would dare resist his spiritual monarch on almost any point, and especially when disobedience was supposed to entail the burnings of a physical hell forever and ever? So celibacy was re-established as a law of the Christian Church at the bidding of that far-seeing genius who had devised the means of spiritual despotism. That law – so gloomy, so unnatural, so fraught with evil – has never been repealed; it still rules the Catholic priesthood of Europe and America. Nor will it be repealed so long as the ideas of the Middle Ages have more force than enlightened reason. It is an abominable law, but who can doubt its efficacy in cementing the power of the popes?

But simony, or the sale of ecclesiastical benefices, was a still more alarming evil to the mind of Gregory. It was the great scandal of the Church and age. Here we honor the Pope for striving to remove it. And yet its abolition was no easy thing. He came in contact with the selfishness of barons and kings. He found it an easier matter to take away the wives of priests than the purses of princes. Priests who had vowed obedience might consent to the repudiation of their wives, but would great temporal robbers part with their spoils? The sale of benefices was one great source of royal and baronial revenues. Bishoprics, once conferred for wisdom and piety, had become prizes for the rapacious and ambitious. Bishops and abbots were most frequently chosen from the ranks of the great. Powerful Sees were the gifts of kings to their favorites or families, or were bought by the wealthy; so that worldly or incapable men were made overseers of the Church of Christ. The clergy were in danger of being hopelessly secularized. And the evil spread to the extremities of the clerical body. The princes and barons were getting control of the Church itself. Bishops often possessed a plurality of Sees. Children were elevated to episcopal thrones. Sycophants, courtiers, jesters, imbecile sons of princes, became great ecclesiastical dignitaries. Who can wonder at the degeneracy of the clergy when they held their cures at the hands of lay patrons, to whom they swore allegiance for the temporalities of their benefices? Even the ring and the crozier, the emblems of spiritual authority, – once received at the hand of metropolitan archbishops alone, were now bestowed by temporal sovereigns, who claimed thereby fealty and allegiance; so that princes had gradually usurped the old rights of the Church, and Gregory resolved to recover them. So long as emperors and kings could fill the rich bishoprics and abbacies with their creatures, the papal dominion was weakened in its most vital point, and might become a dream. This evil was rapidly undermining the whole ecclesiastical edifice, and it required a hero of prodigious genius, energy, and influence to reform it.

Hildebrand saw and comprehended the whole extent and bearing of the evil, and resolved to remove it or die in the attempt. It was not only undermining his throne, but was secularizing the Church and destroying the real power of the clergy. He made up his mind to face the difficulty in its most dreaded quarters. He knew that the attempt to remove this scandal would entail a desperate conflict with the princes of the earth. Before this, popes and princes were generally leagued together; they played into each other's hands: but now a battle was to be fought between the temporal and spiritual powers. He knew that princes would never relinquish so lucrative a source of profit as the sale of powerful Sees, unless the right to sell them were taken away by some tremendous conflict. He therefore prepared for the fight, and forged his weapons and gathered together his forces. Nor would he waste time by idle negotiations; it was necessary to act with promptness and vigor. No matter how great the danger; no matter how powerful his enemies. The Church was in peril; and he resolved to come to the rescue, cost what it might. What was his life compared with the sale of God's heritage? For what was he placed in the most exalted post of the Church, if not to defend her in an alarming crisis?'

In resolving to separate forever the spiritual from the temporal power, Hildebrand followed in the footsteps of Ambrose. But he had also deeper designs. He resolved to raise, if possible, the spiritual *above* the temporal power. Kings should be subject to the Church, not the Church to the kings of the earth. He believed that he was the appointed vicar of the Almighty to rule the world in peace, on the principles of eternal love; that Christ had established a new theocracy, and had delegated his power to the Apostle Peter, which had descended to the Pope as the Apostle's legitimate successor.

I say nothing here of this monstrous claim, of this ingenious falsehood, on which the monarchical power of the Papacy rests. It is the great fraud of the Middle Ages. And yet, but for this theocratic idea, it is difficult to see how the external unity of the Church could have been preserved among the semi-barbarians of Europe. And what a necessary thing it was – in ages of superstition, ignorance, and anarchy – to preserve the unity of the Church, to establish a spiritual power which should awe and control barbaric princes! There are two sides to the supremacy of the popes as head of the Church, when we consider the aspect and state of society in those iron and lawless times. Would Providence have permitted such a power to rule for a thousand years had it not been a necessity? At any rate, this is too complicated a question for me to discuss. It is enough for me to describe the conflict for principles, not to attempt to settle them. In this matter I am not a partisan, but a painter. I seek to describe a battle, not to defend either this cause or that. I have my opinions, but this is no place to present them. I seek to describe simply the great battle of the Middle Ages, and you can draw your own conclusions as to the merits of the respective causes. I present the battle of heroes, – a battle worthy of the muse of Homer.

Hildebrand in this battle disdained to fight with any but great and noble antagonists. As the friend of the poor man, crushed and mocked by a cold and unfeeling nobility; as the protector of the Church, in danger of being subverted by the unhallowed tyranny and greed of princes; as the consecrated monarch of a great spiritual fraternity, – he resolved to face the mightiest monarchs, and suffer, and if need be die, for a cause which he regarded as the hope and salvation of Europe. Therefore he convened another council, and prohibited, under the terrible penalty of excommunication, – for that was his mighty weapon, – the investiture of bishoprics and abbacies at the hands of laymen: only he himself should give to ecclesiastics the ring and the crozier, – the badges of spiritual authority. And he equally threatened with eternal fire any bishop or abbot who should receive his dignity from the hand of a prince.

This decree was especially aimed against the Emperor of Germany, to whom, as liege lord, the Pope himself owed fealty and obedience. Henry IV was one of the mightiest monarchs of the Franconian dynasty, – a great warrior and a great man, beloved by his subjects and feared by the princes of Europe. But he, as well as Gregory, was resolved to maintain the rights of his predecessors. He also perceived the importance of the approaching contest. And what a contest! The spiritual and temporal powers were now to be arrayed against each other in a fierce antagonism. The apparent object of contention changed. It was not merely simony; it was as to who should be the supreme master of Germany and Italy, the emperor or the pope. To whom, in the eyes of contemporaries, would victory incline, – to the son of a carpenter, speaking in the name of the Church, and holding in his hands the consecrated weapon of excommunication; or the most powerful monarch of his age, armed with the secular sword, and seeking to restore the dignity of Roman emperors? The Pope is supported by the monks, the inferior clergy, and the vast spiritual powers universally supposed to be delegated to him by Christ, as the successor of Saint Peter; the Emperor is supported by large feudal armies, and all the prestige of the successors of Charlemagne. If the Pope appeals to an ancient custom of the Church, the Emperor appeals to a general feudal custom which required bishops and abbots to pay their homage to him for the temporalities of their Sees. The Pope has the canons of the Church on his side; the Emperor the laws of feudalism, – and both the canons of the Church and feudal principles are binding obligations. Hitherto they have not clashed. But now feudalism, very generally established, and papal absolutism, rapidly culminating, are to meet in angry collision. Shall the kings of the earth prevail, assisted by feudal armies and outward grandeur, and sustained by such powerful sentiments as loyalty and chivalry; or shall a priest, speaking in the name of God Almighty, and appealing to the future fears of men?

What conflict grander and more sublime than this, in the whole history of society? What conflict proved more momentous in its results?

I need not trace all the steps of that memorable contest, or describe the details, from the time when the Pope sent out his edicts and excommunicated all who dared to disobey him, – including some of the most eminent German prelates and German princes. Henry at this time was engaged in a desperate war with the Saxons, and Gregory seized this opportunity to summon the Emperor – his emperor – to appear before him at Rome and answer for alleged crimes against the Saxon Church. Was there ever such audacity? How could Henry help giving way to passionate indignation; he – the successor of the Roman Caesars, sovereign lord of Germany and Italy – summoned to the bar of a priest, and that priest his own subject, in a temporal sense? He was filled with wrath and defiance, and at once summoned a council of German bishops at Worms, "who denounced the Pope as a usurper, a simonist, a murderer, a worshipper of the Devil, and pronounced upon him the empty sentence of a deposition"

"The aged Hildebrand," in the words of Stephen, "was holding a council in the second week of Lent, 1076, beneath the sculptured roof of the Vatican, arrayed in the rich and mystic vestments of pontifical dominion, and the papal choir were chanting those immortal anthems which had come down from blessed saints and martyrs, when the messenger of the Emperor presented himself before the assembled hierarchy of Rome, and with insolent demeanor and abrupt speech delivered the sentence of the German council." He was left unharmed by the indignant pontiff; but the next day ascending his throne, and in presence of the dignitaries of his Church, thus invoked the assistance of the pretended founder of his empire: –

> "Saint Peter! lend us your ears, and listen to your servant whom you have cherished from his infancy; and all the saints also bear witness how the Roman Church raised me by force and against my will to this high dignity, although I should have preferred to spend my days in a continual pilgrimage than to ascend thy pulpit for any human motive. And inasmuch as I think it will be grateful to you that those intrusted to my care should obey me; therefore, supported by these hopes, and for the honor and defence of the Church, in the name of the Omnipotent God, – Father, Son, and Holy Ghost, – by my authority and power, I prohibit King Henry, who with unheard-of pride has raised himself against your Church, from governing the kingdoms of Germany and Italy; I absolve all Christians from the oath they have taken to him, and I forbid all men to yield to him that service which is due unto a king. Finally, I bind him with the bonds of anathema, that all people may know that thou art Peter, and that upon thee the Son of God hath built His Church, against which the gates of hell cannot prevail."

This was an old-fashioned excommunication; and we in these days have but a faint idea what a dreadful thing it was, especially when accompanied with an interdict. The churches were everywhere shut; the dead were unburied in consecrated ground; the rites of religion were suspended; gloom and fear sat on every countenance; desolation overspread the land. The king was regarded as guilty and damned; his ministers looked upon him as a Samson shorn of his locks; his very wife feared contamination from his society; his children, as a man blasted with the malediction of Heaven. When a man was universally supposed to be cursed in the house and in the field; in the wood and in the church; in eating or drinking; in fasting or sleeping; in working or resting; in his arms, in his legs, in his heart, and in his head; living or dying; in this world and in the next, – what could he do?

And what could Henry do, with all his greatness? His victorious armies deserted him; a rival prince laid claim to his throne; his enemies multiplied; his difficulties thickened; new dangers surrounded him on every side. If loyalty – that potent principle – had summoned one hundred thousand warriors to his camp, a principle much more powerful than loyalty – the fear of hell – had dispersed them. Even his friends joined the Pope. The sainted Agnes, his own mother, acquiesced in the sentence. The Countess Matilda, the richest lady in the world, threw all her treasures at the feet of her spiritual monarch. The moral sentiments of his own subjects were turned against him; he was regarded as justly condemned. The great princes of Germany sought his deposition. The world rejected him, the Church abandoned him, and God had forsaken him. He was prostrate, helpless, disarmed, ruined. True, he made superhuman efforts: he traversed his empire with the hope of rallying his subjects; he flew from city to city, – but all in vain. Every convent, every castle, every city of his vast dominions beheld in him the visitation of the Almighty. The diadem was obscured by the tiara, and loyalty itself yielded to the superior potency of religious fear. Only Bertha, his neglected wife, was faithful and trusting in that gloomy day; all else had defrauded and betrayed him. How bitter his humiliation! And yet his haughty foe was not contented with the punishment he had inflicted. He declared that if the sun went down on the 23d of February, 1077, before Henry was restored to the bosom of the Church, his crown should be transferred to another. That inexorable old pontiff laid claim to the right of giving and taking away imperial crowns. Was ever before seen such arrogance and audacity in a priest? And yet he knew that he would be sustained. He knew that his supremacy was based on a universally recognized idea. Who can resist the ideas of his age? Henry might have resisted, if resistance had been possible. Even he must yield to irresistible necessity. He was morally certain that he would lose his crown, and be in danger of losing his soul, unless he made his peace with his dangerous enemy. It was necessary that the awful curse should be removed. He had no remedy; only one course was before him. He must yield; not to man alone, but to an idea which had the force of fate. Wonder not that he made up his mind to submit. He was great, but not greater than his age. How few men are! Mohammed could renounce prevailing idolatries; Luther could burn a papal bull; but the Emperor of Germany could not resist the supposed vicegerent of the Almighty.

Behold, then, the melancholy, pitiable spectacle of this mighty monarch in the depth of winter – and a winter of unprecedented severity – crossing, in the garb of a pilgrim, the frozen Alps, enduring the greatest privations and fatigues and perils, and approaching on foot the gloomy fortress of Canossa (beyond the Po), in which Hildebrand had intrenched himself. Even then the angry pontiff refused to see him. Henry had to stoop to a still deeper degradation, – to stand bareheaded and barefooted for three days, amid the blasts of winter, in the court-yard of the castle, before the Pope would promise absolution, and then only at the intercession of the Countess Matilda.

What are we to think of such a fall, such a humiliation on the part of a sovereign? What are we to think of such haughtiness on the part of a priest, – his subject? We are filled with blended pity and indignation. We are inclined to say that this was the greatest blunder that any monarch ever made; that Henry – humbled and deserted and threatened as he was – should not have stooped to this; that he should have lost his crown and life rather than handed over his empire to a plebeian priest, – for he was an acknowledged hero; he was monarch of half of Europe. And yet we are bound to consider Henry's circumstances and the ideas with which he had to contend. His was the error of the Middle Ages; the feeblest of his modern successors would have killed the Pope if he could, rather than have disgraced himself by such an ignominy.

True it is that Henry came to himself; that he repented of his step. But it was too late. Gregory had gained the victory; and it was all the greater because it was a moral one. It was known to all Europe and all the world, and would be known to all posterity, that the Emperor of Germany had bowed in submission to a foreign priest. The temporal power had yielded to the spiritual; the State had conceded the supremacy of the Church. The Pope had triumphed over the mightiest monarch of the age, and his successors would place their feet over future prostrate kings. What a victory! What mighty consequences were the result of it! On what a throne did this moral victory seat the future pontiffs of the Eternal City! How august their dominion, for it was over the minds and souls of men! Truly to the Pope were given the keys of Heaven and Hell; and so long as the ideas of that age were accepted, who could resist a man armed with the thunders of Omnipotence?

It mattered nothing that the Emperor was ashamed of his weakness; that he retracted; that he vowed vengeance; that he marched at the head of new armies. No matter that his adherents were indignant; that all Germany wept; that loyalty rallied to his aid; that he gained victories proportionate with his former defeats; that he chased Gregory from city to city, and castle to castle, and convent to convent, while his generals burned the Pope's palaces and wasted his territories. No matter that Gregory – broken, defeated, miserable, outwardly ruined – died prematurely in exile; no matter that he did not, in his great reverses, anticipate the fruits of his firmness and heroism. His principles survived him; they have never been lost sight of by his successors; they gained strength through successive generations. Innocent III reaped what he had sown. Kings dared not resist Innocent III, who realized those three things to which the more able Gregory had aspired, – "independent sovereignty, control over the princes of the earth, and the supremacy of the Church." Innocent was the greater pope, but Hildebrand was the greater man.

Yet, like so many of the great heroes of the world, he was not destined in his own person to reap the fruits of his heroism. "I have loved righteousness and hated iniquity, and therefore I die in exile," – these were his last bitter words. He fancied he had failed. But did he fail? What did he leave behind? He left his great example and his still greater ideas. He left a legacy to his successors which makes them still potent on the earth, in spite of reformations and revolutions, and all the triumphs of literature and science. How mighty his deeds! How great his services to his Church! "He found," says an eloquent and able Edinburgh reviewer, "the papacy dependent on the emperor; he sustained it by alliances almost commensurate with the Italian peninsula. He found the papacy electoral by the Roman people and clergy; he left it electoral by papal nomination. He found the emperor the virtual patron of the Roman See; he wrenched that power from his hands. He found the secular clergy the allies and dependents of the secular power; he converted them into inalienable auxiliaries of his own. He found the patronage of the Church the desecrated spoil and merchandise of princes; he reduced it to his own dominion. He is celebrated as the reformer of the impure and profane abuses of his age; he is more justly entitled to the praise of having left the impress of his gigantic character on all the ages which have succeeded him."

Such was the great Hildebrand; a conqueror, however, by the force of recognized ideas more than by his own strength. How long, you ask, shall his empire last? We cannot tell who can predict the fortunes of such a power. It is not for me to speculate or preach. In considering his life and career, I have simply attempted to paint one of the most memorable moral contests of the world; to show the power of genius and will in a superstitious age, – and, more, the majestic force of ideas over the minds and souls of men, even though these ideas cannot be sustained by reason or Scripture.

AUTHORITIES

Epistles of Gregory VII
Baronius's *Annals*
Dupin's *Ecclesiastical History*
Voigt, in his *Hildebrand als Gregory VII*
Guizot's *Lectures on Civilization*
Sir James Stephens's article on *Hildebrand*, in *Edinburgh Review*
Dugdale's *Monasticon*
Hallam's *Middle Ages*
Digby's *Ages of Faith*
Jaffe's *Regesta Pontificum Romanorum*
Mignet's series of articles on *La Lutte des Papes contre les Empereurs d'Allemagne*
M. Villemain's *Histoire de Grégoire VII*
Bowden on the *Life and Times of Hildebrand*
Milman's *Latin Christianity*
Watterich's *Romanorum Pontificum ab Aequalibus Conscriptae*
Platina's *Lives of the Popes*
Stubbs's *Constitutional History*
Lee's *History of Clerical Celibacy*

Cardinal Newman's Essays
Lecky's *History of European Morals*
Dr. Döllinger's *Church History*
Neander's *Church History*
Contemporary Review articles of July and August, 1882, on the Turning Point of the Middle Ages.

Chapter 4

SAINT BERNARD: MONASTIC INSTITUTIONS

A.D. 1091-1153

One of the oldest institutions of the Church is that which grew out of monastic life. It had its seat, at a remote period, in India. It has existed, in different forms, in other Oriental countries. It has been modified by Brahminical, Buddhistic, and Persian theogonies, and extended to Egypt, Syria, and Asia Minor. Go where you will in the East, and you see traces of its mighty influence. We cannot tell its remotest origin, but we see everywhere the force of its ideas. Its fundamental principle appears to be the desire to propitiate the Deity by penances and ascetic labors as an atonement for sin, or as a means of rising to a higher religious life. It has sought to escape the polluting influences of demoralized society by lofty contemplation and retirement from the world. From the first, it was a protest against materialism, luxury, and enervating pleasures. It recognized something higher and nobler than devotion to material gains, or a life of degrading pleasure. In one sense it was an intellectual movement, while in another it was an insult to the human understanding. It attempted a purer morality, but abnegated obvious and pressing duties. It was always a contradiction, – lofty while degraded, seeking to comprehend the profoundest mysteries, yet debased by puerile superstitions.

The consciousness of mankind, in all ages and countries, has ever accepted retribution for sin – more or less permanent – in this world or in the next. And it has equally accepted the existence of a Supreme Intelligence and Power, to whom all are responsible, and in connection with whom human destinies are bound up. The deeper we penetrate into the occult wisdom of the East, – on which light has been shed by modern explorations, monumental inscriptions, manuscripts, historical records, and other things which science and genius have deciphered, – the surer we feel that the esoteric classes of India, Egypt, and China were more united in their views of Supreme Power and Intelligence than was generally supposed fifty years ago. The higher intellects of Asia, in all countries and ages, had more lofty ideas of God than we have a right to infer from the superstitions of the people generally. They had unenlightened ideas as to the grounds of forgiveness. But of the necessity of forgiveness and the favor of the Deity they had no doubt.

The philosophical opinions of these sages gave direction to a great religious movement. Matter was supposed to be inherently evil, and mind was thought to be inherently good. The seat of evil was placed in the body rather than in the heart and mind. Not the thoughts of men were evil, but the passions and appetites of the body. Hence the first thing for a good man to do was to bring the body – this seat of evil – under subjection, and, if possible, to eradicate the passions and appetites which enslave the body; and this was to be done by self-flagellations, penances, austerities, and solitude, – flight from the contaminating influences of the world. All Oriental piety assumed this ascetic form. The transition was easy to the sundering of domestic ties, to the suppression of natural emotions and social enjoyments. The devotee became austere, cold, inhuman, unsocial. He shunned the habitations of men. And the more desirous he was to essay a high religious life and thus rise in favor with God, the more severe and revengeful and unforgiving he made the Deity he adored, – not a compassionate Creator and Father, but an irresistible Power bent on his destruction. This degrading view of the Deity, borrowed from Paganism, tinged the subsequent theology of the Christian monks, and entered largely into the theology of the Middle Ages.

Such was the prevailing philosophy, or theosophy – both lofty and degraded – with which the Christian convert had to contend; not merely the shameless vices of the people, so open and flagrant as to call out disgust and indignation, but also the views which the more virtuous and religious of Pagan saints accepted and promulgated: and not saints alone, but those who made the greatest pretension to intellectual culture, like the Gnostics and Manicheans; those men who were the first to ensnare Saint Augustine, – specious, subtle, sophistical, as acute as the Brahmins of India. It was Eastern philosophy, false as we regard it, which created the most powerful institution that existed in Europe for above a thousand years, – an institution which all the learning and eloquence of the Reformers of the sixteenth century could not subvert, except in Protestant countries.

Now what, more specifically, were the ideas which the early monks borrowed from India, Persia, and Egypt, which ultimately took such a firm hold of the European mind?

One was the superior virtue of a life devoted to purely religious contemplation, and for the same end that animated the existence of fakirs and sofis. It was to escape the contaminating influence of matter, to rise above the wants of the body, to exterminate animal passions and appetites, to hide from a world which luxury corrupted. The Christian recluses were thus led to bury themselves in cells among the mountains and deserts, in dreary and uncomfortable caverns, in isolated retreats far from the habitation of men, – yea, among wild beasts, clothing themselves in their skins and eating their food, in order to commune with God more effectually, and propitiate His favor. Their thoughts were diverted from the miseries which they ought to have alleviated and the ignorance which they ought to have removed, and were concentrated upon themselves, not upon their relatives and neighbors. The cries of suffering humanity were disregarded in a vain attempt to practise doubtful virtues. How much good those pious recluses might have done, had their piety taken a more practical form! What missionaries they might have made, what self-denying laborers in the field of active philanthropy, what noble teachers to the poor and miserable! The conversion of the world to Christianity did not enter into their minds so much as the desire to swell the number of their communities. They only aimed at a dreamy pietism, – at best their own individual salvation, rather than the salvation of others. Instead of reaching to the beatific vision, they became ignorant, narrow, and visionary; and, when learned, they fought for words and not for things. They were advocates of subtile and metaphysical distinctions in theology, rather than of those practical duties and simple faith which primitive Christianity enjoined. Monastic life, no less than the schools of Alexandria, was influential in creating a divinity which gave as great authority to dogmas that are the result of intellectual deductions, as those based on direct and original declarations. And these deductions were often gloomy, and colored by the fears which were inseparable from a belief in divine wrath rather than divine love. The genius of monasticism, ancient and modern, is the propitiation of the Divinity who seeks to punish rather than to forgive. It invented Purgatory, to escape the awful burnings of an everlasting hell of physical sufferings. It pervaded the whole theology of the Middle Ages, filling hamlet and convent alike with an atmosphere of fear and wrath, and creating a cruel spiritual despotism. The recluse, isolated and lonely, consumed himself with phantoms, fancied devils, and "chimeras dire." He could not escape from himself, although he might fly from society. As a means of grace he sought voluntary solitary confinement, without nutritious food or proper protection from the heat and cold, clad in a sheepskin filled with dirt and vermin. What life could be more antagonistic to enlightened reason? What mistake more fatal to everything like self-improvement, culture, knowledge, happiness? And all for what? To strive after an impossible perfection, or the solution of insoluble questions, or the favor of a Deity whose attributes he misunderstood.

But this unnatural, unwise retirement was not the worst evil in the life of a primitive monk, with all its dreamy contemplation and silent despair. It was accompanied with the most painful austerities, – self-inflicted scourgings, lacerations, dire privations, to propitiate an angry deity, or to bring the body into a state which would be insensible to pain, or to exorcise passions which the imaginations inflamed. All this was based on penance, – self-expiation, – which entered so largely into the theogonies of the East, and which gave a gloomy form to the piety of the Middle Ages. This error was among the first to kindle the fiery protests of Luther. The repudiation of this error, and of its logical sequences, was one of the causes of the Reformation. This error cast its dismal shadow on the common life of the Middle Ages. You cannot penetrate the spirit of those centuries without a painful recognition of almost universal darkness and despair. How gloomy was a Gothic church before the eleventh century, with its dark and heavy crypt, its narrow windows, its massive pillars, its low roof, its cold, damp pavement, as if men went into that church to hide themselves and sing mournful songs, – the *Dies Irae* of monastic fear!

But the primitive monks, with all their lofty self-sacrifices and efforts for holy meditation, towards the middle of the fourth century, as their number increased from the anarchies and miseries of a falling empire, became quarrelsome, sometimes turbulent, and generally fierce and fanatical. They had to be governed. They needed some master mind to control them, and confine them to their religious duties. Then arose Basil, a great scholar, and accustomed to civilized life in the schools of Athens and Constantinople, who gave rules and laws to the monks, gathered them into communities and discouraged social isolation, knowing that the demons had more power over men when they were alone and idle.

This Basil was an extraordinary man. His ancestors were honorable and wealthy. He moved in the highest circle of social life, like Chrysostom. He was educated in the most famous schools. He travelled extensively like other young men of rank. His tutor was the celebrated Libanius, the greatest rhetorician of the day. He exhausted Antioch, Caesarea, and Constantinople, and completed his studies at Athens, where he formed a famous friendship with Gregory Nazianzen, which was as warm and devoted as that between Cicero and Atticus: these young men were the talk and admiration of Athens. Here, too, he was intimate with young Julian, afterwards the "Apostate" Emperor of Rome. Basil then visited the schools of Alexandria, and made the acquaintance of the great Athanasius, as well as of those monks who sought a retreat amid Egyptian solitudes. Here his conversion took place, and he parted with his princely patrimony for the benefit of the poor. He then entered the Church, and was successively ordained deacon and priest, while leading a monastic life. He retired among the mountains of Armenia, and made choice of a beautiful grove, watered with crystal streams, where he gave himself to study and meditation. Here he was joined by his friend Gregory Nazianzen and by enthusiastic admirers, who formed a religious fraternity, to whom he was a spiritual father. He afterwards was forced to accept the great See of Caesarea, and was no less renowned as bishop and orator than he had been as monk. Yet it is as a monk that he left the most enduring influence, since he made the first great change in monastic life, – making it more orderly, more industrious, and less fanatical.

He instituted or embodied, among others, the three great vows, which are vital to monastic institutions, – Poverty, Obedience, and Chastity. In these vows he gave the institution a more Christian and a less Oriental aspect. Monachism became more practical and less visionary and wild. It approximated nearer to the Christian standard. Submission to poverty is certainly a Christian virtue, if voluntary poverty is not. Chastity is a cardinal duty. Obedience is a necessity to all civilized life. It is the first condition of all government.

Moreover, these three vows seem to have been called for by the condition of society, and the prevalence of destructive views. Here Basil, – one of the commanding intellects of his day, and as learned and polished as he was pious, – like Jerome after him, proved himself a great legislator and administrator, including in his comprehensive view both Christian principles and the necessities of the times, and adapting his institution to both.

One of the most obvious, flagrant, and universal evils of the day was devotion to money-making in order to purchase sensual pleasures. It pervaded Roman life from the time of Augustus. The vow of poverty, therefore, was a stern, lofty, disdainful protest against the most dangerous and demoralizing evil of the Empire. It hurled scorn, hatred, and defiance on this overwhelming evil, and invoked the aid of Christianity. It was simply the earnest affirmation and belief that money could not buy the higher joys of earth, and might jeopardize the hopes of heaven. It called to mind the greatest examples; it showed that the great teachers of mankind, the sages and prophets of history, had disdained money as the highest good; that riches exposed men to great temptation, and lowered the standard of morality and virtue, – "how hardly shall they who have riches enter into the kingdom of God!" It appealed to the highest form of self-sacrifice; it arrayed itself against a vice which was undermining society. And among truly Christian people this new application of Christ's warnings against the dangers of wealth excited enthusiasm. It was like enlisting in the army of Christ against his greatest enemies. Make any duty clear and imperious to Christian people, and they will generally conform to it. So the world saw one of the most impressive spectacles of all history, – the rich giving up their possessions to follow the example and injunctions of Christ. It was the most signal test of Christian obedience. It prompted Paula, the richest lady of Christian antiquity, to devote the revenues of an entire city, which she owned, to the cause of Christ; and the approbation of Jerome, her friend, was a sufficient recompense.

The vow of Chastity was equally a protest against one of the characteristic vices of the day, as well as a Christian virtue. Luxury and pleasure-seeking lives had relaxed the restraints of home and the virtues of earlier days. The evils of concubinage were shameless and open throughout the empire, which led to a low estimate of female virtue and degraded the sex. The pagan poets held up woman as a subject of scorn and sarcasm. On no subject were the apostles more urgent in their exhortations than to a life of purity. To no greater temptation were the converts to Christianity subjected than the looseness of prevailing sentiments in reference to this vice. It stared everybody in the face. Basil took especial care to guard the monks from this prevailing iniquity, and made chastity a transcendent and fundamental virtue. He aimed to remove the temptation to sin. The monks were enjoined to shun the very presence of women. If they carried the system of non-intercourse too far, and became hard and unsympathetic, it was to avoid the great scandal of the age, – a still greater evil. To the monk was denied even the blessing of the marriage ties. Celibacy became a fundamental law of monachism. It was not to cement a spiritual despotism that Basil forbade marriage, but to attain a greater sanctity, – for a monk was consecrated to what was supposed to be the higher life. This law of celibacy was abused, and gradually was extended to all the clergy, secular as well as regular, but not till the clergy were all subordinated to the rule of an absolute Pope. It is the fate of all human institutions to become corrupt; but no institution of the Church has been so fatally perverted as that pertaining to the marriage of the clergy. Founded to promote purity of personal life, it was used to uphold the arms of spiritual despotism. It was the policy of Hildebrand.

The vow of Obedience, again, was made in special reference to the disintegration of society, when laws were feebly enforced and a central power was passing away. The discipline even of armies was relaxed. Mobs were the order of the day, even in imperial cities. Moreover, monks had long been insubordinate; they obeyed no head, except nominally; they were with difficulty ruled in their communities. Therefore obedience was made a cardinal virtue, as essential to the very existence of monastic institutions. I need not here allude to the perversion of this rule, – how it degenerated into a fearful despotism, and was made use of by ambitious popes, and finally by the generals of the Mendicant Friars and the Jesuits. All the rules of Basil were perverted from their original intention; but in his day they were called for.

About a century later the monastic system went through another change or development, when Benedict, a remarkable organizer, instituted on Monte Cassino, near Naples, his celebrated monastery (529, A.D.), which became the model of all the monasteries of the West. He reaffirmed the rules of Basil, but with greater strictness. He gave no new principles to monastic life; but he adapted it to the climate and institutions of the newly founded Gothic kingdoms of Europe. It became less Oriental; it was made more practical; it was invested with new dignity. The most visionary and fanatical of all the institutions of the East was made useful. The monks became industrious. Industry was recognized as a prime necessity even for men who had retired from the world. No longer were the labors of monks confined to the weaving of baskets, but they were extended to the comforts of ordinary life, – to the erection of stately buildings, to useful arts, the systematic cultivation of the land, to the accumulation of wealth, – not for individuals, but for their monasteries. Monastic life became less dreamy, less visionary, but more useful, recognizing the bodily necessities of men. The religious duties of monks were still dreary, monotonous, and gloomy, – long and protracted singing in the choir, incessant vigils, an unnatural silence at the table, solitary walks in the cloister, the absence of social pleasures, confinement to the precincts of their convents; but their convents became bee-hives of industry, and their lands were highly cultivated. The monks were hospitable; they entertained strangers, and gave a shelter to the persecuted and miserable. Their monasteries became sacred retreats, which were respected by those rude warriors who crushed beneath their feet the glories of ancient civilization. Nor for several centuries did the monks in their sacred enclosures give especial scandal. Their lives were spent in labors of a useful kind, alternated and relieved by devotional duties.

Hence they secured the respect and favor of princes and good men, who gave them lands and rich presents of gold and silver vessels. Their convents were unmolested and richly endowed, and these became enormously multiplied in every European country. Gradually they became so rich as to absorb the wealth of nations. Their abbots became great personages, being chosen from the ranks of princes and barons. The original poverty and social insignificance of monachism passed away, and the institution became the most powerful organization in Europe. It then aspired to political influence, and the lord abbots became the peers of princes and the ministers of kings. Their abbey churches, especially, became the wonder and the admiration of the age, both for size and magnificence. The abbey church of Cluny, in Burgundy, was five hundred and thirty feet long, and had stalls for two hundred monks. It had the appointment of one hundred and fifty parish priests. The church of Saint Albans, in England, is said to have been six hundred feet long; and that of Glastonbury, the oldest in England, five hundred and thirty. Peterborough's was over five hundred. The kings of England, both Saxon and Norman, were especial patrons of these religious houses. King Edgar founded forty-seven monasteries and richly endowed them; Henry I founded one hundred and fifty; and Henry II as many more. At one time there were seven hundred Benedictine abbeys in England, some of which were enormously rich, – like those of Westminster, St. Albans, Glastonbury, and Bury St. Edmunds, – and their abbots were men of the highest social and political distinction. They sat in Parliament as peers of the realm; they coined money, like feudal barons; they lived in great state and dignity. The abbot of Monte Cassino was duke and prince, and chancellor of the kingdom of the Two Sicilies. Tins celebrated convent had the patronage of four bishoprics, sixteen hundred and sixty-two churches, and possessed or controlled two hundred and fifty castles, four hundred and forty towns, and three hundred and thirty-six manors. Its revenues exceeded five hundred thousand ducats, so that the lord-abbot was the peer of the greatest secular princes. He was more powerful and wealthy, probably, than any archbishop in Europe. One of the abbots of St. Gall entered Strasburg with one thousand horsemen in his train. Whiting, of Glastonbury, entertained five hundred people of fashion at one time, and had three hundred domestic servants. "My vow of poverty," said another of these lordly abbots, – who generally rode on mules with gilded bridles and with hawks on their wrists, – "has given me ten thousand crowns a year; and my vow of obedience has raised me to the rank of a sovereign prince."

Among the privileges of these abbots was exemption from taxes and tolls; they were judges in the courts; they had the execution of all rents, and the supreme control of the income of the abbey lands. The revenues of Westminster and Glastonbury were equal to half a million of dollars a year in our money, considering the relative value of gold and silver. Glastonbury owned about one thousand oxen, two hundred and fifty cows, and six thousand sheep. Fontaine abbey possessed forty thousand acres of land. The abbot of Augia, in Germany, had a revenue of sixty thousand crowns, – several millions, as money is now measured. At one time the monks, with the other clergy, owned half of the lands of Europe. If a king was to be ransomed, it was they who furnished the money; if costly gifts were to be given to the Pope, it was they who made them. The value of the vessels of gold and silver, the robes and copes of silk and velvet, the chalices, the altar-pieces, and the shrines enriched with jewels, was inestimable. The feasts which the abbots gave were almost regal. At the installation of the abbot of St. Augustine, at Canterbury, there were consumed fifty-eight tuns of beer, eleven tuns of wine, thirty-one oxen, three hundred pigs, two hundred sheep, one thousand geese, one thousand capons, six hundred rabbits, nine thousand eggs, while the guests numbered six thousand people. Of the various orders of the Benedictines there have been thirty-seven thousand monasteries and one hundred and fifty thousand abbots. From the monks, twenty-one thousand have been chosen as bishops and archbishops, and twenty-eight have been elevated to the papal throne.

From these things, and others which may seem too trivial to mention, we infer the great wealth and power of monastic institutions, the most flourishing days of which were from the sixth century to the Crusades, beginning in the eleventh, when more than one hundred thousand monks acknowledged the rule of Saint Benedict. During this period of prosperity, when the vast abbey churches were built, and when abbots were great temporal as well as spiritual magnates, quite on an equality with the proudest feudal barons, we notice a marked decline in the virtues which had extorted the admiration of Europe. The Benedictines retained their original organization, they were bound by the same vows (as individuals, the monks were always poor), they wore the same dress, as they did centuries before, and they did not fail in their duties in the choir, – singing their mournful chants from two o'clock in the morning. But discipline was relaxed; the brothers strayed into unseemly places; they indulged in the pleasures of the table; they were sensual in their appearance; they were certainly ignorant, as a body; and they performed more singing than preaching or teaching. They lived for themselves rather than for the people. They however remained hospitable to the last. Their convents were hotels as well as bee-hives; any stranger could remain two nights at a convent without compensation and without being questioned. The brothers dined together at the refectory, according to the rules, on bread, vegetables, and a little meat; although it was noticed that they had a great variety in cooking eggs, which were turned and roasted and beaten up, and hardened and minced and fried and stuffed. It is said that subsequently they drank enormous quantities of beer and wine, and sometimes even to disgraceful excess. Their rules required them to keep silence at their meals; but their humanity got the better of them, and they have been censured for their hilarious and frivolous conversation, – for jests and stories and puns. Bernard accused the monks of degeneracy, of being given to the pleasures of the table, of loving the good things which they professed to scorn, – rare fish, game, and elaborate cookery.

That the monks sadly degenerated in morals and discipline, and even became objects of scandal, is questioned by no respectable historian. No one was more bitter and vehement in his denunciations of this almost universal corruption of monastic life than Saint Bernard himself, – the impersonation of an ideal monk. Hence reforms were attempted; and the Cluniacs and Cistercians and other orders arose, modelled after the original institution on Monte Cassino. These were only branches of the Benedictines. Their vows and habits and duties were the same. It would seem that the prevailing vices of the Benedictines, in their decline, were those which were fostered by great wealth, and consequent idleness and luxury. But at their worst estate the monks, or regular clergy, were no worse than the secular clergy, or parish priests, in their ordinary lives, and were more intelligent, – at least more learned. The ignorance of the secular clergy was notorious and scandalous. They could not even write letters of common salutation; and what little knowledge they had was extolled and exaggerated. It was confined to the acquisition of the Psalter by heart, while a little grammar, writing, and accounts were regarded as extraordinary. He who could write a few homilies, drawn from the Fathers, was a wonder and a prodigy. There was a total absence of classical literature.

But the monks, ignorant and degenerate as they were, guarded what little literature had escaped the ruin of the ancient civilization. They gave the only education the age afforded. There was usually a school attached to every convent, and manual labor was shortened in favor of students. Nor did the monks systematically and deliberately shut the door of knowledge against those inclined to study, for at that time there was no jealousy of learning; there was only indifference to it, or want of appreciation. The age was ignorant, and life was hard, and the struggle for existence occupied the thoughts of all. The time of the monks was consumed in alternate drudgeries and monotonous devotions. There was such a general intellectual torpor that scholars (and these were very few) were left at liberty to think and write as they pleased on the great questions of theology. There was such a general unanimity of belief, that the popes were not on the look-out for heresy. Nobody thought of attacking their throne. There was no jealousy about the reading of the Scriptures. Every convent had a small library, mostly composed of Lives of the saints, and of devout meditations and homilies; and the Bible was the greatest treasure of all, – the Vulgate of Saint Jerome, which was copied and illuminated by busy hands. In spite of the general ignorance, the monks relieved their dull lives by some attempts at art. This was the age of the most beautiful illuminated manuscripts. There was but little of doctrinal controversy, for the creed of the Church was settled; but pious meditations and the writings of noted saints were studied and accepted, – especially the works of Saint Augustine, who had fixed the thinking of the West for a thousand years. Pagan literature had but little charm until Aristotle was translated by Arabian scholars. The literature of the Church was puerile and extravagant, yet Christian, – consisting chiefly of legends of martyrs and Lives of saints. That literature has no charm to us, and can never be revived, indeed is already forgotten and neglected, as well it may be; but it gave unity to Christian belief, and enthroned the Christian heroes on the highest pedestal of human greatness. In the monasteries some one of the fraternity read aloud these Lives and Meditations, while the brothers worked or dined. There was no discussion, for all thought alike; and all sought to stimulate religious emotions rather than to quicken intellectual activity.

About half the time of the monks, in a well-regulated monastery, was given to singing and devotional exercises and religious improvement, and the other half to labors in the fields, or in painting or musical composition. So far as we know, the monks lived in great harmony, and were obedient to the commands of their superiors. They had a common object to live for, and had few differences in opinion on any subject. They did not enjoy a high life, but it was free from distracting pleasures. They affected great humility, with which spiritual pride was mingled, – not the arrogant pride of the dialectician, but the self-satisfied pride of the devotee. There was no religious hatred, except towards Turks and Saracens. The monk, in his narrowness and ignorance, may be repulsive to an enlightened age: he was not repulsive to his own, for he was not behind it either in his ideas or in his habits of life. In fact, the more repulsive the monk of the dark ages is to this generation, the more venerated he was by bishops and barons seven hundred years ago; which fact leads us to infer that the degenerate monk might be to us most interesting when he was most condemned by the reformers of his day, since he was more humane, genial, and free than his brethren, chained to the rigid discipline of his convent. Even a Friar Tuck is not so repulsive to us as an unsocial, austere, narrow-minded, and ignorant fanatic of the eleventh century.

But the monks were not to remain forever imprisoned in the castles of ignorance and despair. With the opening of the twelfth century light began to dawn upon the human mind. The intellectual monk, long accustomed to devout meditations, began to speculate on those subjects which had occupied his thoughts, – on God and His attributes, on the nature and penalty of sin, on redemption, on the Saviour, on the power of the will to resist evil, and other questions that had agitated the early Fathers of the Church. Then arose such men as Erigena, Roscelin, Bérenger, Lanfranc, Anselm, Bernard, and others, – all more or less orthodox, but inquiring and intellectual. It was within the walls of the cloister that the awakening began and the first impulse was given to learning and philosophy. The abbey of Bec, in Normandy, was the most distinguished of new intellectual centres, while Clairvaux and other princely abbeys had inmates as distinguished for meditative habits as for luxury and pride.

It was at this period, when the convents of Europe rejoiced in ample possessions, and their churches rivalled cathedrals in size and magnificence, and their abbots were lords and princes, – the palmy age of monastic institutions, chiefly of the Benedictine order, – that Saint Bernard, the greatest and best representative of Mediaeval monasticism, was born, 1091, at Fontaine, in Burgundy. He belonged to a noble family. His mother was as remarkable as Monica or Nonna. She had six sons and a daughter, whom she early consecrated to the Lord. Bernard was the third son. Like Luther, he was religiously inclined from early youth, and panted for monastic seclusion. At the age of twenty-three he entered the new monastery at Citeaux, which had been founded a few years before by Stephen Harding, an English saint, who revived the rule of Saint Benedict with still greater strictness, and was the founder of the Cistercian order, – a branch of the Benedictines. He entered this gloomy retreat, situated amid marshes and morasses, with no outward attractions like Cluny, but unhealthy and miserably poor, – the dreariest spot, perhaps, in Burgundy; and he entered at the head of thirty young men, of the noble class, among whom were four of his brothers who had been knights, and who presented themselves to the abbot as novices, bent on the severest austerities that human nature could support.

Bernard himself was a beautiful, delicate, refined young man, – tall, with flaxen hair, fair complexion, blue eyes from which shone a superhuman simplicity and purity. His noble birth would have opened to him the highest dignities of the Church, but he sought only to bear the yoke of Christ, and to be nailed to the cross; and he really became a common laborer wrapped in a coarse cowl, digging ditches and planting fields, – for such were the labors of the monks of Citeaux when not performing their religious exercises. But his disposition was as beautiful as his person, and he soon won the admiration of his brother monks, as he had won the affection of the knights of Burgundy. Such was his physical weakness that "nearly everything he took his stomach rejected;" and such was the rigor of his austerities that he destroyed the power of appetite. He could scarcely distinguish oil from wine. He satisfied his hunger with the Bible, and quenched his thirst with prayer. In three years he became famous as a saint, and was made Abbot of Clairvaux, – a new Cistercian convent, in a retired valley which had been a nest of robbers.

But his intellect was as remarkable as his piety, and his monastery became not only a model of monastic life, to which flocked men from all parts of Europe to study its rules, but the ascetic abbot himself became an oracle on all the questions of the day. So great was his influence that when he died, in 1153, he left behind one hundred and sixty monasteries formed after his model. He became the counsellor of kings and nobles, bishops and popes. He was summoned to attend councils and settle quarrels. His correspondence exceeded that of Jerome or Saint Augustine. He was sought for as bishop in the largest cities of France and Italy. He ruled Europe by the power of learning and sanctity. He entered into all the theological controversies of the day. He was the opponent of Abélard, whose condemnation he secured. He became a great theologian and statesman, as well as churchman. He incited the princes of Europe to a new crusade. His eloquence is said to have been marvellous; even the tones of his voice would melt to pity or excite to rage. With a long neck, like that of Cicero, and a trembling, emaciated frame, he preached with passionate intensity. Nobody could resist his eloquence. He could scarcely stand upright from weakness, yet he could address ten thousand men. He was an outspoken man, and reproved the greatest dignitaries with as much boldness as did Savonarola. He denounced the gluttony of monks, the avarice of popes, and the rapacity of princes. He held heresy in mortal hatred, like the Fathers of the fifth century. His hostility to Abélard was direful, since he looked upon him as undermining Christianity and extinguishing faith in the world. In his defence of orthodoxy he was the peer of Augustine or Athanasius. He absolutely abhorred the Mohammedans as the bitterest foes of Christendom, – the persecutors of pious pilgrims. He wandered over Europe preaching a crusade. He renounced the world, yet was compelled by the unanimous voice of his contemporaries to govern the world. He gave a new impulse to the order of Knights Templars. He was as warlike as he was humble. He would breathe the breath of intense hostility into the souls of crusaders, and then hasten back to the desolate and barren country in which Clairvaux was situated, rebuild his hut of leaves and boughs, and soothe his restless spirit with the study of the Song of Songs. Like his age, and like his institution, he was a great contradiction. The fiercest and most dogmatic of controversialists was the most gentle and loving of saints. His humanity was as marked as his fanaticism, and nothing could weaken it, – not even the rigors of his convent life. He wept at the sorrows of all who sought his sympathy or advice. On the occasion of his brother's death he endeavored to preach a sermon on the Canticles, but broke down as Jerome did at the funeral of Paula. He kept to the last the most vivid recollection of his mother; and every night, before he went to bed, he recited the seven Penitential Psalms for the benefit of her soul.

In his sermons and exhortations Bernard dwelt equally on the wrath of God and the love of Christ. Said he to a runaway Cistercian, "Thou fearest watchings, fasts, and manual labor, but these are light to one who thinks on eternal fire. The remembrance of the outer darkness takes away all horror from solitude. Place before thine eyes the everlasting weeping and gnashing of teeth, the fury of those flames which can never be extinguished" (the essence of the theology of the Middle Ages, – the fear of Hell, of a physical and eternal Hell of bodily torments, by which fear those ages were controlled). Bernard, the loveliest impersonation of virtue which those ages saw, was not beyond their ideas. He impersonated them, and therefore led the age and became its greatest oracle. The passive virtues of the Sermon on the Mount were united with the fiercest passions of religious intolerance and the most repulsive views of divine vengeance. That is the soul of monasticism, even as reformed by Harding, Alberic, and Bernard in the twelfth century, less human than in the tenth century, yet more intellectual.

Figure 5. St. Bernard Counselling Conrad III. *After the painting by Adolph Maria Mucha.*

The monks of Citeaux, of Morimond, of Pontigny, of Clairvaux, amid the wastes of a barren country, with their white habits and perpetual vigils and haircloth shirts and root dinners and hard labors in the field, were yet the counsellors and ministers of kings and the creators of popes, and incited the nations to the most bloody and unfortunate wars in the whole history of society, – I mean the Crusades. Some were great intellectual giants, yet all repelled scepticism as life repels death; all dwelt on the sufferings of the cross as a door through which the penitent and believing could surely enter heaven, yet based the justice of the infinite Father of Love on what, when it appeals to consciousness, seems to be the direst injustice. We cannot despise the Middle Ages, which produced such beatific and exalted saints, but we pity those dismal times when the great mass of the people had so little pleasure and comfort in this life, and such gloomy fears of the world to come; when life was made a perpetual sacrifice and abnegation of all the pleasures that are given us to enjoy, – to use and not to pervert. Hence monasticism was repulsive, even in its best ages, to enlightened reason, and fatal to all progress among nations, although it served a useful purpose when men were governed by fear alone, and when violence and strife and physical discomfort and ignorance and degrading superstitions covered the fairest portion of the earth with a funereal pall for more than a thousand years.

The thirteenth century saw a new development of monastic institutions in the creation of the Mendicant Friars, – especially the Dominicans and Franciscans, – monks whose mission it was to wander over Europe as preachers, confessors, and teachers. The Benedictines were too numerous, wealthy, and corrupt to be reformed. They had become a scandal; they had lost the confidence of good men. There were needed more active partisans of the Pope to sustain his authority; the new universities required abler professors; the cities sought more popular preachers; the great desired more intelligent confessors. The Crusades had created a new field of enterprise, and had opened to the eye of Europe a wider horizon of knowledge. The universities which had grown up around the cathedral schools had kindled a spirit of inquiry. Church architecture had become lighter, more cheerful, and more symbolic. The Greek philosophy had revealed a new method. The doctrines of the Church, if they did not require a new system, yet needed, or were supposed to need, the aid of philosophy, for the questions which the schoolmen discussed were so subtle and intricate that only the logic of Aristotle could make them clear.

Now the Mendicant orders entered with a zeal which has never been equalled, except by the Jesuits, into all the inquiries of the schools, and kindled a new religious life among the people, like the Methodists of the last century. They were somewhat similar to the Temperance reformers of the last fifty years. They were popular, zealous, intelligent, and religious. So great were their talents and virtues that they speedily spread over Europe, and occupied the principal pulpits and the most important chairs in the universities. Bonaventura, Albertus Magnus, Thomas Aquinas, and Duns Scotus were the great ornaments of these new orders. Their peculiarity – in contrast with the old orders – was, that they wandered from city to city and village to village at the command of their superiors. They had convents, like the other monks; but they professed absolute poverty, went barefooted, and submitted to increased rigors. Their vows were essentially those of the Benedictines. In less than a century, however, they too had degenerated, and were bitterly reproached for their vagabond habits and the violation of their vows. Their convents had also become rich, like those of the Benedictines. It was these friars whom Chaucer ridiculed, and against whose vices Wyclif declaimed. Yet they were retained by the popes for their services in behalf of ecclesiastical usurpation. It was they who were especially chosen to peddle indulgences. Their history is an impressive confirmation of the tendency of all human institutions to degenerate. It would seem that the mission of the Benedictines had been accomplished in the thirteenth century, and that of the Dominicans and Franciscans in the fourteenth.

But monasticism, in any of its forms, ceased to have a salutary influence on society when the darkness of the Middle Ages was dispersed. It is peculiarly a Mediaeval institution. As a Mediaeval institution, it conferred many benefits on the semi-barbarians of Europe. As a whole, considering the shadows of ignorance and superstition which veiled Christendom, and the evils which violence produced, its influence was beneficent.

Among the benefits which monastic institutions conferred, at least indirectly, may be mentioned the counteracting influence they exerted against the turbulence and tyranny of baronial lords, whose arrogance and extortion they rebuked; they befriended the peasantry; they enabled poor boys to rise; they defended the doctrine that the instructors of mankind should be taken from all classes alike; they were democratic in their sympathies, while feudal life produced haughtiness and scorn; they welcomed scholars from the humblest ranks; they beheld in peasants' children souls which could be ennobled. Though abbots were chosen generally from the upper classes, yet the ordinary monks sprang from the peasantry. For instance, a peasant's family is deprived of its head; he has been killed while fighting for a feudal lord. The family are doomed to misery and hardship. No aristocratic tears are shed for them; they are no better than dogs or cattle. The mother is heartbroken. Not one of her children can ordinarily rise from their abject position; they can live and breathe the common air, and that is all. They are unmolested in their mud huts, if they will toil for the owner of their village at the foot of the baronial castle. But one of her sons is bright and religious. He attracts the attention of a sympathetic monk, whose venerable retreat is shaded with trees, adorned with flowers, and seated perhaps on the side of a murmuring stream, whose banks have been made fertile by industry and beautiful with herds of cattle and flocks of sheep. He urges the afflicted mother to consecrate him to the service of the Church; and the boy enters the sanctuary and is educated according to the fashion of the age, growing up a sad, melancholy, austere, and pharisaical member of the fraternity, whose spirit is buried in a gloomy grave of ascetic severities, He passes from office to office. In time he becomes the prior of his convent, – possibly its abbot, the equal of that proud baron in whose service his father lost his life, the controller of innumerable acres, the minister of kings. How, outside the Church, could he thus have arisen? But in the monastery he is enabled, in the most aristocratic age of the world, to rise to the highest of worldly dignities. And he is a man of peace and not of war. He hates war; he seeks to quell dissensions and quarrels. He believes that there is a higher than the warrior's excellence. Monachism recognized what feudalism did not, – the claims of man as man. In this respect it was human and sympathetic. It furnished a retreat from misery and oppression. It favored contemplative habits and the passive virtues, so much needed in turbulent times. Whatever faults the monks had, it must be allowed that they alleviated sufferings, and presented the only consolation that their gloomy and iron age afforded. In an imperfect manner their convents answered the purpose of our modern hotels, hospitals, and schools. It was benevolence, charity, and piety which the monks aimed to secure, and which they often succeeded in diffusing among people more wretched and ignorant than themselves.

AUTHORITIES

Saint Bernard's Works, especially the Epistles
Mabillon
Hélyot's *Histoire des Ordres Monastiques*
Dugdale's *Monasticon*
Döring's *Geschichte der Monchsorden*
Montalembert's *Les Moines d'Occident*
Milman's *Latin Christianity*
Morison's *Life and Times of Saint Bernard*
Lives of the English Saints
Stephen Harding
Histoire d'Abbaye de Cluny, par M.P. Lorain
Neander's *Church History*
Butler's *Lives of the Saints*
Vaughan's *Life of Thomas Aquinas*
Digby's *Ages of Faith*.

Chapter 5

SAINT ANSELM: MEDIAEVAL THEOLOGY

A.D. 1033-1109

The Middle Ages produced no more interesting man than Anselm, Abbot of Bec and Archbishop of Canterbury, – not merely a great prelate, but a great theologian, resplendent in the virtues of monastic life and in devotion to the interests of the Church. He was one of the first to create an intellectual movement in Europe, and to stimulate theological inquiries.

Anselm was born at Aosta, in Italy, 1033, and he died in 1109, at the age of 76. He was therefore the contemporary of Hildebrand, of Lanfranc, of Bérenger, of Roscelin, of Henry IV of Germany, of William the Conqueror, of the Countess Matilda, and of Urban II. He saw the first Crusade, the great quarrel about investitures and the establishment of the Normans in England. Aosta was on the confines of Lombardy and Burgundy, in a mountainous district, amid rich cornfields and fruitful vines and dark, waving chestnuts, in sight of lofty peaks with their everlasting snow. Anselm belonged to a noble but impoverished family; his father was violent and unthrifty, but his mother was religious and prudent. He was by nature a student, and early was destined to monastic life, – the only life favorable to the development of the intellect in a rude and turbulent age. I have already alluded to the general ignorance of the clergy in those times. There were no schools of any note at this period, and no convents where learning was cultivated beyond the rudiments of grammar and arithmetic and the writings of the Fathers. The monks could read and talk in Latin, of a barbarous sort, – which was the common language of the learned, so far as any in that age could be called learned.

The most famous place in Europe, at that time, where learning was cultivated, was the newly-founded abbey of Bec in Normandy, under the superintendence of the Archbishop of Rouen, of which Lanfranc of Pavia was the prior. It was the first abbey in Normandy to open the door of learning to the young and inquiring minds of Western Europe. It was a Benedictine abbey, as severe in its rules as that of Clairvaux. It would seem that the fame of this convent, and of Lanfranc its presiding genius (afterwards the great Archbishop of Canterbury), reached the ears of Anselm; so that on the death of his parents he wandered over the Alps, through Burgundy, to this famous school, where the best teaching of the day was to be had. Lanfranc cordially welcomed his fellow-countryman, then at the age of twenty-six, to his retreat; and on his removal three years afterwards to the more princely abbey of St. Stephen in Caen, Anselm succeeded him as prior. Fifteen years later he became abbot, and ruled the abbey for fifteen years, during which time Lanfranc – the mutual friend of William the Conqueror and the great Hildebrand – became Archbishop of Canterbury.

During this seclusion of thirty years in the abbey of Bec, Anselm gave himself up to theological and philosophical studies, and became known both as a profound and original thinker and a powerful supporter of ecclesiastical authority. The scholastic age, – that is, the age of dialectics, when theology invoked the aid of philosophy to establish the truths of Christianity, – had not yet begun; but Anselm may be regarded as a pioneer, the precursor of Thomas Aquinas, since he was led into important theological controversies to establish the creed of Saint Augustine. It was not till several centuries after his death, however, that his remarkable originality of genius was fully appreciated. He anticipated Descartes in his argument to prove the existence of God. He is generally regarded as the profoundest intellect among the early schoolmen, and the most original that appeared in the Church after Saint Augustine. He was not a popular preacher like Saint Bernard, but he taught theology with marvellous lucidity to the monks who sought the genial quiet of his convent. As an abbot he was cheerful and humane, almost to light-heartedness, frank and kind to everybody, – an exception to most of the abbots of his day, who were either austere and rigid, or convivial and worldly. He was a man whom everybody loved and trusted, yet one not unmindful of his duties as the supreme ruler of his abbey, enforcing discipline, while favoring relaxation. No monk ever led a life of higher meditation than he; absorbed not in a dreamy and visionary piety, but in intelligent inquiries as to the grounds of religious belief. He was a true scholar of the Platonic and Augustinian school; not a dialectician like Albertus Magnus and Abélard, but a man who went beyond words to things, and seized on realities rather than forms; not given to disputations and the sports of logical tournaments, but to solid inquiries after truth. The universities had not then arisen, but a hundred years later he would have been their ornament, like Thomas Aquinas and Bonaventura.

Like other Norman abbeys, the abbey of Bec had after the Conquest received lands in England, and it became one of the duties of the abbot to look after its temporal interests. Hence Anselm was obliged to make frequent visits to England, where his friendship with Lanfranc was renewed, and where he made the acquaintance of distinguished prelates and abbots and churchmen, among others of Eadmer, his future biographer. It seems that he also won the hearts of the English nobility by his gentleness and affability, so that they rendered to him uncommon attentions, not only as a great ecclesiastic who had no equal in learning, but as a man whom they could not help loving.

The life of Anselm very nearly corresponded with that of the Conqueror, who died in 1087, being five years older; and he was Abbot of Bec during the whole reign of William as King of England. There was nothing particularly memorable in his life as abbot aside from his theological studies. It was not until he was elevated to the See of Canterbury, on the death of Lanfranc, that his memorable career became historical. He anticipated Thomas Becket in his contest to secure the liberties of the Church against the encroachments of the Norman kings. The cause of the one was the cause of the other; only, Anselm was trained in monastic seclusion, and Becket amid the tumults and intrigues of a court. The one was essentially an ecclesiastic and theologian; the other a courtier and statesman. The former was religious, and the latter secular in his habits and duties. Yet both fought the same great battle, the essential principle of which was the object of contention between the popes and the emperors of Germany, – that pertaining to the right of investiture, which may be regarded, next to the Crusades, as the great outward event of the twelfth century. That memorable struggle for supremacy was not brought to a close until Innocent III made the kings of the earth his vassals, and reigned without a rival in Christendom. Gregory VII had fought heroically, but he died in exile, leaving to future popes the fruit of his transcendent labors.

Lanfranc died in 1089, – the ablest churchman of the century next to the great Hildebrand, his master. It was through his influence that England was more closely allied with Rome, and that those fetters were imposed by the popes which the ablest of the Norman kings were unable to break. The Pope had sanctioned the atrocious conquest of England by the Normans – beneficially as it afterwards turned out – only on the condition that extraordinary powers should be conferred on the Archbishop of Canterbury, his representative in enforcing the papal claims, who thus became virtually independent of the king, – a spiritual monarch of such dignity that he was almost equal to his sovereign in authority. There was no such See in Germany and France as that of Canterbury. Its mighty and lordly metropolitan had the exclusive right of crowning the king. To him the Archbishop of York, once his equal, had succumbed. He was not merely primate, but had the supreme control of the Church in England. He could depose prelates and excommunicate the greatest personages; he enjoyed enormous revenues; he was vicegerent of the Pope.

Loth was William to concede such great powers to the Pope, but he could not be King of England without making a king of Canterbury. So he made choice of Lanfranc – then Abbot of St. Stephen, the most princely of the Norman convents – for the highest ecclesiastical dignity in his realm, and perhaps in Europe after the papacy itself. Lanfranc was his friend, and also the friend of Hildebrand; and no collision took place between them, for neither could do without the other. William was willing to waive some of his prerogatives as a sovereign for such a kingdom as England, which made him the most powerful monarch in Western Europe, since he ruled the fairest part of France and the whole British realm, the united possession of both Saxons and Danes, with more absolute authority than any feudal sovereign at that time possessed. His victorious knights were virtually a standing army, bound to him with more than feudal loyalty, since he divided among them the lands of the conquered Saxons, and gave to their relatives the richest benefices of the Church. With the aid of an Italian prelate, bound in allegiance to the Pope, he hoped to cement his conquest. Lanfranc did as he wished, – removed the Saxon bishops, and gave their sees to Normans. Since Dunstan, no great Saxon bishop had arisen. The Saxon bishops were feeble and indolent, and were not capable of making an effective resistance. But Lanfranc was even more able than Dunstan, – a great statesman as well as prelate. He ruled England as grand justiciary in the absence of the monarch, and was thus viceregent of the kingdom. But while he despoiled the Saxon prelates, he would suffer no royal spoliation of the Norman bishops. He even wrested away from Odo, half-brother of the Conqueror, the manors he held as Count of Kent, which originally belonged to the See of Canterbury. Thus was William, with all his greed and ambition, kept in check by the spiritual monarch he had himself made so powerful.

On the death of this great prelate, all eyes were turned to Anselm as his successor, who was then Abbot of Bec, absorbed in his studies. But William Rufus, who had in the meantime succeeded to the throne of the Conqueror, did not at once appoint anyone to the vacant See, since he had seized and used its revenues to the scandal of the nation and the indignation of the Church. For five years there was no primate in England and no Archbishop of Canterbury. At last, what seemed to be a mortal sickness seized the King, and in the near prospect of death he summoned Anselm to his chamber and conferred upon him the exalted dignity, – which Anselm refused to accept, dreading the burdens of the office, and preferring the quiet life of a scholar in his Norman abbey. Like Thomas Aquinas, in the next century, who refused the archbishopric of Naples to pursue his philosophical studies in Paris, Anselm declined the primacy of the Church in England, with its cares and labors and responsibilities, that he might be unmolested in his theological inquiries. He understood the position in which he should be placed, and foresaw that he should be brought in collision with his sovereign if he would faithfully guard the liberties and interests of the Church. He was a man of peace and meditation, and hated conflict, turmoil, and active life. He knew that one of the requirements of a great prelate is to have business talents, more necessary perhaps than eloquence or learning. At last, however, on the pressing solicitation of the Pope, the King, and the clergy, he consented to mount the throne of Lanfranc, on condition that the temporalities, privileges, and powers of the See of Canterbury should not be attacked. The crafty and rapacious, but now penitent monarch, thinking he was about to die, and wishing to make his peace with Heaven, made all the concessions required; and the quiet monk and doctor, whom everybody loved and revered, was enthroned and consecrated as the spiritual monarch of England.

Anselm's memorable career as bishop began in peace, but was soon clouded by a desperate quarrel with his sovereign, as he had anticipated. This learned and peace-loving theologian was forced into a contest which stands out in history like the warfare between Hildebrand and Henry IV. It was the beginning of that fierce contest in England which was made memorable by the martyrdom of Becket. Anselm, when consecrated, was sixty years of age, – a period of life when men are naturally timid, cautious, and averse to innovations, quarrels, and physical discomforts.

The friendly relations between William Rufus and Anselm were disturbed when the former sought to exact large sums of money from his subjects to carry on war against his brother Robert. Among those who were expected to make heavy contributions, in the shape of presents, was the Archbishop of Canterbury, whose revenues were enormous, – perhaps the largest in the realm next to those of the King. Anselm offered as his contribution five hundred marks, what would now be equal to £10,000, – a large sum in those days, but not as much as the Norman sovereign expected. In indignation he refused the present, which seemed to him meagre, especially since it was accompanied with words of seeming reproof; for Anselm had said that "a free gift, which he meant this to be, was better than a forced and servile contribution." The King then angrily bade him begone;

"that he wanted neither his money nor his scolding." The courtiers tried to prevail on the prelate to double the amount of his present, and thus regain the royal favor; but he firmly refused to do this, since it looked to him like a corrupt bargain. Anselm, having distributed among the poor the money which the King had refused, left the court as soon as the Christmas festival was over and retired to his diocese, preserving his independence and dignity.

A breach had not been made, but the irritation was followed by coolness; and this was increased when Anselm desired to have the religious posts filled the revenues of which the King had too long enjoyed, and when, in addition, he demanded a council of bishops to remedy the disorders and growing evils of the kingdom. This council the angry King refused with a sneer, saying, "he would call the council when he himself pleased, not when Anselm pleased." As to the filling the vacancies of the abbeys, he further replied: "What are abbeys to *you*? Are they not *mine*? Go and do what you like with your farms, and I will do what I please with my abbeys." So they parted, these two potentates, the King saying to his companions, "I hated him yesterday; I hate him more to-day; and I shall hate him still more to-morrow. I refuse alike his blessings and his prayers." His chief desire now was to get rid of the man he had elevated to the throne of Canterbury. It may be observed that it was not the Pope who made this appointment, but the King of England. Yet, by the rules long established by the popes and accepted by Christendom, it was necessary that an archbishop, before he could fully exercise his spiritual powers, should go to Rome and receive at the hands of the Pope his *pallium*, or white woolen stole, as the badge of his office and dignity. Lanfranc had himself gone to Rome for this purpose, – and a journey from Canterbury to Rome in the eleventh century was no small undertaking, being expensive and fatiguing. But there were now at Rome two rival popes. Which one should Anselm recognize? France and Normandy acknowledged Urban. England was undecided whether it should be Urban or Clement. William would probably recognize the one that Anselm did not, for a rupture was certain, and the King sought for a pretext.

So when the Archbishop asked leave of the King to go to Rome, according to custom, William demanded to know to which of these two popes he would apply for his pallium. "To Pope Urban," was the reply.

"But," said the King, "him I have not acknowledged; and no man in England may acknowledge a pope without my leave." At first view the matter was a small one comparatively, whether Urban was or was not the true pope. The real point was whether the King of England should accept as pope the man whom the Archbishop recognized, or whether the Archbishop should acknowledge him whom the King had accepted. This could be settled only by a grand council of the nation, to whom the matter should be submitted, – virtually a parliament. This council, demanded by Anselm, met in the royal castle of Rockingham, 1095, composed of nobles, bishops, and abbots. A large majority of the council were in the interests of the King, and the subject at issue was virtually whether the King or the prelate was supreme in spiritual matters, – a point which the Conqueror had ceded to Lanfranc and Hildebrand. This council insulted and worried the primate, and sought to frighten him into submission. But submission was to yield up the liberties of the Church. The intrepid prelate was not prepared for this, and he appealed from the council to the Pope, thereby putting himself in antagonism to the King and a majority of the peers of the realm. The King was exasperated, but foiled, while the council was perplexed. The Bishop of Durham saw no solution but in violence; but violence to the metropolitan was too bold a measure to be seriously entertained. The King hoped that Anselm would resign, as his situation was very unpleasant.

But resignation would be an act of cowardice, and would result in the appointment of an archbishop favorable to the encroachments of the King, who doubtless aimed at the subversion of the liberties of the Church and greater independence. Five centuries later the sympathies of England would have been on his side. But the English nation felt differently in the eleventh century. All Christendom sympathized with the Pope; for this resistance of Anselm to the King was the cause of the popes themselves against the monarchs of Europe. Anselm simply acted as the vicegerent of the Pope. To submit to the dictation of the King in a spiritual matter was to undermine the authority of Rome. I do not attempt to settle the merits of the question, but only to describe the contest. To settle the merits of such a question is to settle the question whether the papal power in its plenitude was good or evil for society in the Middle Ages.

One thing seems certain, that the King was thus far foiled by the firmness of a churchman, – the man who had passed the greater part of his life in a convent, studying and teaching theology; one of the mildest and meekest men ever elevated to high ecclesiastical office. Anselm was sustained by the power of conscience, by an imperative sense of duty, by allegiance to his spiritual head. He indeed owed fealty to the King, but only for the temporalities of his See. His paramount obligations as an archbishop were, according to all the ideas of his age, to the supreme pontiff of Christendom. Doubtless his life would have been easier and more pleasant had he been more submissive to the King. He could have brought all the bishops, as well as barons, to acknowledge the King's supremacy; but on his shoulders was laid the burden of sustaining ecclesiastical authority in England. He had anticipated this burden, and would have joyfully been exempted from its weight. But having assumed it, perhaps against his will, he had only one course to pursue, according to the ideas of the age; and this was to maintain the supreme authority of the Pope in England in all spiritual matters. It was remarkable that at this stage of the contest the barons took his side, and the bishops took the side of the King. The barons feared for their own privileges should the monarch be successful; for they knew his unscrupulous and tyrannical character, – that he would encroach on these and make himself as absolute as possible. The bishops were weak and worldly men, and either did not realize the gravity of the case or wished to gain the royal favor. They were nearly all Norman nobles, who had been under obligations to the crown.

The King, however, understood and appreciated his position. He could not afford to quarrel with the Pope; he dared not do violence to the primate of the realm. So he dissembled his designs and restrained his wrath, and sought to gain by cunning what he could not openly effect by the exercise of royal power. He sent messengers and costly gifts to Rome, such as the needy and greedy servants of the servants of God rarely disdained. He sought to conciliate the Pope, and begged, as a favor, that the pallium should be sent to him as monarch, and given by him, with the papal sanction, to the Archbishop, – the name of Anselm being suppressed. This favor, being bought by potent arguments, was granted unwisely, and the pallium was sent to William with the greatest secrecy. In return, the King acknowledged the claims of Urban as pope. So Anselm did not go to Rome for the emblem of his power.

The King, having succeeded thus far, then demanded of the Pope the deposition of Anselm. He could not himself depose the archbishop. He could elevate him, but not remove him; he could make, but not unmake. Only he who held the keys of Saint Peter, who was armed with spiritual omnipotence, could reverse his own decrees and rule arbitrarily. But for any king to expect that the Pope would part with the ablest defender of the liberties of the Church, and disgrace him for being faithful to papal interests, was absurd. The Pope may have used smooth words, but was firm in the uniform policy of all his predecessors.

Meanwhile political troubles came so thick and heavy on the King, some of his powerful nobles being in open rebellion, that he felt it necessary to dissemble and defer the gratification of his vengeance on the man he hated more than any personage in England. He pretended to restore Anselm to favor. "Bygones should be bygones." The King and the Archbishop sat at dinner at Windsor with friends and nobles, while an ironical courtier pleasantly quoted the Psalmist, "Behold, how good and how pleasant it is for brethren to dwell together in unity!"

The King now supposed that Anselm would receive the pallium at his royal hands, which the prelate warily refused to accept. The subject was carefully dropped, but as the pallium was Saint Peter's gift, it was brought to Canterbury and placed upon the altar, and the Archbishop condescended, amid much pomp and ceremony, to take it thence and put it on, – a sort of puerile concession for the sake of peace. The King, too, wishing conciliation for the present, until he had gained the possession of Normandy from his brother Robert, who had embarked in the Crusades, and feeling that he could ill afford to quarrel with the highest dignitary of his kingdom until his political ambition was gratified, treated Anselm with affected kindness, until his ill success with the Celtic Welsh put him in a bad humor and led to renewed hostility. He complained that Anselm had not furnished his proper contingent of forces for the conquest of Wales, and summoned him to his court. In a secular matter like this, Anselm as a subject had no remedy.

Refusal to appear would be regarded as treason and rebellion. Yet he neglected to obey the summons, perhaps fearing violence, and sought counsel from the Pope. He asked permission to go to Rome. The request was angrily refused. Again he renewed his request, and again it was denied him, with threats if he departed without leave. The barons, now against him, thought he had no right to leave his post; the bishops even urged him not to go. To all of whom he replied: "You wish me to swear that I will not appeal to Saint Peter. To swear this is to forswear Saint Peter; to forswear Saint Peter is to forswear Christ." At last it seems that the King gave a reluctant consent, but with messages that were insulting; and Anselm, with a pilgrim's staff, took leave of his monks, for the chapter of Canterbury was composed of monks, set out for Dover, and reached the continent in safety.

"Thus began," says Church, "the system of appeals to Rome, and of inviting foreign interference in the home affairs of England; and Anselm was the beginning of it." But however unfortunate it ultimately proved, it was in accordance with the ideas and customs of the Middle Ages, without which the papal power could not have been so successfully established. And I take the ground that the Papacy was an institution of which very much may be said in its favor in the dark ages of European society, especially in restraining the tyranny of kings and the turbulence of nobles. Governments are based on expediencies and changing circumstances, not on immutable principles or divine rights. If this be not true, we are driven to accept as the true form of government that which was recognized by Christ and his disciples. The feudal kings of Europe claimed a "divine right," and professed to reign by the "grace of God." Whence was this right derived? If it can be substantiated, on what claim rests the sovereignty of the people? Are not popes and kings and bishops alike the creation of circumstances, good or evil inventions, as they meet the wants of society?

Anselm felt himself to be the subject of the Pope as well as of the King, but that, as a priest, his supreme allegiance should be given to the Pope, as the spiritual head of the Church and vicegerent of Christ upon the earth. We differ from him in his view of the claims of the Pope, which he regarded as based on immutable truth and the fiat of Almighty power, – even as Richelieu looked upon the imbecile king whom he served as reigning by divine right. The Protestant Reformation demolished the claims of the spiritual potentate, as the French Revolution swept away the claims of the temporal monarch. The "logic of events" is the only logic which substantiates the claims of rulers; and this logic means, in our day, constitutional government in politics and private judgment in religion, – the free choice of such public servants, whatever their titles of honor, in State and Church, as the exigencies and circumstances of society require. The haughtiest of the popes, in the proudest period of their absolute ascendancy, never rejected their early title, – "servant of the servants of God." Wherever there is real liberty among the people, whose sovereignty is acknowledged as the source of power, the ruler *is* a servant of the people and not their tyrant, however great the authority which they delegate to him, which they alone may continue or take away. Absolute authority, delegated to kings or popes by God, was the belief of the Middle Ages; limited authority, delegated to rulers by the people, is the idea of our times. What the next invention in government may be no one can tell; but whatever it be, it will be in accordance with the ideas and altered circumstances of progressive ages. No one can anticipate or foresee the revolutions in human thought, and therefore in human governments, "till He shall come whose right it is to reign."

Taking it, then, to be the established idea of the Middle Ages that all ecclesiastics owed supreme allegiance to the visible head of the Church, no one can blame Anselm for siding with the Pope, rather than with his sovereign, in spiritual matters. He would have been disloyal to his conscience if he had not been true to his clerical vows of obedience. Conscience may be unenlightened, yet take away the power of conscience and what would become of our world? What is a man without a conscience? He is a usurper, a tyrant, a libertine, a spendthrift, a robber, a miser, an idler, a trifler, – whatever he is tempted to be; a supreme egotist, who says in his heart, "There is no God." The Almighty Creator placed this instinct in the soul of man to prevent the total eclipse of faith, and to preserve some allegiance to Him, some guidance in the trials and temptations of life. We lament a perverted conscience; yet better this than no conscience at all, a voice silenced by the combined forces of evil. A man *must* obey this voice. It is the wisdom of the ages to make it harmonious with eternal right; it is the power of God to remove or weaken the assailing forces which pervert or silence it.

See, then, this gentle, lovable, and meditative scholar – not haughty like Dunstan, not arrogant like Becket, not sacerdotal like Ambrose, not passionate like Chrysostom, but meek as Moses is said to have been before Pharaoh (although I never could see this distinguishing trait in the Hebrew leader) – yet firmly and heroically braving the wrath of the sovereign who had elevated him, and pursuing his toilsome journey to Rome to appeal to justice against injustice, to law against violence. He reached the old capital of the world in midwinter, after having spent Christmas in that hospitable convent where Hildebrand had reigned, and which was to shield the persecuted Abélard from the wrath of his ecclesiastical tormentors. He was most honorably received by the Pope, and lodged in the Lateran, as the great champion of papal authority. Vainly did he beseech the Pope to relieve him from his dignities and burdens; for such a man could not be spared from the exalted post in which he had been placed. Peace-loving as he was, his destiny was to fight battles.

In the following year Pope Urban died; and in the following year William Rufus himself was accidentally killed in the New Forest. His death was not much lamented, he having proved hard, unscrupulous, cunning, and tyrannical. At this period the kings of England reigned with almost despotic power, independent of barons and oppressive to the people. William had but little regard for the interests of the kingdom. He built neither churches nor convents, but Westminster Hall was the memorial of his iron reign.

Much was expected of Henry I, who immediately recalled Anselm from Lyons, where he was living in voluntary exile. He returned to Canterbury, with the firm intention of reforming the morals of the clergy and resisting royal encroachments. Henry was equally resolved on making bishops as well as nobles subservient to him. Of course harmony and concord could not long exist between such men, with such opposite views. Even at the first interview of the King with the Archbishop at Salisbury, he demanded a renewal of homage by a new act of investiture, which was virtually a continuance of the quarrel. It was, however, mutually agreed that the matter should be referred to the new pope. Anselm, on his part, knew that the appeal was hopeless; while the King wished to gain time. It was not long before the answer of Pope Pascal came. He was willing that Henry should have many favors, but not this. Only the head of the Church could bestow the emblems of spiritual authority. On receiving the papal reply the King summoned his nobles and bishops to his court, and required that Anselm should acknowledge the right of the King to invest prelates with the badges of spiritual authority. The result was a second embassy to the Pope, of more distinguished persons, – the Archbishop of York and two other prelates. The Pope, of course, remained inflexible. On the return of the envoys a great council was assembled in London, and Anselm again was required to submit to the King's will. It seems that the Pope, from motives of policy (for all the popes were reluctant to quarrel with princes), had given the envoys assurance that, so long as Henry was a good king, he should not be disturbed, and that oral declarations were contrary to his written documents.

This contradiction and double dealing required a new embassy to Rome; but in the meantime the King gave the See of Salisbury to his chancellor, and that of Hereford to the superintendent of his larder. When the answer of the Pope was finally received, it was found that he indignantly disavowed the verbal message, and excommunicated the three prelates as liars. But the King was not disconcerted. He suddenly appeared at Canterbury, and told Anselm that further opposition would be followed by the royal enmity; yet, mollifying his wrath, requested Anselm himself to go to Rome and do what he could with the Pope. Anselm assured him that he could do nothing to the prejudice of the Church. He departed, however, the King obviously wishing him out of the way.

The second journey of Anselm to Rome was a perpetual ovation, but was of course barren of results. The Pope remained inflexible, and Anselm prepared to return to England; but, from the friendly hints of the prelates who accompanied him, he sojourned again at Lyons with his friend the archbishop. Both the Pope and the King had compromised; Anselm alone was straightforward and fearless. As a consequence his revenues were seized, and he remained in exile. He had been willing to do the Pope's bidding, had he made an exception to the canons; but so long as the law remained in force he had nothing to do but conform to it. He remained in

Lyons a year and a half, while Henry continued his negotiations with Pascal; but finding that nothing was accomplished, Anselm resolved to excommunicate his sovereign. The report of this intention alarmed Henry, then preparing for a decisive conflict with his brother Robert. The excommunication would at least be inconvenient; it might cost him his crown. So he sought an interview with Anselm at the castle of l'Aigle, and became outwardly reconciled, and restored to him his revenues.

Figure 6. Canterbury Cathedral. *From a photograph*.

"The end of the dreary contest came at last, in 1107, after vexatious delays and intrigues." It was settled by compromise, – as most quarrels are settled, as most institutions are established. Outwardly the King yielded. He agreed, in an assembly of nobles, bishops, and abbots at London, that henceforth no one should be invested with bishopric or abbacy, either by king or layman, by the customary badges of ring and crosier. Anselm, on his part, agreed that no prelate should be refused consecration who was nominated by the King. The appointment of bishops remained with the King;

but the consecration could be withheld by the primate, since he alone had the right to give the badges of office, without which spiritual functions could not be lawfully performed. It was a moral victory to the Church, but the victory of an unpopular cause. It cemented the power of the Pope, while freedom from papal interference has ever been dear to the English nation.

When Anselm had fought this great fight he died, 1109, in the sixteenth year of his reign as primate of the Church in England, and was buried, next to Lanfranc, in his abbey church. His career outwardly is memorable only for this contest, which was afterwards renewed by Thomas Becket with a greater king than either William Rufus or Henry I. It is interesting, since it was a part of the great struggle between the spiritual and temporal powers for two hundred years, – from Hildebrand to Innocent III. This was only one of the phases of the quarrel, – one of the battles of a long war, – not between popes and emperors, as in Germany and Italy, but between a king and the vicegerent of a pope; a king and his subject, the one armed with secular, the other with spiritual, weapons. It was only brought to an end by an appeal to the fears of men, – the dread of excommunication and consequent torments in hell, which was the great governing idea of the Middle Ages, the means by which the clergy controlled the laity. Abused and perverted as this idea was, it indicates and presupposes a general belief in the personality of God, in rewards and punishments in a future state, and the necessity of conforming to the divine laws as expounded and enforced by the Christian Church. Hence the dark ages have been called "Ages of Faith."

It now remains to us to contemplate Anselm as a theologian and philosopher, – a more interesting view, for in this aspect his character is more genial, and his influence more extended and permanent. He is one of the first who revived theological studies in Europe. He did not teach in the universities as a scholastic doctor, but he was one who prepared the way for universities by the stimulus he gave to philosophy. It was in his abbey of Bec that he laid the foundation of a new school of theological inquiry. In original genius he was surpassed by no scholastic in the Middle Ages, although both Abélard and Thomas Aquinas enjoyed a greater fame. It was for his learning and sanctity that he was canonized, – and singularly enough by Alexander VI, the worst pope who ever reigned. Still more singular is it that the last of his successors, as abbot of Bec, was the diplomatist Talleyrand, – one of the most worldly and secular of all the ecclesiastical dignitaries of an infidel age.

The theology of the Middle Ages, of which Anselm was one of the greatest expounders, certainly the most profound, was that which was systematized by Saint Augustine from the writings of Paul. Augustine was the oracle of the Latin Church until the Council of Trent, and nominally his authority has never been repudiated by the Catholic Church. But he was no more the father of the Catholic theology than he was of the Protestant, as taught by John Calvin: these two great theologians were in harmony in all essential doctrines as completely as were Augustine and Anselm, or Augustine and Thomas Aquinas. The doctrines of theology, as formulated by Augustine, were subjects of contemplation and study in all the convents of the Middle Ages. In spite of the prevailing ignorance, it was impossible that inquiring men, "secluded in gloomy monasteries, should find food for their minds in the dreary and monotonous duties to which monks were doomed, – a life devoted to alternate manual labor and mechanical religious services." There would be some of them who would speculate on the lofty subjects which were the constant themes of their meditations. Bishops were absorbed in their practical duties as executive rulers. Village priests were too ignorant to do much beyond looking after the wants of hinds and peasants. The only scholarly men were the monks. And although the number of these was small, they have the honor of creating the first intellectual movement since the fall of the Roman Empire. They alone combined leisure with brainwork. These intellectual and inquiring monks, as far back as the ninth century speculated on the great subjects of Christian faith with singular boldness, considering the general ignorance which veiled Europe in melancholy darkness. Some of them were logically led "to a secret mutiny and insurrection" against the doctrines which were universally received. This insurrection of human intelligence gave great alarm to the orthodox leaders of the Church; and to suppress it the Church raised up conservative dialecticians as acute and able as those who strove for emancipation. At first they used the weapons of natural reason, but afterwards employed the logic and method of Aristotle, as translated into Latin from the Arabic, to assist them in their intellectual combats. Gradually the movement centred in the scholastic philosophy, as a bulwark to Catholic theology. But this was nearly a hundred years after the time of Anselm, who himself was not enslaved by the technicalities of a complicated system of dialectics.

Naturally the first subject which was suggested to the minds of inquiring monks was the being and attributes of God. He was the beginning and end of their meditations. It was to meditate upon God that the Oriental recluse sought the deserts of Asia Minor and Egypt. Like the Eastern monk of the fourth century, he sought to know the essence and nature of the Deity he worshipped. There arose before his mind the great doctrines of the trinity, the incarnation, and redemption. Closely connected with these were predestination and grace, and then "fixed fate, free-will, foreknowledge absolute." On these mysteries he could not help meditating; and with meditation came speculation on unfathomable subjects pertaining to God and his relations with man, to the nature of sin and its penalty, to the freedom of the will, and eternal decrees.

The monk became first a theologian and then a philosopher, whether of the school of Plato or of Aristotle he did not know. He began to speculate on questions which had agitated the Grecian schools, – the origin of evil and of matter; whether the world was created or uncreated; whether there is a distinction between things visible and invisible; whether we derive our knowledge from sensation or reflection; whether the soul is necessarily immortal; how free-will is to be reconciled with God's eternal decrees, or what the Greeks called Fate; whether ideas are eternal, or are the creation of our own minds. These, and other more subtle questions – like the nature of angels – began to agitate the convent in the ninth century.

It was then that the monk Gottschalk revived the question of predestination, which had slumbered since the time of Saint Augustine. Although the Bishop of Hippo was the oracle of the Church, and no one disputed his authority, it would seem that his characteristic doctrine, – that of grace; the essential doctrine of Luther also, – was never a favorite one with the great churchmen of the Middle Ages. They did not dispute Saint Augustine, but they adhered to penances and expiations, which entered so largely into the piety of the Middle Ages. The idea of penances and expiations, pushed to their utmost logical sequence, was salvation by works and not by faith. Grace, as understood by the Fathers, was closely allied to predestination; it disdained the elaborate and cumbrous machinery of ecclesiastical discipline, on which the power of the clergy was based. Grace was opposed to penance, while penance was the form which religion took; and as predestination was a theological sequence of grace, it was distasteful to the Mediaeval Church. Both grace and predestination tended to undermine the system of penance then universally accepted. The great churchmen of the Middle Ages were plainly at war with their great oracle in this matter, without being fully aware of their real antagonism. So they made an onslaught on Gottschalk, as opposed to those ideas on which sacerdotal power rested, – especially did Hincmar, Archbishop of Rheims, the greatest prelate of that age. Persecuted, Gottschalk appealed to reason rather than authority, thus anticipating Luther by five hundred years, – an immense heresy in the Middle Ages. Hincmar, not being able to grapple with the monk in argument, summoned to his aid the brightest intellect of that century, – the first man who really gave an impulse to philosophical inquiries in the Middle Ages, the true founder of scholasticism.

This man was John Scotus Erigena, – or John the Erin-born, – who was also a monk, and whose early days had been spent in some secluded monastery in Ireland, or the Scottish islands. Somehow he attracted the attention of Charles the Bald, A.D. 843, and became his guest and chosen companion. And yet, while he lived in the court, he spent the most of his time in intellectual seclusion. As a guest of the king he may have become acquainted with Hincmar, or his acquaintance with Hincmar may have led to his friendship with Charles. He was witty, bright, and learned, like Abélard, a favorite with the great. In his treatise on Predestination, in which he combated the views of Gotschalk, he probably went further than Hincmar desired or expected: he boldly asserted the supremacy of reason, and threw off the shackles of authority. He combated Saint Augustine as well as Gottschalk. He even aspired to reconcile free-will with the divine sovereignty, – the great mistake of theologians in every age, the most hopeless and the most ambitious effort of human genius, – a problem which cannot be solved. He went even further than this: he attempted to harmonize philosophy with religion, as Abélard did afterwards. He brought all theological questions to the test of dialectical reasoning. Thus the ninth century saw a rationalist and a pantheist at the court of a Christian king. Like Democritus, he maintained the eternity of matter. Like a Buddhist, he believed that God is all things and all things are God. Such doctrines were not to be tolerated, even in an age when theological speculations did not usually provoke persecution. Religious persecution for opinions was the fruit of subsequent inquiries, and did not reach its height until the Dominicans arose in the thirteenth century. But Erigena was generally denounced; he fell under the censure of the Pope, and was obliged to fly, taking refuge about the year 882 in England, – it is said at Oxford, where there was probably a cathedral school, but not as yet a university, with its professors' chairs and scholastic honors. Others suppose that he died in Paris, 891.

A spirit of inquiry having been thus awakened among a few intellectual monks, they began to speculate about those questions which had agitated the Grecian schools: whether *genera* and *species* – called "universals," or ideas – have a substantial and independent existence, or whether they are the creation of our own minds; whether, if they have a real existence, they are material or immaterial essences; whether they exist apart from objects perceptible by the senses. It is singular that such questions should have been discussed in the ninth century, since neither Plato nor Aristotle were studied. That age was totally ignorant of Greek. It may be doubted whether there was a Greek scholar in Western Europe, – or even in Rome.

No very remarkable man arose with a rationalizing spirit, after Erigena, until Berengar of Tours in the eleventh century, who maintained that in the Sacrament the presence of the body of Christ involves no change in the nature and essence of the bread and wine. He was opposed by Lanfranc. But the doctrine of transubstantiation was too deeply grounded in the faith of Christendom to be easily shaken. Controversies seemed to centre around the doctrine of the real existence of ideas, – what are called "universals," – which doctrine was generally accepted. The monks, in this matter, followed Saint Augustine, who was a realist, as were also the orthodox leaders of the

Church generally from his time to that of Saint Bernard. It was a sequence of the belief in the doctrine of the Trinity.

No one of mark opposed the Realism which had now become one of the accepted philosophical opinions of the age, until Roscelin, in the latter part of the eleventh century, denied that universals have a real existence. It was Plato's doctrine that universals have an independent existence apart from individual objects, and that they exist before the latter (*universalia* ANTE *rem*, – the thought *before* the thing); while Aristotle maintained that universals, though possessing a real existence, exist only in individual objects (*universalia* IN *re*, – the thought *in* the thing). Nominalism is the doctrine that individuals only have real existence (*universalia* POST *rem*, – the thought *after* the thing).

It is not probable that this profound question about universals would have excited much interest among the intellectual monks of the eleventh century, had it not been applied to theological subjects, in which chiefly they were absorbed. Now Roscelin advanced the doctrine, that, if the three persons in the Trinity were one thing, it would follow that the Father and the Holy Ghost must have entered into the flesh together with the Son; and as he believed that only individuals exist in reality, it would follow that the three persons of the Godhead are three substances, in fact three Gods. Thus Nominalism logically led to an assault on the received doctrine of the Trinity – the central point in the theology of the Church. This was heresy. The foundations of Christian belief were attacked, and no one in that age was strong enough to come to the rescue but Anselm, then Abbot of Bec.

His great service to the cause of Christian theology, and therefore to the Church universal, was his exposition of the logical results of the Nominalism of Roscelin, – to whom universals, or ideas, were merely creations of the mind, or conventional phrases, having no real existence. Hence such things as love, friendship, beauty, justice, were only conceptions. Plato and Augustine maintained that they are eternal verities, not to be explained by definitions, appealing to consciousness, in the firm belief in which the soul sustains itself; that there can be no certain knowledge without a recognition of these; that from these only sound deductions of moral truth can be drawn; that without a firm belief in these eternal certitudes there can be no repose and no lofty faith. These ideas are independent of us. They do not vary with our changing sensations; they have nothing to do with sensation. They are not creations of the brain; they inherently exist, from all eternity. The substance of these ideas is God; without these we could not conceive of God. Augustine especially, in the true spirit of Platonism, abhorred doctrines which made the existence of God depend upon our own abstractions. To him there was a reality in love, in friendship, in justice, in beauty; and he repelled scepticism as to their eternal existence, as life repels death.

Roscelin took away the platform from whose lofty heights Socrates and Plato would survey the universe. He attacked the citadel in which Augustine intrenched himself amid the desolations of a dissolving world; he laid the axe at the root of the tree which sheltered all those who would fly from uncertainty and despair.

But if these ideas were not true, what was true; on what were the hopes of the world to be based; where was consolation for the miseries of life to be found? "There are many goods," says Anselm, "which we desire, – some for utility, and others for beauty; but all these goods are relative, – more or less good, – and imply something absolutely good. This absolute good – the *summum bonum* – is God. In like manner all that is great and high are only relatively great and high; and hence there must be something absolutely great and high, and this is God. There must exist at least one being than which no other is higher; hence there must be but one such being, – and this is God."

It was thus that Anselm brought philosophy to the support of theology. He would combat the philosophical reasonings of Roscelin with still keener dialectics. He would conquer him on his own ground and with his own weapons.

Let it not be supposed that this controversy about universals was a mere dialectical tournament, with no grand results. It goes down to the root of almost every great subject in philosophy and religion. The denial of universal ideas is rationalism and materialism in philosophy, as it is Pelagianism and Arminianism in theology. The Nominalism of Roscelin reappeared in the Rationalism of Abélard; and, carried out to its severe logical sequences, is the refusal to accept any doctrine which cannot be proved by reason. Hence nothing is to be accepted which is beyond the province of reason to explain; and hence nothing is to be received by faith alone. Christianity, in the hands of fearless and logical nominalists, would melt away, – that is, what is peculiar in its mysterious dogmas. Its mysterious dogmas were the anchors of belief in ages of faith. It was these which animated the existence of such men as Augustine, Bernard, Anselm, and Thomas Aquinas. Hence their terrible antagonism even to philosophical doctrines which conflicted with the orthodox belief, on which, as they thought, the salvation of mankind rested.

But Anselm did not rest with combating the Nominalism of Roscelin. In the course of his inquiries and arguments he felt it necessary to establish the belief in God – the one great thing from which all other questions radiated – by a new argument, and on firmer ground than that on which it had hitherto rested. He was profoundly devotional as well as logical, and original as he was learned. Beyond all the monks of his age he lived in the contemplation of God. God was to him the essence of all good, the end of all inquiries, the joy and repose of his soul He could not understand unless he *first* believed; knowledge was the *fruit* of faith, not its *cause*. The idea of God in the mind of man is the highest proof of the existence of God. That only is real which appeals to consciousness. He did not care to reason about a thing when reasoning would not strengthen his convictions, perhaps involve him in doubts and perplexities. Reason is finite and clouded and warped. But that which directly appeals to consciousness (as all that is eternal must appeal), and to that alone, like beauty and justice and love, – ultimate ideas to which reasoning and definitions add nothing, – is to be received as a final certitude. Hence, absolute certainty of the existence of God, as it appeals to consciousness, – like the "*Cogito, ergo sum.*" In this argument he anticipated Descartes, and proved himself the profoundest thinker of his century, perhaps of five centuries.

The deductions which Anselm made from the attributes of God and his moral government seem to have strengthened the belief of the Middle Ages in some theological aspects which are repulsive to consciousness, – his stronghold; thereby showing how one-sided any deductions are apt to be when pushed out to their utmost logical consequences; how they may even become a rebuke to human reason in those grand efforts of which reason is most proud, for theology, it must be borne in mind, is a science of deductions from acknowledged truths of revelation. Hence, from the imperfections of reason, or from disregard of other established truths, deductions may be pushed to absurdity even when logical, and may be made to conflict with the obvious meaning of primal truths from which these deductions are made, or at least with those intuitions which are hard to be distinguished from consciousness itself. There may be no flaw in the argument, but the argument may land one in absurdity and contradiction. For instance, from the acknowledged sinfulness of human nature – one of the cardinal declarations of Scripture, and confirmed by universal experience – and the equally fundamental truth that God is infinite, Anselm assumed the dogma that the guilt of men as sinners against an infinite God is infinitely great. From this premise, which few in his age were disposed to deny, for it was in accordance with Saint Augustine, it follows that infinite sin, according to eternal justice, could only be atoned for by an infinite punishment. Hence all men deserve eternal punishment, and must receive it, unless there be made an infinite satisfaction or atonement, since not otherwise can divine love be harmonized with divine justice. Hence it was necessary that the eternal Son should become man, and make, by his voluntary death on the cross, the necessary atonement for human sins. Pushed out to the severest logical consequences, it would follow, that, as an infinite satisfaction has atoned for sin, *all* sinners are pardoned. But the Church shrank from such a conclusion, although logical, and included in the benefits of the atonement only the *believing* portion of mankind. The discrepancy between the logical deductions and consciousness, and I may add Scripture, lies in assuming that human guilt *is infinitely* great. It is thus that theology became complicated, even gloomy, and in some points false, by metaphysical reasonings, which had such a charm both to the Fathers and the Schoolmen. The attempt to reconcile divine justice with divine love by metaphysics and abstruse reasoning proved as futile as the attempt to reconcile free-will with predestination; for divine justice was made by deduction, without reference to other attributes, to conflict with those ideas of justice which consciousness attests, – even as a fettered will, of which all are conscious (that is, a will fettered by sin), was pushed out by logical deductions into absolute slavery and impotence.

Anselm did not carry out metaphysical reasonings to such lengths as did the Schoolmen who succeeded him, – those dialecticians who lived in universities in the thirteenth century. He was a devout man, who meditated on God and on revealed truth with awe and reverence, without any desire of system-making or dialectical victories. This desire more properly marked the Scholastic doctors of the universities in a subsequent age, when, though philosophy had been invoked by Anselm to support theology, they virtually made theology subordinate to philosophy. It was his main effort to establish, on rational grounds, the existence of God, and afterwards the doctrines of the Trinity and the Incarnation. And yet with Anselm and Roscelin the Scholastic age began. They were the founders of the Realists and the Nominalists, – those two schools which divided the Church in the twelfth and thirteenth centuries, and which will probably go on together, under different names, as long as men shall believe and doubt. But this subject, on which I have only entered, must be deferred to the next lecture.

AUTHORITIES

Church's *Life of Saint Anselm*
Neander's *Church History*
Milman's *History of the Latin Church*
Stockl's *History of the Philosophy of the Middle Ages*
Ueberweg's *History of Philosophy*
Wordsworth's *Ecclesiastical Biography*
Trench's *Mediaeval Church History*
Digby's *Ages of Faith*
Fleury's *Ecclesiastical History*
Dupin's *Ecclesiastical History*
Biographie Universelle
M. Rousselot's *Histoire de la Philosophic du Moyen Age*
Newman's *Mission of the Benedictine Order*

Dugdale's *Monasticon*
Hallam's *Literature of Europe*
Hampden's article on the *Scholastic Philosophy*, in *Encyclopaedia Metropolitana*.

Chapter 6

THOMAS AQUINAS:
THE SCHOLASTIC PHILOSOPHY

A.D. 1225(7)-1274

We have seen how the cloister life of the Middle Ages developed meditative habits of mind, which were followed by a spirit of inquiry on deep theological questions. We have now to consider a great intellectual movement, stimulated by the effort to bring philosophy to the aid of theology, and thus more effectually to battle with insidious and rising heresies. The most illustrious representative of this movement was Thomas of Aquino, generally called Thomas Aquinas. With him we associate the Scholastic Philosophy, which, though barren in the results at which it aimed, led to a remarkable intellectual activity, and hence, indirectly, to the emancipation of the mind. It furnished teachers who prepared the way for the great lights of the Reformation.

Anselm had successfully battled with the rationalism of Roscelin, and also had furnished a new argument for the existence of God. He secured the triumph of Realism for a time and the apparent extinction of heresy. But a new impulse to thought was given, soon after his death, by a less profound but more popular and brilliant man, and, like him, a monk. This was the celebrated Peter Abélard, born in the year 1079, in Brittany, of noble parents, and a boy of remarkable precocity. He was a sort of knight-errant of philosophy, going from convent to convent and from school to school, disputing, while a mere youth, with learned teachers, wherever he could find them. Having vanquished the masters in the provincial schools, he turned his steps to Paris, at that time the intellectual centre of Europe. The university was not yet established, but the cathedral school of Notre Dame was presided over by William of Champeaux, who defended the Realism of Anselm.

To this famous cathedral school Abélard came as a pupil of the veteran dialectician at the age of twenty, and dared to dispute his doctrines. He soon set up as a teacher himself; but as Notre Dame was interdicted to him he retired to Melun, ten leagues from Paris, where enthusiastic pupils crowded to his lecture room, for he was witty, bold, sarcastic, acute, and eloquent. He afterwards removed to Paris, and so completely discomfited his old master that he retired from the field. Abélard then applied himself to the study of divinity, and attended the lectures of Anselm of Laon, who, though an old man, was treated by Abélard with great flippancy and arrogance. He then began to lecture on divinity as well as philosophy, with extraordinary *éclat*. Students flocked to his lecture room from all parts of Germany, Italy, France, and England. It is said that five thousand young men attended his lectures, among whom one hundred were destined to be prelates, including that brilliant and able Italian who afterwards reigned as Innocent III. It was about this time, 1117, when he was thirty-eight, that he encountered Héloïse, – a passage of his life which will be considered in a later volume of this work. His unfortunate love and his cruel misfortune led to a temporary seclusion in a convent, from which, however, he issued to lecture with renewed popularity in a desert place in Champagne, where he constructed a vast edifice and dedicated it to the Paraclete. It was here that his most brilliant days were spent. It is said that three thousand pupils followed him to this wilderness. He was doubtless the most brilliant and successful lecturer that the Middle Ages ever saw. He continued the controversy which was begun by Roscelin respecting universals, the reality of which he denied.

Abélard was not acquainted with the Greek, but in a Latin translation from the Arabic he had studied Aristotle, whom he regarded as the great master of dialectics, although not making use of his method, as did the great Scholastics of the succeeding century. Still, he was among the first to apply dialectics to theology. He maintained a certain independence of the patristic authority by his "Sic et Non," in which treatise he makes the authorities neutralize each other by placing side by side contradictory assertions. He maintained that the natural propensity to evil, in consequence of the original transgression, is not in itself sin; that sin consists in consenting to evil. "It is not," said he, "the temptation to lust that is sinful, but the acquiescence in the temptation;" hence, that virtue cannot be tested without temptations; consequently, that moral worth can only be truly estimated by God, to whom motives are known, – in short, that sin consists in the intention, and not in act. He admitted with Anselm that faith, in a certain sense, precedes knowledge, but insisted that one must know why and what he believes before his faith is established; hence, that faith works itself out of doubt by means of rational investigation.

The tendency of Abélard's teachings was rationalistic, and therefore he arrayed against himself the great champion of orthodoxy in his day, – Saint Bernard, Abbot of Clairvaux, the most influential churchman of his age, and the most devout and lofty. His immense influence was based on his learning and sanctity; but he was dogmatic and intolerant. It is probable that the intellectual arrogance of Abélard, his flippancy and his sarcasms, offended more than the matter of his lectures. "It is not by industry," said he, "that I have reached the heights of philosophy, but by force of genius." He was more admired by young and worldly men than by old men. He was the admiration of women, for he was poet as well as philosopher. His love-songs were scattered over Europe. With a proud and aristocratic bearing, severe yet negligent dress, beautiful and noble figure, musical and electrical voice, added to the impression he made by his wit and dialectical power, no man ever commanded greater admiration from those who listened to him. But he excited envy as well as admiration, and was probably misrepresented by his opponents. Like all strong and original characters, he had bitter enemies as well as admiring friends; and these enemies exaggerated his failings and his heretical opinions. Therefore he was summoned before the Council of Soissons, and condemned to perpetual silence. From this he appealed to Rome, and Rome sided with his enemies. He found a retreat, after his condemnation, in the abbey of Cluny, and died in the arms of his friend Peter the Venerable, the most benignant ecclesiastic of the century, who venerated his genius and defended his orthodoxy, and whose influence procured him absolution from the Pope.

But whatever were the faults of Abélard; however selfish he was in his treatment of Héloïse, or proud and provoking to adversaries, or even heretical in many of his doctrines, especially in reference to faith, which he is accused of undermining, although he accepted in the main the received doctrines of the Church, certainly in his latter days, when he was broken and penitent (for no great man ever suffered more humiliating misfortunes), – one thing is clear, that he gave a stimulus to philosophical inquiries, and awakened a desire of knowledge, and gave dignity to human reason, beyond any man in the Middle Ages.

The dialectical and controversial spirit awakened by Abélard led to such a variety of opinions among the inquiring young men who assembled in Paris at the various schools, some of which were regarded as rationalistic in their tendency, or at least a departure from the patristic standard, that Peter Lombard, Bishop of Paris, collected in four books the various sayings of the Fathers concerning theological dogmas. He was also influenced to make this exposition by the "Sic et Non" of Abélard, which tended to unsettle belief. This famous manual, called the "Book of Sentences," appeared about the middle of the twelfth century, and had an immense influence. It was the great text-book of the theological schools.

About the time this book appeared the works of Aristotle were introduced to the attention of students, translated into Latin from the Saracenic language. Aristotle had already been commented upon by Arabian scholars in Spain, – among whom Averroes, a physician and mathematician of Cordova, was the most distinguished, – who regarded the Greek philosopher as the founder of scientific knowledge. His works were translated from the Greek into the Arabic in the early part of the ninth century.

Thomas Aquinas: The Scholastic Philosophy　　　　　　121

The introduction of Aristotle led to an extension of philosophical studies. From the time of Charlemagne only grammar and elementary logic and dogmatic theology had been taught, but Abélard introduced dialectics into theology. A more complete method was required than that which the existing schools furnished, and this was supplied by the dialectics of Aristotle. He became, therefore, at the close of the twelfth century, an acknowledged authority, and his method was adopted to support the dogmas of the Church.

Meanwhile the press of students at Paris, collected into various schools, – the chief of which were the theological school of Notre Dame, and the school of logic at Mount Geneviève, where Abélard had lectured, – demanded a new organization. The teachers and pupils of these schools then formed a corporation called a university (*Universitas Magistrorum et Scholarium*), under the control of the chancellor and chapter of Notre Dame, whose corporate existence was secured from Innocent III a few years afterwards.

Thus arose the University of Paris at the close of the twelfth century, or about the beginning of the thirteenth, soon followed in different parts of Europe by other universities, the most distinguished of which were those of Oxford, Bologna, Padua, and Salamanca. But that of Paris took the lead, this city being the intellectual centre of Europe even at that early day. Thither flocked young men from Germany, England, and Italy, as well as from all parts of France, to the number of twenty-five or thirty thousand. These students were a motley crowd: some of them were half-starved youth, with tattered clothes, living in garrets and unhealthy cells; others again were rich and noble, – but all were eager for knowledge. They came to Paris as pilgrims flocked to Jerusalem, being drawn by the fame of the lecturers. The old sleepy schools of the convents were deserted, for who would go to Fulda or York or Citeaux, when such men as Abélard, Albert, and Victor were dazzling enthusiastic youth by their brilliant disputations? These young men also seem to have been noisy, turbulent, and dissipated for the most part, "filling the streets with their brawls and the taverns with the fumes of liquor. There was no such thing as discipline among them. They yelled and shouted and brandished daggers, fought the townspeople, and were free with their knocks and blows." They were not all youth; many of them were men in middle life, with wives and children. At that time no one finished his education at twenty-one; some remained scholars until the age of thirty-five.

Some of these students came to study medicine, others law, but more theology and philosophy. The headquarters of theology was the Sorbonne, opened in 1253, – a college founded by Robert Sorbon, chaplain of the king, whose aim was to bring together the students and professors, heretofore scattered throughout the city. The students of this college, which formed a part of the university, under the rule of the chancellor of Notre Dame, it would seem were more orderly and studious than the other students. They arose at five, assisted at Mass at six, studied till ten, – the dinner hour; from dinner till five they studied or attended lectures; then went to supper, – the principal meal; after which they discussed problems till nine or ten, when they went to bed. The students were divided into *hospites* and *socii*, the latter of whom carried on the administration. The lectures were given in a large hall, in the middle of which was the chair of the master or doctor, while immediately below him sat his assistant, the bachelor, who was going through his training for a professorship. The chair of theology was the most coveted honor of the university, and was reached only by a long course of study and searching examinations, to which no one could aspire but the most learned and gifted of the doctors. The students sat around on benches, or on the straw. There were no writing-desks. The teaching was oral, principally by questions and answers. Neither the master nor the bachelor used a book. No reading was allowed. The students rarely took notes or wrote in shorthand; they listened to the lectures and wrote them down afterwards, so far as their memory served them. The usual text-book was the "Book of Sentences," by Peter Lombard. The bachelor, after having previously studied ten years, was obliged to go through a three years' drill, and then submit to a public examination in presence of the whole university before he was thought fit to teach. He could not then receive his master's badge until he had successfully maintained a public disputation on some thesis proposed; and even then he stood no chance of being elevated to a professor's chair unless he had lectured for some time with great *éclat* Even Albertus Magnus, fresh with the laurels of Cologne, was compelled to go through a three years' course as a sub-teacher at Paris before he received his doctor's cap, and to lecture for some years more as master before his transcendent abilities were rewarded with a professorship. The dean of the faculty of theology was chosen by the suffrages of the doctors.

The *Organum* (philosophy of first principles) of Aristotle was first publicly taught in 1215. This was certainly in advance of the seven liberal arts which were studied in the old Cathedral schools, – grammar, rhetoric, and dialectic (Trivium); and arithmetic, geometry, music, and astronomy (Quadrivium), – for only the elements of these were taught. But philosophy and theology, under the teaching of the Scholastic doctors (*Doctores Scholastici*), taxed severely the intellectual powers. When they introduced dialectics to support theology a more severe method was required. "The method consisted in connecting the doctrine to be expounded with a commentary on some work chosen for the purpose. The contents were divided and subdivided, until the several propositions of which it was composed were reached. Then these were interpreted, questions were raised in reference to them, and the grounds of affirming or denying were presented. Then the decision was announced, and in case this was affirmative, the grounds of the negative were confuted."

Aristotle was made use of in order to reduce to scientific form a body of dogmatic teachings, or to introduce a logical arrangement. Platonism, embraced by the early Fathers, was a collection of abstractions and theories, but was deficient in method. It did not furnish the weapons to assail heresy with effect. But Aristotle was logical and precise and passionless. He examined the nature of language, and was clear and accurate in his definitions. His logic was studied with the sole view of learning to use polemical weapons. For this end the syllogism was introduced, which descends from the universal to the particular, by deduction, – connecting the general with the special by means of a middle term which is common to both. This mode of reasoning is opposite to the method by induction, which rises to the universal from a comparison of the single and particular, or, as applied in science, from a collection and collation of facts sufficient to form a certainty or high probability. A sound special deduction can be arrived at only by logical inference from true and certain general principles.

This is what Anselm essayed to do; but the Schoolmen who succeeded Abélard often drew dialectical inferences from what appeared to be true, while some of them were so sophistical as to argue from false premises. This syllogistic reasoning, in the hands of an acute dialectician, was very efficient in overthrowing an antagonist, or turning his position into absurdity, but not favorable for the discovery of truth, since it aimed no higher than the establishment of the particulars which were included in the doctrine assumed or deduced from it. It was reasoning in perpetual circles; it was full of quibbles and sophistries; it was ingenious, subtle, acute, very attractive to the minds of that age, and inexhaustible from divisions and subdivisions and endless ramifications. It made the contests of the schools a dialectical display of remarkable powers in which great interest was felt, yet but little knowledge was acquired. In one respect the Scholastic doctors rendered a service: they demolished all dreamy theories and poured contempt on mystical phrases. They insisted, like Socrates, on a definite meaning to words. If they were hair-splitting in their definitions and distinctions, they were at least clear and precise. Their method was scientific. Such terms and expressions as are frequently used by our modern transcendental philosophers would have been laughed to scorn by the Schoolmen. No system of philosophy can be built up when words have no definite meaning. This Socrates was the first to inculcate, and Aristotle followed in his steps.

With the Crusades arose a new spirit, which gave an impulse to philosophy as well as to art and enterprise. "The *primum mobile* of the new system was Motion, in distinction from the Rest which marked the old monastic retreats." An immense enthusiasm for knowledge had been kindled by Abélard, which was further intensified by the Scholastic doctors of the thirteenth century, especially such of them as belonged to the Dominican and Franciscan friars.

These celebrated Orders arose at a great crisis in the Papal history, when rival popes aspired to the throne of Saint Peter, when the Church was rent with divisions, when princes were contending for the right of investiture, and when heretical opinions were defended by men of genius. At this crisis a great Pope was called to the government of the Church, – Innocent III, under whose able rule the papal power culminated. He belonged to an illustrious Roman family, and received an unusual education, being versed in theology, philosophy, and canon law. His name was Lothario, of the family of the Conti; he was nephew of a pope, and counted three cardinals among his relatives. At the age of twenty-one, about the year 1181, he was one of the canons of Saint Peter's Church; at twenty-four he was sent by the Pope on important missions. In 1188 he was created cardinal by his uncle, Clement III; and in 1198 he was elected Pope, at the age of thirty-eight, when the Crusades were at their height, when the south of France was agitated by the opinions of the Albigenses, and the provinces on the Rhine by those of the Waldenses. It was a turbulent age, full of tumults, insurrections, wars, and theological dissensions. The old Benedictine monks had lost their influence, and were disgraced by idleness and gluttony, while the secular clergy were ignorant and worldly. Innocent cast his eagle eye into all the abuses which disgraced the age and Church, and made fearless war upon those princes who usurped his prerogatives. He excommunicated princes, humbled the Emperor of Germany and the King of England, put kingdoms under interdict, exempted abbots from the jurisdiction of bishops, punished heretics, formed crusades, laid down new canons, regulated taxes, and directed all ecclesiastical movements. His activity was ceaseless, and his ambition was boundless. He instituted important changes, and added new orders of monks to the Church. It was this Pope who instituted auricular confession, and laid the foundation of a more dreadful spiritual despotism in the form of inquisitions.

Yet while he ruled tyrannically, his private life was above reproach. His habits were simple and his tastes were cultivated. He was charitable and kind to the poor and unfortunate. He spent his enormous revenues in building churches, endowing hospitals, and rewarding learned men; and otherwise showed himself the friend of scholars, and the patron of benevolent movements. He was a reformer of abuses, publishing the most severe acts against venality, and deciding quarrels on principles of justice. He had no dramatic conflicts like Hildebrand, for his authority was established. As the supreme guardian of the interests of the Church he seldom made demands which he had not the power to enforce. John of England attempted resistance, but was compelled to submit. Innocent even gave the archbishopric of Canterbury to one of his cardinals, Stephen Langton, against the wishes of a Norman king. He took away the wife of Philip Augustus; he nominated an emperor to the throne of Constantine; he compelled France to make war on England, and incited the barons to rebellion against John. Ten years' civil war in Germany was the fruit of his astute policy, and the only great failure of his administration was that he could not exempt Italy from the dominion of the Emperors of Germany, thus giving rise to the two great political parties of the thirteenth and fourteenth centuries, – the Guelphs and Ghibellines.

To cement his vast spiritual power he encouraged what doubtless seemed even to him a great fanaticism, but which he found could be turned to his advantage, – that of the Mendicant Friars, established by Saint Francis of Assisi, and Saint Dominic of the great family of the Guzmans in Spain. These men made substantially the same offers to the Pope that Ignatius Loyola did in after times, – to go where they were sent as teachers, preachers, and missionaries without condition or reward. They renounced riches, professed absolute poverty, and wandered from village to city barefooted, and subsisting entirely on alms as beggars. The Dominican friar in his black habit, and the Franciscan in his gray, became the ablest and most effective preachers of the thirteenth century. The Dominicans confined their teachings to the upper classes, and became their favorite confessors. They were the most learned men of the thirteenth century, and also the most reproachless in morals. The Franciscans were itinerary preachers to the common people, and created among them the same religious revival that the Methodists did later in England under the guidance of Wesley. The founder of the Franciscans was a man who seemed to be "inebriated with love," so unquenchable was his charity, rapt his devotions, and supernal his sympathy. He found his way to Rome in the year 1215, and in twenty-two years after his death there were nine thousand religious houses of his Order. In a century from his death the friars numbered one hundred and fifty thousand. The increase of the Dominicans was not so rapid, but more illustrious men belonged to this institution. It is affirmed that it produced seventy cardinals, four hundred and sixty bishops, and four popes.

It was in the palmy days of these celebrated monks, before corruption had set in, that the Dominican Order was recruited with one of the most extraordinary men of the Middle Ages. This man was Saint Thomas, born 1225 or 1227, son of a Count of Aquino in the kingdom of Naples, known in history as Thomas Aquinas, "the most successful organizer of knowledge," says Archbishop Trench, "the world has known since Aristotle." He was called "the angelical doctor," exciting the enthusiasm of his age for his learning and piety and genius alike. He was a prodigy and a marvel of dialectical skill, and Catholic writers have exhausted language to find expressions for their admiration. Their Lives of him are an unbounded panegyric for the sweetness of his temper, his wonderful self-control, his lofty devotion to study, his indifference to praises and rewards, his spiritual devotion, his loyalty to the Church, his marvelous acuteness of intellect, his industry, and his unparalleled logical victories. When he was five years of age his father, a noble of very high rank, sent him to Monte Cassino with the hope that he would become a Benedictine monk, and ultimately abbot of that famous monastery, with the control of its vast revenues and patronage. Here he remained seven years, until the convent was taken and sacked by the soldiers of the Emperor Frederic in his war with the Pope. The young Aquino returned to his father's castle, and was then sent to Naples to be educated at the university, living in a Benedictine abbey, and not in lodgings like other students. The Dominicans and Franciscans held chairs in the university, one of which was filled with a man of great ability, whose preaching and teaching had such great influence on the youthful Thomas that he resolved to join the Order, and at the age of seventeen became a Dominican friar, to the disappointment of his family. His mother Theodora went to Naples to extricate him from the hands of the Dominicans, who secretly hurried him off to Rome and immured him in their convent, from which he was rescued by violence. But the youth persisted in his intentions against the most passionate entreaties of his mother, made his escape, and was carried back to Naples. The Pope, at the solicitation of his family, offered to make him Abbot of Monte Cassino, but he remained a poor Dominican. His superior, seeing his remarkable talents, sent him to Cologne to attend the lectures of Albertus Magnus, then the most able expounder of the Scholastic

Philosophy, and the oracle of the universities, who continued his lectures after he was made a bishop, and even until he was eighty-five. When Albertus was transferred from Cologne to Paris, where the Dominicans held two chairs of theology, Thomas followed him, and soon after was made bachelor. Again was Albert sent back to Cologne, and Thomas was made his assistant professor. He at once attracted attention, was ordained priest, and became as famous for his sermons as for his lectures. After four years at Cologne Thomas was ordered back to Paris, travelling on foot, and begging his way, yet stopping to preach in the large cities. He was still magister and Albert professor, but had greatly distinguished himself by his lectures.

Figure 7. St. Thomas Aquinas in the School of Albertus Magnus. *After the painting by H. Lerolle.*

His appearance at this time was marked. His body was tall and massive, but spare and lean from fasting and labor. His eyes were bright, but their expression was most modest. His face was oblong, his complexion sallow; his forehead depressed, his head large, his person erect.

His first great work was a commentary of about twelve hundred pages on the "Book of Sentences," in the Parma edition, which was received with great admiration for its logical precision, and its opposition to the rationalistic tendencies of the times. In it are discussed all the great theological questions treated by Saint Augustine, – God, Christ, the Holy Spirit, grace, predestination, faith, free-will, Providence, and the like, – blended with metaphysical discussions on the soul, the existence of evil, the nature of angels, and other subjects which interested the Middle Ages. Such was his fame and dialectical skill that he was taken away from his teachings and sent to Rome to defend his Order and the cause of orthodoxy against the slanders of William of Saint Amour, an aristocratic doctor, who hated the Mendicant Friars and their wandering and begging habits. William had written a book called "Perils," in which he exposed the dangers to be apprehended from the new order of monks, in which he proved himself a true prophet, for ultimately the Mendicant Friars became subjects of ridicule and reproach. But the Pope came to the rescue of his best supporters.

On the return of Thomas to Paris he was made doctor of theology, at the same time with Bonaventura the Franciscan, called "the seraphic doctor," between whom and Thomas were intimate ties of friendship. He had now reached the highest honor that the university could bestow, which was conferred with such extraordinary ceremony that it would seem to have been a great event in Paris at that time.

His fame chiefly rests on the ablest treatise written in the Middle Ages, – the "Summa Theologica," – in which all the great questions in theology and philosophy are minutely discussed, in the most exhaustive manner. He took the side of the Realists, his object being to uphold Saint Augustine. He was more a Platonist in his spirit than an Aristotelian, although he was indebted to Aristotle for his method. He appealed to both reason and authority. He presented the Christian religion in a scientific form. His book is an assimilation of all that is precious in the thinking of the Church. If he learned many things at Paris, Cologne, and Naples, he was also educated by Chrysostom, by Augustine, and Ambrose. "It is impossible," says Cardinal Newman, and no authority is higher than his, "to read the *Catena* of Saint Thomas without being struck by the masterly skill with which he put it together. A learning of the highest kind, – not mere literary book knowledge which may have supplied the place of indexes and tables in ages destitute of these helps, and when they had to be read in unarranged and fragmentary manuscripts, but a thorough acquaintance with the whole range of ecclesiastical antiquity, so as to be able to bring the substance of all that had been written on any point to bear upon the text which involved it, – a familiarity with the style of each writer so as to compress in a few words the pith of the whole page, and a power of clear and orderly arrangement in this mass of knowledge, are qualities which make this *Catena* nearly perfect as an interpretation of Patristic literature." Dr. Vaughan, in eulogistic language, says: "The 'Summa Theologica' may be likened to one of the great cathedrals of the Middle Ages, infinite in detail but massive in the grouping of pillars and arches, forming a complete unity that must have taxed the brain of the architect to its greatest extent. But greater as work of intellect is this digest of all theological richness for one thousand years, in which the thread of discourse is never lost sight of, but winds through a labyrinth of important discussions and digressions, all bearing on the fundamental truths which Paul declared and Augustine systematized."

This treatise would seem to be a thesaurus of both Patristic and Mediaeval learning; not a dictionary of knowledge, but a system of truth severely elaborated in every part, – a work to be studied by the Mediaeval students as Calvin's "Institutes" were by the scholars of the Reformation, and not far different in its scope and end; for the Patristic, the Mediaeval, and the Protestant divines did not materially differ in reference to the fundamental truths pertaining to God, the Incarnation, and Redemption. The Catholic and Protestant divines differ chiefly on the ideas pertaining to government and ecclesiastical institutions, and the various inventions of the Middle Ages to uphold the authority of the Church, not on dogmas strictly theological. A student in theology could even in our times sit at the feet of Thomas Aquinas, as he could at the feet of Augustine or Calvin; except that in the theology which Thomas Aquinas commented upon there is a cumbrous method, borrowed from Aristotle, which introduced infinite distinctions and questions and definitions and deductions and ramifications which have no charm to men who have other things to occupy their minds than Scholastic subtilties, acute and logical as they may be. Thomas Aquinas was raised to combat, with the weapons most esteemed in his day, the various forms of Rationalism, Pantheism, and Mysticism which then existed, and were included in the Nominalism of his antagonists. And as long as universities are centres of inquiry the same errors, under other names, will have to be combated, but probably not with the same methods which marked the teachings of the "angelical doctor." In demolishing errors and systematizing truth he was the greatest benefactor to the cause of "orthodoxy" that appeared in Europe for several centuries, admired for his genius as much as Spencer and other great lights of science are in our day, but standing preeminent and lofty over all, like a beacon light to give both guidance and warning to inquiring minds in every part of Christendom. Nor could popes and sovereigns render too great honor to such a prodigy of genius. They offered him the abbacy of Monte Cassino and the archbishopric of Naples, but he preferred the life of a quiet student, finding in knowledge and study, for their own sake, the highest reward, and pursuing his labors without the *impedimenta* of those high positions which involve ceremonies and cares and pomps, yet which most ambitious men love better than freedom, placidity, and intellectual repose. He lived not in a palace, as he might have lived, surrounded with flatterers, luxuries, and dignities, but in a cell, wearing his simple black gown, and walking barefooted wherever he went, begging his daily bread according to the rules of his Order. His black gown was not an academic badge, but the Dominican dress. His only badge of distinction was the doctors' cap.

Dr. Vaughan, in his heavy and unartistic life of Thomas Aquinas, has drawn a striking resemblance between Plato and the Mediaeval doctor: "Both," he says, "were nobly born, both were grave from youth, both loved truth with an intensity of devotion. If Plato was instructed by Socrates, Aquinas was taught by Albertus Magnus; if Plato travelled into Italy, Greece, and Egypt, Aquinas went to Cologne, Naples, Bologna, and Rome;

if Plato was famous for his erudition, Aquinas was no less noted for his universal knowledge. Both were naturally meek and gentle; both led lives of retirement and contemplation; both loved solitude; both were celebrated for self-control; both were brave; both held their pupils spell-bound by their brilliant mental gifts; both passed their time in lecturing to the schools (what the Pythagoreans were to Plato, the Benedictines were to the angelical); both shrank from the display of self; both were great dialecticians; both reposed on eternal ideas; both were oracles to their generation." But if Aquinas had the soul of Plato, he also had the scholastic gifts of Aristotle, to whom the Church is indebted for method and nomenclature as it was to Plato for synthesis and that exalted Realism which went hand in hand with Christianity. How far he was indebted to Plato it is difficult to say. He certainly had not studied his dialectics through translations or in the original, but had probably imbibed the spirit of this great philosopher through Saint Augustine and other orthodox Fathers who were his admirers.

Although both Plato and Aristotle accepted "universals" as the foundation of scientific inquiry, the former arrived at them by consciousness, and the other by reasoning. The spirit of the two great masters of thought was as essentially different as their habits and lives. Plato believed that God governed the world; Aristotle believed that it was governed by chance. The former maintained that mind is divine and eternal; the latter that it is a form of the body, and consequently mortal. Plato thought that the source of happiness was in virtue and resemblance to God; while Aristotle placed it in riches and outward prosperity. Plato believed in prayer; but Aristotle thought that God would not hear or answer it, and therefore that it was useless. Plato believed in happiness after death; while Aristotle supposed that death ended all pleasure. Plato lived in the world of abstract ideas; Aristotle in the realm of sense and observation. The one was religious; the other secular and worldly. With both the passion for knowledge was boundless, but they differed in their conceptions of knowledge; the one basing it on eternal ideas and the deductions to be drawn from them, and the other on physical science, – the phenomena of Nature, – those things which are cognizable by the senses. The spiritual life of Plato was "a longing after love and of eternal ideas, by the contemplation of which the soul sustains itself and becomes participant in immortality." The life of Aristotle was not spiritual, but intellectual. He was an incarnation of mere intellect, the architect of a great temple of knowledge, which received the name of *Organum*, or the philosophy of first principles.

Thomas Aquinas, we may see from what has been said, was both Platonic and Aristotelian. He resembled Plato in his deep and pious meditations on the eternal realities of the spiritual world, while in the severity of his logic he resembled Aristotle, from whom he learned precision of language, lucidity of statement, and a syllogistic mode of argument well calculated to confirm what was already known, but not to make attainments in new fields of thought or knowledge. If he was gentle and loving and pious like Plato, he was also as calm and passionless as Aristotle.

This great man died at the age of forty-eight, in the year 1274, a few years after Saint Louis, before his sum of theology was completed. He died prematurely, exhausted by his intense studies; leaving, however, treatises which filled seventeen printed folio volumes, – one of the most voluminous writers of the world. His fame was prodigious, both as a dialectician and a saint, and he was in due time canonized as one of the great pillars of the Church, ranking after Chrysostom, Jerome, Augustine, and Gregory the Great, – the standard authority for centuries of the Catholic theology.

The Scholastic Philosophy, which culminated in Thomas Aquinas, maintained its position in the universities of Europe until the Reformation, but declined in earnestness. It descended to the discussion of unimportant and often frivolous questions. Even the "angelical doctor" is quoted as discussing the absurd question as to how many angels could dance together on the point of a needle. The play of words became interminable. Things were lost sight of in a barbarous jargon about questions which have no interest to humanity, and which are utterly unintelligible. At the best, logical processes can add nothing to the ideas from which they start. When these ideas are lofty, discussion upon them elevates the mind and doubtless strengthens its powers. But when the subjects themselves are frivolous, the logical tournaments in their defence degrade the intellect and narrow it. Nothing destroys intellectual dignity more effectually than the waste of energies in the defence of what is of no practical utility, and which cannot be applied to the acquisition of solid knowledge. Hence the Scholastic Philosophy did not advance knowledge, since it did not seek the acquisition of new truths, but only the establishment of the old. Its utility consisted in training the human mind to logical reasonings. It exercised the intellect and strengthened it, as gymnastics do the body, without enlarging it. It was nothing but barren dialectics, – "dry bones," a perpetual fencing. The soul cries out for bread; the Scholastics gave it a stone.

We are amazed that intellectual giants, equal to the old Greeks in acuteness and logical powers, could waste their time on the frivolous questions and dialectical subtilties to which they devoted their mighty powers. However interesting to them, nothing is drier and duller to us, nothing more barren and unsatisfying, than their logical sports. Their treatises are like trees with endless branches, each leading to new ramifications, with no central point in view, and hence never finished, and which might be carried on *ad infinitum*. To attempt to read their disquisitions is like walking in labyrinths of ever-opening intricacies. By such a method no ultimate truth could be arrived at, beyond what was assumed. There is now and then a man who professes to have derived light and wisdom from those dialectical displays, since they were doubtless marvels of logical precision and clearness of statement. But in a practical point of view those "masterpieces of logic" are utterly useless to most modern inquirers. These are interesting only as they exhibit the waste of gigantic energies; they do not even have the merit of illustrative rhetoric or eloquence. The earlier monks were devout and spiritual, and we can still read their lofty meditations with profit, since they elevate the soul and make it pant for the beatitudes of spiritual communion with God. But the writings of the Scholastic doctors are cold, calm, passionless, and purely intellectual, – logical without being edifying. We turn from them, however acute and able, with blended disappointment and despair. They are fig-trees, bearing nothing but leaves, such as our Lord did curse. The distinctions are simply metaphysical, and not moral.

Why the whole force of an awakening age should have been devoted to such subtilties and barren discussion it is difficult to see, unless they were found useful in supporting a theology made up of metaphysical deductions rather than an interpretation of the meaning of Scripture texts. But there was then no knowledge of Greek or Hebrew; there was no exegetical research; there was no science and no real learning. There was nothing but theology, with the exception of Lives of the Saints. The horizon of human inquiries was extremely narrow. But when the minds of very intellectual men were directed to one particular field, it would be natural to expect something remarkable and marvelously elaborate of its kind. Such was the Scholastic Philosophy. As a mere exhibition of dialectical acumen, minute distinctions, and logical precision in the use of words, it was wonderful. The intricacy and detail and ramifications of this system were an intellectual feat which astonishes us, yet which does not instruct us, certainly outside of a metaphysical divinity which had more charm to the men of the Middle Ages than it can have to us, even in a theological school where dogmatic divinity is made the most important study. The day will soon come when the principal chair in the theological school will be for the explanation of the Scripture texts on which dogmas are based; and for this, great learning and scholarship will be indispensable. To me it is surprising that metaphysics have so long retained their hold on the minds of Protestant divines. Nothing is more unsatisfactory, and to many more repulsive, than metaphysical divinity. It is a perversion of the spirit of Christian teachings. "What says our Lord?" should be the great inquiry in our schools of theology; not, What deductions can be drawn from them by a process of ingenious reasoning which often, without reference to other important truths, lands one in absurdities, or at least in one-sided systems?

But the metaphysical divinity of the Schoolmen had great attractions to the students of the Middle Ages. And there must have been something in it which we do not appreciate, or it would not have maintained itself in the schools for three hundred years. Perhaps it was what those ages needed, – the discipline through which the mind must go before it could be prepared for the scientific investigations of our own times. In an important sense the Scholastic doctors were the teachers of Luther and Bacon. Certainly their unsatisfactory science was one of the marked developments of the civilization of Europe, through which the Gothic nations must need pass. It has been the fashion to ridicule it and depreciate it in our modern times, especially among Protestants, who have ridiculed and slandered the papal power and all the institutions of the Middle Ages. Yet scholars might as well ridicule the text-books they were required to study fifty years ago, because they are not up to our times. We should not disdain the early steps by which future progress is made easy. We cannot despise men who gave up their lives to the contemplation of subjects which demand the highest tension of the intellectual faculties, even if these exercises were barren of utilitarian results. Some future age may be surprised at the comparative unimportance of questions which interest this generation. The Scholastic Philosophy cannot indeed be utilized by us in the pursuit of scientific knowledge; nor (to recur to Vaughan's simile for the great work of Aquinas) can a mediaeval cathedral be utilized for purposes of oratory or business. But the cathedral is nevertheless a grand monument, suggesting lofty sentiments, which it would be senseless and ruthless barbarism to destroy or allow to fall into decay, but which should rather be preserved as a precious memento of what is most poetic and attractive in the Middle Ages. When any modern philosopher shall rear so gigantic and symmetrical a monument of logical disquisitions as the "Summa Theologica" is said to be by the most competent authorities, then the sneers of a Macaulay or a Lewes will be entitled to more consideration. It is said that a new edition of this great Mediaeval work is about to be published under the direct auspices of the Pope, as the best and most comprehensive system of Christian theology ever written by man.

AUTHORITIES

Dr. Vaughan's *Life of Thomas Aquinas*
Histoire de la Vie et des Écrits de St. Thomas d'Aquin, par l'Abbé Bareille
Lacordaire's *Life of Saint Dominic*
Dr. Hampden's *Life of Thomas Aquinas*
Thomas Aquinas, in *London Quarterly* article, July, 1881
Summa Theologica Neander, Milman, Fleury, Dupin, and Ecclesiastical Histories generally

Biographic Universelle
Werner's *Leben des Heiligen Thomas von Aquino*
Trench's *Lectures on Mediaeval History*
Ueberweg & Rousselot's *History of Philosophy*. Dr. Hampden's article, in the *Encyclopaedia Metropolitana*, on Thomas Aquinas and the Scholastic Philosophy, is regarded by Hallam as the ablest view of this subject which has appeared in English.

Chapter 7

THOMAS BECKET: PRELATICAL POWER

A.D. 1118-1170

A great deal has been written of late years on Thomas Becket, Archbishop of Canterbury in the reign of Henry II, – some historians writing him up, and others writing him down; some making him a martyr to the Church, and others representing him as an ambitious prelate who encroached on royal authority, – more of a rebel than a patriot. His history has become interesting, in view of this very discrepancy of opinion, – like that of Oliver Cromwell, one of those historical puzzles which always have attraction to critics. And there is abundant material for either side we choose to take. An advocate can make a case in reference to Becket's career with more plausibility than about any other great character in English history, – with the exception of Queen Elizabeth, Cromwell, and Archbishop Laud.

The cause of Becket was the cause of the Middle Ages. He was not the advocate of fundamental principles, as were Burke and Bacon. He fought either for himself, or for principles whose importance has in a measure passed away. He was a high-churchman, who sought to make the temporal power subordinate to the spiritual. He appears in an interesting light only so far as the principles he sought to establish were necessary for the elevation of society in his ignorant and iron age. Moreover, it was his struggles which give to his life its chief charm, and invest it with dramatic interest. It was his energy, his audacity, his ability in overcoming obstacles, which made him memorable, – one of the heroes of history, like Ambrose and Hildebrand; an ecclesiastical warrior who fought bravely, and died without seeing the fruits of his bravery.

There seems to be some discrepancy among historians as to Becket's birth and origin, some making him out a pure Norman, and others a Saxon, and others again half Saracen. But that is, after all, a small matter, although the critics make a great thing of it. They always are inclined to wrangle over unimportant points. Michelet thinks he was a Saxon, and that his mother was a Saracen lady of rank, who had become enamored of the Saxon when taken prisoner while on a pilgrimage to the Holy Land, and who returned with him to England, embraced his religion, and was publicly baptized in Saint Paul's Cathedral, her beauty and rank having won attention; but Mr. Froude and Milman regard this as a late legend.

It would seem, however, that he was born in London about the year 1118 or 1119, and that his father, Gilbert Becket, was probably a respectable merchant and sheriff, or portreeve, of London, and was a Norman. His parents died young, leaving him not well provided for; but being beautiful and bright he was sent to school in an abbey, and afterwards to Oxford. From Oxford he went into a house of business in London for three years, and contrived to attract the notice of Theobald, Archbishop of Canterbury, who saw his talents, sent him to Paris, and thence to Bologna to study the canon law, which was necessary to a young man who would rise in the world. He was afterwards employed by Theobald in confidential negotiations. The question of the day in England was whether Stephen's son (Eustace) or Matilda's son (Henry of Anjou) was the true heir to the crown, it being settled that Stephen should continue to rule during his lifetime, and that Henry should peaceably follow him; which happened in a little more than a year. Becket had espoused the side of Henry.

The reign of Henry II, during which Becket's memorable career took place, was an important one. He united, through his mother Matilda, the blood of the old Saxon kings with that of the Norman dukes. He was the first truly English sovereign who had sat on the throne since the Conquest. In his reign (1154-1189) the blending of the Norman and Saxon races was effected. Villages and towns rose around the castles of great Norman nobles and the cathedrals and abbeys of Norman ecclesiastics. Ultimately these towns obtained freedom. London became a great city with more than a hundred churches. The castles, built during the disastrous civil wars of Stephen's usurped reign, were demolished. Peace and order were restored by a legitimate central power.

Between the young monarch of twenty-two and Thomas, as a favorite of Theobald and as Archdeacon of Canterbury, an intimacy sprang up. Henry II was the most powerful sovereign of Western Europe, since he was not only King of England, but had inherited in France Anjou and Touraine from his father, and Normandy and Maine from his mother. By his marriage with Eleanor of Aquitaine, he gained seven other provinces as her dower. The dominions of Louis were not half so great as his, even in France. And Henry was not only a powerful sovereign by his great territorial possessions, but also for his tact and ability. He saw the genius of Becket and made him his chancellor, loading him with honors and perquisites and Church benefices.

The power of Becket as chancellor was very great, since he was prime minister, and the civil administration of the kingdom was chiefly intrusted to him, embracing nearly all the functions now performed by the various members of the Cabinet. As chancellor he rendered great services. He effected a decided improvement in the state of the country; it was freed from robbers and bandits, and brought under dominion of the law. He depressed the power of the feudal nobles; he appointed the most deserving people to office; he repaired the royal palaces, increased the royal revenues, and promoted agricultural industry. He seems to have pursued a peace policy. But he was unscrupulous and grasping. His style of life when chancellor was for that age magnificent: Wolsey, in after times, scarcely excelled him. His dress was as rich as barbaric taste could make it, – for the more barbarous the age, the more gorgeous is the attire of great dignitaries. "The hospitalities of the chancellor were unbounded. He kept seven hundred horsemen completely armed. The harnesses of his horses were embossed with gold and silver. The most powerful nobles sent their sons to serve in his household as pages; and nobles and knights waited in his antechamber. There never passed a day when he did not make rich presents." His expenditure was enormous. He rivalled the King in magnificence. His sideboard was loaded with vessels of gold and silver. He was doubtless ostentatious, but his hospitality was free, and his person was as accessible as a primitive bishop. He is accused of being light and frivolous; but this I doubt. He had too many cares and duties for frivolity. He doubtless unbent. All men loaded down with labors must unbend somewhere. It was nothing against him that he told good stories at the royal table, or at his own, surrounded by earls and barons. These relaxations preserved in him elasticity of mind, without which the greatest genius soon becomes a hack, a plodding piece of mechanism, a stupid lump of learned dullness. But he was stained by no vices or excesses. He was a man of indefatigable activity, and all his labors were in the service of the Crown, to which, as chancellor, he was devoted, body and soul.

Is it strange that such a man should have been offered the See of Canterbury on the death of Theobald? He had been devoted to his royal master and friend; he enjoyed rich livings, and was Archdeacon of Canterbury; he had shown no opposition to the royal will. Moreover Henry wanted an able man for that exalted post, in order to carry out his schemes of making himself independent of priestly influence and papal interference.

So Becket was made archbishop and primate of the English Church at the age of forty-four, the clergy of the province acquiescing, – perhaps with secret complaints, for he was not even priest; merely deacon, and the minister of an unscrupulous king. He was ordained priest only just before receiving the primacy, and for that purpose.

Nothing in England could exceed the dignity of the See of Canterbury. Even the archbishopric of York was subordinate. Becket as metropolitan of the English Church was second in rank only to the King himself. He could depose any ecclesiastic in the realm. He had the exclusive privilege of crowning the king. His decisions were final, except an appeal to Rome. No one dared disobey his mandates, for the law of clerical obedience was one of the fundamental ideas of the age. Through his clergy, over whom his power was absolute, he controlled the people. His law courts had cognizance of questions which the royal courts could not interfere with. No ecclesiastical dignitary in Europe was his superior, except the Pope.

The Archbishop of Canterbury had been a great personage under the Saxon kings. Dunstan ruled England as the prime minister of Edward the Martyr, but his influence would have been nearly as great had he been merely primate of the Church. Nor was the power of the archbishop reduced by the Norman kings. William the Conqueror might have made the spiritual authority subordinate to the temporal, if he had followed his inclinations. But he dared not quarrel with the Pope, – the great Hildebrand, by whose favor he was unmolested in the conquest of the Saxons. He was on very intimate terms of friendship with Lanfranc, whom he made Archbishop of Canterbury, – a wily and ambitious Italian, who was devoted to the See of Rome and his spiritual monarch. The influence of Hildebrand and Lanfranc combined was too great to be resisted. Nor did he attempt resistance; he acquiesced in the necessity of making a king of Canterbury. His mind was so deeply absorbed with his conquest and other state matters that he did not seem to comprehend the difficulties which might arise under his successors, in yielding so much power to the primate. Moreover Lanfranc, in the quiet enjoyment of his ecclesiastical privileges, gave his powerful assistance in imposing the Norman yoke. He filled the great sees with Norman prelates. He does not seem to have had much sympathy with the Saxons, or their bishops, who were not so refined or intellectual as the bishops of France. The Normans were a superior race to the Saxons in executive ability and military enthusiasm. The chivalric element of English society, among the higher classes, came from the Normans, not from the Saxons. In piety, in passive virtues, in sustained industry, in patient toil, in love of personal freedom, the Saxons doubtless furnished a finer material for the basis of an agricultural, industrial, and commercial nation. The sturdy yeomen of England were Saxons: the noble and great administrators were Normans. In pride, in ambition, and in executive ability the Normans bore a closer resemblance to the old heroic Romans than did the Saxons.

The next archbishop after Lanfranc was Anselm, appointed by William Rufus. Anselm was a great scholar, the profoundest of the early Schoolmen; a man of meditative habits, who it was presumed would not interfere with royal encroachments. William Rufus never dreamed that the austere and learned monk, who had spent most of his days in the abbey of Bec in devout meditations and scholastic inquiries, would interfere with his rapacity. But, as we have already seen, Anselm was conscientious, and became the champion of the high-church party in the West. He occupied two distinct spheres, – he was absorbed in philosophical speculations, yet took an interest in all mundane questions. His resolve to oppose the king's usurpations in the spiritual realm caused the bitter quarrel already described, which ended in a compromise.

When Henry I came to the throne, he appointed Theobald, a feeble but good man, to the See of Canterbury, – less ambitious than Lanfranc, more inoffensive than Anselm; a Norman disinclined to quarrel with his sovereign. He died during the reign of Henry II, and this great monarch, as we have seen, appointed Becket to the vacant See, thinking that in the double capacity of chancellor and archbishop he would be a very powerful ally. But he was amazingly deceived in the character of his Chancellor. Becket had not sought the office, – the office had sought him. It would seem that he accepted it unwillingly. He knew that new responsibilities and duties would be imposed upon him, which, if he discharged conscientiously like Anselm, would in all probability alienate his friend the King, and provoke a desperate contest. And when the courtly and luxurious Chancellor held out, in Normandy, the skirts of his gilded and embroidered garments to show how unfit he was for an archbishop, Henry ought to have perceived that a future estrangement was a probability.

Better for Henry had Becket remained in the civil service. But Henry, with all his penetration, had not fathomed the mind of his favorite. Becket may have been a dissembler, or a great change may have been wrought in his character. Probably the new responsibilities imposed upon him as Primate of the English Church pressed upon his conscience. He knew that supreme allegiance was due to the Pope as head of the Church, and that if compelled to choose between the Pope and the King, he must obey the Pope. He was ambitious, doubtless; but his subsequent career shows that he preferred the liberties of his Church to the temporal interests of the sovereign. He was not a theologian, like Lanfranc and Anselm. Of all the great characters who preceded him, he most resembles Ambrose. Ambrose the governor, and a layman, became Archbishop of Milan. Becket the minister of a king, and only deacon, became Archbishop of Canterbury. The character of both these great men changed on their elevation to high ecclesiastical position. They both became high-churchmen, and defended the prerogatives of the clergy. But Ambrose was superior to Becket in his zeal to defend the doctrines of the Church. It does not appear that Becket took much interest in doctrines. In his age there was no dissent. Everybody, outwardly at least, was orthodox. In England, certainly, there were no heretics. Had Becket remained chancellor, in all probability he would not have quarreled with Henry. As archbishop he knew what was expected of him; and he knew also the infamy in store for him should he betray his cause. I do not believe he was a hypocrite. Every subsequent act of his life shows his sincerity and his devotion to his Church against his own interests.

Becket was no sooner ordained priest and consecrated as archbishop than he changed his habits. He became as austere as Lanfranc. He laid aside his former ostentation. He clothed himself in sackcloth; he mortified his body with fasts and laceration; he associated only with the pious and the learned; he frequented the cloisters and places of meditation; he received into his palace the needy and the miserable; he washed the feet of thirteen beggars every day; he conformed to the standard of piety in his age; he called forth the admiration of his attendants by his devotion to clerical duties. "He was," says James Stephen, "a second Moses entering the tabernacle at the accepted time for the contemplation of his God, and going out from it in order to perform some work of piety to his neighbor. He was like one of God's angels on the ladder, whose top reached the heavens, now descending to lighten the wants of men, now ascending to behold the divine majesty and the splendor of the Heavenly One. His prime councilor was reason, which ruled his passions as a mistress guides her servants. Under her guidance he was conducted to virtue, which, wrapped up in itself, and embracing everything within itself, never looks forward for anything additional."

This is the testimony of his biographer, and has not been explained away or denied, although it is probably true that Becket did not purge the corruptions of the Church, or punish the disorders and vices of the clergy, as Hildebrand did. But I only speak of his private character. I admit that he was no reformer. He was simply the high-churchman aiming to secure the ascendency of the spiritual power. Becket is not immortal for his reforms, or his theological attainments, but for his intrepidity, his courage, his devotion to his cause, – a hero, and not a man of progress; a man who fought a fight. It should be the aim of an historian to show for what he was distinguished; to describe his warfare, not to abuse him because he was not a philosopher and reformer. He lived in the twelfth century.

One of the first things which opened the eyes of the King was the resignation of the Chancellor. The King doubtless made him primate of the English hierarchy in order that he might combine both offices. But they were incompatible, unless Becket was willing to be the unscrupulous tool of the King in everything. Of course Henry could not long remain the friend of the man who he thought had duped him. Before a year had passed, his friendship was turned to secret but bitter enmity. Nor was it long before an event occurred, – a small matter, – which brought the King and the Prelate into open collision.

The matter was this: A young nobleman, who held a clerical office, committed a murder. As an ecclesiastic, he was brought before the court of the Bishop of Lincoln, and was sentenced to pay a small fine. But public justice was not satisfied, and the sheriff summoned the canon, who refused to plead before him. The matter was referred to the King, who insisted that the murderer should be tried in the civil court, – that a sacred profession should not screen a man who had committed a crime against society. While the King had, as we think, justice on his side, yet in this matter he interfered with the jurisdiction of the spiritual courts, which had been in force since Constantine. Theodosius and Justinian had confirmed the privilege of the Church, on the ground that the irregularities of a body of men devoted to the offices of religion should be veiled from the common eye; so that ecclesiastics were sometimes protected when they should be punished. But if the ecclesiastical courts had abuses, they were generally presided over by good and wise men, – more learned than the officers of the civil courts, and very popular in the Middle Ages; and justice in them was generally administered. So much were they valued in a dark age, when the clergy were the most learned men of their times, that much business came gradually to be transacted in them which previously had been settled in the civil courts,

– as tithes, testaments, breaches of contract, perjuries, and questions pertaining to marriage. But Henry did not like these courts, and was determined to weaken their jurisdiction, and transfer their power to his own courts, in order to strengthen the royal authority. Enlightened jurists and historians in our times here sympathize with Henry. High-Church ecclesiastics defend the jurisdiction of the spiritual courts, since they upheld the power of the Church, so useful in the Middle Ages. The King began the attack where the spiritual courts were weakest, – protection afforded to clergymen accused of crime. So he assembled a council of bishops and barons to meet him at Westminster. The bishops at first were inclined to yield to the King, but Becket gained them over, and would make no concession. He stood up for the privileges of his order. It was neither justice nor right which he defended, but his Church, at all hazards, – not her doctrines, but her prerogatives. He would present a barrier against royal encroachments, even if they were for the welfare of the realm. He would defend the independence of the clergy, and their power, – perhaps as an offset to royal power. In his rigid defence of the privileges of the clergy we see the churchman, not the statesman; we see the antagonist, not the ally, of the King. Henry was of course enraged. Who can wonder? He was bearded by his former favorite, – by one of his subjects.

If Becket was narrow, he probably was conscientious. He may have been ambitious of wielding unlimited spiritual authority. But it should be noted that, had he not quarreled with the King, he could have been both archbishop and chancellor, and in that double capacity wielded more power; and had he been disposed to serve his royal master, had he been more gentle, the King might not have pushed out his policy of crippling the spiritual courts, – might have waived, delayed, or made concessions. But now these two great potentates were in open opposition, and a deadly warfare was at hand. It is this fight which gives to Becket all his historical importance. It is not for me to settle the merits of the case, if I could, – only to describe the battle. The lawyers would probably take one side, and Catholic priests would take the other, and perhaps all high-churchmen. Even men like Mr. Froude and Mr. Freeman, both very learned and able, are totally at issue, not merely as to the merits of the case, but even as to the facts. Mr. Froude seems to hate Becket and all other churchmen as much as Mr. Freeman loves them. I think one reason why Mr. Froude exalts so highly Henry VIII is because he put his foot on the clergy and took away their revenues. But with the war of partisans I have nothing to do, except the war between Henry II and Thomas Becket.

This war waxed hot when a second council of bishops and barons was assembled at Clarendon, near Winchester, to give their assent to certain resolutions which the King's judges had prepared in reference to the questions at issue, and other things tending to increase the royal authority. They are called in history "The Constitutions of Clarendon." The gist and substance of them were, that during the vacancy of any bishopric or abbey of royal foundation, the estates were to be in the custody of the Crown; that all disputes between laymen and clergymen should be tried in the civil courts; that clergymen accused of crime should, if the judges decided, be tried in the King's court, and, if found guilty, be handed over to the secular arm for punishment; that no officer or tenant of the King should be excommunicated without the King's consent; that no peasant's son should be ordained without permission of his feudal lord; that great ecclesiastical personages should not leave the kingdom without the King's consent.

"Anybody must see that these articles were nothing more nor less than the surrender of the most important and vital privileges of the Church into the hands of the King: not merely her properties, but her liberties; even a surrender of the only weapon with which she defended herself in extreme cases, – that of excommunication." It was the virtual confiscation of the Church in favor of an aggressive and unscrupulous monarch. Could we expect Becket to sign such an agreement, to part with his powers, to betray the Church of which he was the first dignitary in England? When have men parted with their privileges, except upon compulsion? He never would have given up his prerogatives; he never meant for a moment to do so. He was not the man for such a base submission. Yet he was so worried and threatened by the King, who had taken away from him the government of the Prince, his son, and the custody of certain castles; he was so importuned by the bishops themselves, for fear that the peace of the country would be endangered, – that in a weak moment he promised to sign the articles, reserving this phrase: "Saving the honor of his order." With this reservation, he thought he could sign the agreement, for he could include under such a phrase whatever he pleased.

But when really called to fulfil his promise and sign with his own hand those constitutions, he wavered. He burst out in passionate self-reproaches for having made a promise he never intended to keep. "Never, never!" he said; "I will never do it so long as breath is in my body." In his repentance he mortified himself with new self-expiations. He suspended himself from the service of the altar. He was overwhelmed with grief, shame, rage, and penitence. He resolved he would not yield up the privileges of his order, come what might, – not even if the Pope gave him authority to sign.

The dejected and humbled metropolitan advanced to the royal throne with downcast eye but unfaltering voice; accused himself of weakness and folly, and firmly refused to sign the articles. "Miserable wretch that I am," cried he, with bitter tears coursing down his cheeks, "I see the Anglican Church enslaved, in punishment for my sins. But it is all right. I was taken from the court, not the cloister, to fill this station; from the palace of Caesar, not the school of the Saviour. I was a feeder of birds, but suddenly made a feeder of men; a patron of stage-players, a follower of hounds, and I became a shepherd over so many souls. Surely I am rightly abandoned by God."

He then took his departure for Canterbury, but was soon summoned to a grand council at Northampton, to answer serious charges. He was called to account for the sums he had spent as chancellor, and for various alleged injustices. He was found guilty by a court controlled by the King, and sentenced to pay a heavy fine, which he paid. The next day new charges were preferred, and he was condemned to a still heavier fine, which he was unable to pay; but he found sureties. On the next day still heavier charges were made, and new fines inflicted, which would have embarrassed the temporalities of his See. He now perceived that the King was bent on his ruin; that the more he yielded the more he would be expected to yield. He therefore resolved to yield no further, but to stand on his rights.

But before he made his final resistance he armed himself with his crozier, and sought counsel from the bishops assembled in another chamber of the royal castle. The bishops were divided: some for him, some against him. Gilbert Foliot of London put him in mind of the benefits he had received from Henry, and the humble condition from which he was raised, and advised him to resign for sake of peace. Henry of Winchester, a relative of the King, bade him resign. Roger of Worcester was non-committal. "If I advise to resist the King, I shall be put out of the synagogue," said he. "I counsel nothing." The Bishop of Chichester declared that Becket was primate no longer, as he had gone against the laws of the realm. In the midst of this conference the Earl of Leicester entered, and announced the sentence of the peers. Then gathering himself up to his full height, the Primate, with austere dignity, addressed the Earl and the Bishops: "My brethren, our enemies are pressing hard upon us, and the whole world is against us; but I now enjoin you, in virtue of your obedience, and in peril of your orders, not to be present in any cause which may be made against my person; and I appeal to that refuge of the distressed, the Holy See. And I command you as your Primate, and in the name of the Pope, to put forth the censures of the Church in behalf of your Archbishop, should the secular arm lay violent hands upon me; for, be assured, though this frail body may yield to persecution, – since all flesh is weak, – yet shall my spirit never yield."

Then pushing his way, he swept through the chamber, reached the quadrangle of the palace, mounted his horse, reached his lodgings, gave a banquet to some beggars, stole away in disguise and fled, reaching the coast in safety, and succeeding in crossing over to Flanders. He was now out of the King's power, who doubtless would have imprisoned him and perhaps killed him, for he hated him with the intensest hatred. Becket had deceived him, having trifled with him by taking an oath to sign the Constitutions of Clarendon, and then broken his oath and defied his authority, appealing to the Pope, and perhaps involving the King in a quarrel with the supreme spiritual power of Christendom. Finally he had deserted his post and fled the kingdom. He had defeated the King in his most darling schemes.

But although Becket was an exile, a fugitive, and a wanderer, he was still Archbishop of Canterbury. He was the head of the English Church, and all the clergy of the kingdom owed him spiritual obedience. He still had the power of excommunicating the King, and the sole right of crowning his successor. If the Pope should take his side, and the King of France, and other temporal powers, Becket would be no unequal match for the King. It was a grand crisis which Henry comprehended, and he therefore sent some of his most powerful barons and prelates to the Continent to advance his cause and secure the papal interposition.

Becket did not remain long in Flanders, since the Count was cold and did not take his side. He escaped, and sought shelter and aid from the King of France.

Louis VII was a feeble monarch, but he hated Henry II and admired Becket. He took him under his protection, and wrote a letter to the Pope in his behalf.

That Pope was Alexander III, – himself an exile, living in Sens, and placed in a situation of great difficulty, struggling as he was with an antipope, and the great Frederic Barbarossa, Emperor of Germany. Moreover he was a personal friend of Henry, to whom he had been indebted for his elevation to the papal throne. His course, therefore, was non-committal and dilatory and vacillating, although he doubtless was on the side of the prelate who exalted ecclesiastical authority. But he was obliged from policy to be prudent and conciliatory. He patiently heard both sides, but decided nothing. All he consented to do was to send cardinal legates to England, but intrusted to none but himself the prerogatives of final judgment.

After Henry's ambassadors had left, Becket appeared with a splendid train of three hundred horsemen, the Archbishop of Rheims, the brothers of the King of France, and a long array of bishops. The Pope dared not receive him with the warmth he felt, but was courteous, more so than his cardinals; and Becket unfolded and discussed the Constitutions of Clarendon, which of course found no favor with the Pope. He rebuked Becket for his weakness in promising to sign a paper which curtailed so fundamentally the privileges of the Church. Some historians affirm he did not extend to him the protection he deserved, although he confirmed him in his office. He sent him to the hospitable care of the Abbot of Pontigny. "Go now," he said, "and learn what privation is; and in the company of Christ's humblest servants subdue the flesh to the spirit."

In this Cistercian abbey it would seem that Becket lived in great austerity, tearing his flesh with his nails, and inflicting on himself severe flagellations; so that his health suffered, and his dreams haunted him. He was protected, but he could not escape annoyances and persecutions. Henry, in his wrath, sequestrated the estates of the archbishopric; the incumbents of his benefices were expelled; all his relatives and dependents were banished, – some four hundred people; men, women, and children. The bishops sent him ironical letters, and hoped his fasts would benefit his soul.

The quarrel now was of great interest to all Europe. It was nothing less than a battle between the spiritual and temporal powers, like that, a century before, between Hildebrand and the Emperor of Germany. Although the Pope was obliged from motives of policy, – for fear of being deposed, – to seem neutral and attempt to conciliate, still the war really was carried on in his behalf. "The great, the terrible, the magnificent in the fate of Becket," says Michelet, "arises from his being charged, weak and unassisted, with the interests of the Church Universal, – a post which belonged to the Pope himself." He was still Archbishop; but his revenues were cut off, and had it not been for the bounty of Louis the King of France, who admired him and respected his cause, he might have fared as a simple monk. The Pope allowed him to excommunicate the persons who occupied his estates, but not the King himself. He feared a revolt of the English Church from papal authority, since Henry was supreme in England, and had won over to his cause the English bishops. The whole question became complicated and interesting. It was the common topic of discourse in all the castles and convents of Europe. The Pope, timid and calculating, began to fear he had supported Becket too far, and pressed upon him a reconciliation with Henry, much to the disgust of Becket, who seemed to comprehend the issue better than did the Pope; for the Pope had, in his desire to patch up the quarrel, permitted the son of Henry to be crowned by the Archbishop of York, which was not only an infringement of the privileges of the Primate, but was a blow against the spiritual power. So long as the Archbishop of Canterbury had the exclusive privilege of crowning a king, the King was dependent in a measure on the Primate, and, through him, on the Pope. At this suicidal act on the part of Alexander, Becket lost all patience, and wrote to him a letter of blended indignation and reproach. "Why," said he, "lay in my path a stumbling-block? How can you blind yourself to the wrong which Christ suffers in me and yourself? And yet you call on me, like a hireling, to be silent. I might flourish in power and riches and pleasures, and be feared and honored of all; but since the Lord hath called me, weak and unworthy as I am, to the oversight of the English Church, I prefer proscription, exile, poverty, misery, and death, rather than traffic with the liberties of the Church."

What language to a Pope! What a reproof from a subordinate! How grandly the character of Becket looms up here! I say nothing of his cause. It may have been a right or a wrong one. Who shall settle whether spiritual or temporal power should have the ascendency in the Middle Ages? I speak only of his heroism, his fidelity to his cause, his undoubted sincerity. Men do not become exiles and martyrs voluntarily, unless they are backed by a great cause. Becket may have been haughty, irascible, ambitious. Very likely. But what then? The more personal faults he had, the greater does his devotion to the interests of the Church appear, fighting as it were alone and unassisted. Undaunted, against the advice of his friends, unsupported by the Pope, he now hurls his anathemas from his retreat in France. He excommunicates the Bishop of Salisbury, and John of Oxford, and the Archdeacon of Ilchester, and the Lord Chief-Justice de Luci, and everybody who adhered to the Constitutions of Clarendon. The bishops of England remonstrate with him, and remind him of his plebeian origin and his obligations to the King. To whom he replies: "I am not indeed sprung from noble ancestors, but I would rather be the man to whom nobility of mind gives the advantages of birth than to be the degenerate issue of an illustrious family. David was taken from the sheepfold to be a ruler of God's people, and Peter was taken from fishing to be the head of the Church. I was born under a humble roof, yet, nevertheless, God has intrusted me with the liberties of the Church, which I will guard with my latest breath."

Henry now threatens to confiscate the property of all the Cistercian convents in England; and the Abbot of Pontigny, at the command of his general, is forced to drive Becket away from his sanctuary. Becket retires to Sens, sad at heart and grieved that the excommunications which he had inflicted should have been removed by the Pope. Then Louis, the King of France, made war on Henry, and took Becket under his protection. The Pope rebuked Louis for the war; but Louis retorted by telling Alexander that it was a shame for him not to give up his time-serving policy. In so doing, Louis spoke out the heart of Christendom. The Pope, at last aroused, excommunicated the Archbishop of York for crowning the son of Henry, and threatened Henry himself with an interdict, and recalled his legates. Becket also fulminated his excommunications. There was hardly a prelate or royal chaplain in England who was not under ecclesiastical censure. The bishops began to waver. Henry had reason to fear he might lose the support of his English subjects, and Norman likewise. He could do nothing with the whole Church against him.

The King was therefore obliged to compromise. Several times before, he had sought reconciliation with his dreadful enemy; but Becket always, in his promises, fell back on the phrase, "Saving the honor of his order," or "Saving the honor of God." But now, amid the fire of excommunications, Henry was compelled to make his peace with the man he detested. He himself did not much care for the priestly thunderbolts, but his clergy and his subjects did. The penalty of eternal fire was a dreadful fear to those who believed, as everybody then did, in the hell of which the popes were supposed to hold the keys. This fear sustained the empire of the popes; it was the basis of sacerdotal rule in the Middle Ages. Hence Becket was so powerful, even in exile. His greatness was in his character; his power was in his spiritual weapons.

In the hollow reconciliation at last effected between the King and the Prelate, Henry promised to confirm Becket in his powers and dignities, and molest him no more. But he haughtily refused the customary kiss of peace. Becket saw the omen; so did the King of France. The peace was inconclusive. It was a truce, not a treaty. Both parties distrusted each other.

But Henry was weary with the struggle, and Becket was tired of exile, – never pleasant, even if voluntary. Moreover, the Prelate had gained the moral victory, even as Hildebrand did when the Emperor of Germany stooped as a suppliant in the fortress of Canossa. The King of England had virtually yielded to the Archbishop of Canterbury. Perhaps Becket felt that his mission was accomplished; that he had done the work for which he was raised up. Wearied, sickened with the world, disgusted with the Pope, despising his bishops, perhaps he was willing to die. He had a presentiment that he should die as a martyr. So had the French king and his prelates. But Becket longed to return to his church and celebrate the festivities of Christmas. So he made up his mind to return to England, "although I know, of a truth," he said, "I shall meet my passion there." Before embarking he made a friendly and parting visit to the King of France, and then rode to the coast with an escort of one hundred horsemen. As Dover was guarded by the King's retainers, who might harm him, he landed at Sandwich, his own town. The next day he set out for Canterbury, after an absence of seven years. The whole population lined the road, strewed it with flowers, and rent the air with songs. Their beloved Archbishop had returned. On reaching Canterbury he went directly to his cathedral and seated himself on his throne, and the monks came and kissed him, with tears in their eyes. One Herbert said, "Christ has conquered; Christ is now King!"

From Canterbury Becket made a sort of triumphal progress through the kingdom, with the pretence of paying a visit to the young king at Woodstock, – exciting rather than allaying the causes of discord, scattering his excommunications, still haughty, restless, implacable; so that the Court became alarmed, and ordered him to return to his diocese. He obeyed, as he wished to celebrate Christmas at home; and ascending his long-neglected pulpit preached, according to Michelet, from this singular text: "I am come to die in the midst of you."

Henry at this time was on the Continent, and was greatly annoyed at the reports of Becket's conduct which reached him. Then there arrived three bishops whom the Primate had excommunicated, with renewed complaints and grievances, assuring him there would be no peace so long as Becket lived. Henry was almost wild with rage and perplexity. What could he do? He dared not execute the Archbishop, as Henry VIII would have done. In his age the Prelate was almost as powerful as the King. Violence to his person was the last thing to do, for this would have involved the King in war with the adherents of the Pope, and would have entailed an excommunication. Still, the supremest desire of Henry's soul was to get Becket out of the way. So, yielding to an impulse of passion, he said to his attendants, "Is there no one to relieve me from the insults of this low-born and turbulent priest?"

Among these attendants were four courtiers or knights, of high birth and large estates, who, hearing these reproachful words, left the court at once, crossed the channel, and repaired to the castle of Sir Ranulf de Broc, the great enemy of Becket, who had molested him in innumerable ways. Some friendly person contrived to acquaint Becket with his danger, to whom he paid no heed, knowing it very well himself. He knew he was to die; and resolved to die bravely.

The four armed knights, meanwhile, on the 29th of December, rode with an escort to Canterbury, dined at the Augustinian abbey, and entered the court-yard of the Archbishop's palace as Becket had finished his mid-day meal and had retired to an inner room with his chaplain and a few intimate friends. They then entered the hall and sought the Archbishop, who received them in silence. Sir Reginald Fitzurst then broke the silence with these words: "We bring you the commands of the King beyond the sea, that you repair without delay to the young King's presence and swear allegiance. And further, he commands you to absolve the bishops you have excommunicated." On Becket's refusal, the knight continued: "Since you will not obey, the royal command is that you and your clergy forthwith depart from the realm, never more to return." Becket angrily declared he would never again leave England. The knights then sprang to their feet and departed, enjoining the attendants to prevent the escape of Becket, who exclaimed: "Do you think I shall fly, then? Neither for the King nor any living man will I fly. You cannot be more ready to kill me than I am to die."

He sought, however, the shelter of his cathedral, as the vesper bell summoned him to prayers, – followed by the armed knights, with a company of men-at-arms, driving before them a crowd of monks. The Archbishop was standing on the steps of the choir, beyond the central pillar, which reached to the roof of the cathedral, in the dim light shed by the candles of the altars, so that only the outline of his noble figure could be seen, when the knights closed around him, and Fitzurst seized him, – perhaps meaning to drag him away as a prisoner to the King, or outside the church before despatching him. Becket cried, "Touch me not, thou abominable wretch!" at the same time hurling Tracy, another of the knights, to the ground, who, rising, wounded him in the head with his sword. The Archbishop then bent his neck to the assassins, exclaiming, "I am prepared to die for Christ and His Church."

Figure 8. Murder of St. Thomas à Becket. *After the painting by A. Dawant.*

Such was the murder of Becket, – a martyr, as he has been generally regarded, for the liberties of the Church; but, according to some, justly punished for presumptuous opposition to his sovereign.

The assassination was a shock to Christendom. The most intrepid churchman of his age was slain at his post for doing, as he believed, his duty. No one felt the shock more than the King himself, who knew he would be held responsible for the murder. He dreaded the consequences, and shut himself up for three days in his chamber, refusing food, issuing orders for the arrest of the murderers, and sending ambassadors to the Pope to exculpate himself. Fearing an excommunication and an interdict, he swore on the Gospel, in one of the Norman cathedrals, that he had not commanded nor desired the death of the Archbishop; and stipulated to maintain at his own cost two hundred knights in the Holy Land, to abrogate the Constitutions of Clarendon, to reinvest the See of Canterbury with all he had wrested away, and even to undertake a crusade against the Saracens of Spain if the Pope desired. Amid the calamities which saddened his latter days, he felt that all were the judgments of God for his persecution of the martyr, and did penance at his tomb.

So Becket slew more by his death than he did by his life. His cause was gained by his blood: it arrested the encroachments of the Norman kings for more than three hundred years. He gained the gratitude of the Church and a martyr's crown. He was canonized as a saint. His shrine was enriched with princely offerings beyond any other object of popular veneration in the Middle Ages. Till the time of the Reformation a pilgrimage to that shrine was a common form of penance for people of all conditions, and was supposed to expiate their sins. Even miracles were reputed to be wrought at that shrine, while a drop of Becket's blood would purchase a domain!

Whatever may be said about the cause of Becket, to which there are two sides, there is no doubt about his popularity. Even the Reformation, and the changes made in the English Constitution, have not obliterated the veneration in which he was held for five hundred years. You cannot destroy respect for a man who is willing to be a martyr, whether his cause is right or wrong. If enlightened judgments declare that he was "a martyr of sacerdotal power, not of Christianity; of a caste, and not of mankind;" that he struggled for the authority and privileges of the clergy rather than for the good of his country, – still it will be conceded that he fought bravely and died with dignity. All people love heroism. They are inclined to worship heroes; and especially when an unarmed priest dares to resist an unscrupulous and rapacious king, as Henry is well known to have been, and succeeds in tearing from his hands the spoils he has seized, there must be admiration. You cannot extinguish the tribute of the soul for heroism, any more than that of the mind for genius. The historian who seeks to pull down a hero from the pedestal on which he has been seated for ages plays a losing game. No brilliancy in sophistical pleadings can make men long prefer what is *new* to that which is *true*. Becket is enshrined in the hearts of his countrymen, even as Cromwell is among the descendants of the Puritans; and substantially for the same reason, – because they both fought bravely for their respective causes, – the cause of the people in their respective ages. Both recognized

God Almighty, and both contended against the despotism of kings seeking to be absolute, and in behalf of the people who were ground down by military power. In the twelfth century the people looked up to the clergy as their deliverers and friends; in the seventeenth century to parliaments and lawyers. Becket was the champion of the clergy, even as Cromwell was the champion – at least at first – of the Parliament. Carlyle eulogizes Cromwell as much as Froude abuses Becket; but Becket, if more haughty and repulsive than Cromwell in his private character, yet was truer to his principles. He was a great hero, faithful to a great cause, as he regarded it, however averse this age may justly be to priestly domination. He must be judged by the standard which good and enlightened people adopted seven hundred years ago, – not in semi-barbarous England alone, but throughout the continent of Europe. This is not the standard which reason accepts to-day, I grant; but it is the standard by which Becket must be judged, – even as the standard which justified the encroachments of Leo the Great, or the rigorous rule of Tiberius and Marcus Aurelius, is not that which enthrones Gustavus Adolphus and William of Orange in the heart of the civilized world.

AUTHORITIES

Eadmer's *Life of Anselm*
Historia Novarum
Sir J. Stephen's *Life of Becket*, of William of Malmsbury, and of Henry of Huntington
Correspondence of Thomas Becket, with that of Foliot, Bishop of London, and John of Salisbury
Chronicle of Peter of Peterborough
Chronicle of Ralph Niper, and that of Jocelyn of Brakeland
Dugdale's *Monasticon*
Freeman's *Norman Conquest*
Michelet's *History of France*
Green, Hume, Knight, Stubbs, among the English historians
Encyclopaedia Britannica

Hook's *Lives of the Archbishops of Canterbury*
Lord Littleton on Henry II
Stanley's *Memorials of Canterbury*
Milman's *Latin Christianity*
article by Froude
Morris's *Life of Thomas à Becket*
J. Craigie Robertson's *Life of Thomas Becket.*

Chapter 8

THE FEUDAL SYSTEM

ABOUT A.D. 800-1300

There is no great character with whom Feudalism is especially identified. It was an institution of the Middle Ages, which grew out of the miseries and robberies that succeeded the fall of the Roman Empire.

Before I present the mutual relation between a lord and his vassal, I would call your attention to political anarchies ending in political degradation; to an unformed state of society; to semi-barbarism, with its characteristic vices of plunder, rapine, oppression, and injustice; to wild and violent passions, unchecked by law; to the absence of central power; to the reign of hard and martial nobles; to the miseries of the people, ground down, ignorant, and brutal; to rude agricultural life; to petty wars; to general ignorance, which kept society in darkness and gloom for a thousand years, – all growing out of the eclipse of the old civilization, so that the European nations began a new existence, and toiled in sorrow and fear, with few ameliorations: an iron age, yet an age which was not unfavorable for the development of new virtues and heroic qualities, under the influence of which society emerged from barbarism, with a new foundation for national greatness, and a new material for Christianity and art and literature and science to work upon.

Such was the state of society during the existence of feudal institutions, – a period of about five hundred years, – dating from the dismemberment of Charlemagne's empire to the fifteenth century. The era of its greatest power was from the Norman conquest of England to the reign of Edward III. But there was a long and gloomy period before Feudalism ripened into an institution, – from the dissolution of the Roman Empire to the eighth and ninth centuries. I would assign this period as the darkest and the dreariest in the history of Europe since the Roman conquests, for this reason, – that civilization perished without any one to chronicle the changes, or to take notice of the extinction.

From Charlemagne there had been, with the exception of brief intervals, the birth of new ideas and interests, the growth of a new civilization. Before his day there was a progressive decline. Art, literature, science, alike faded away. There were no grand monuments erected, the voice of the poet was unheard in the universal wretchedness, the monks completed the destruction which the barbarians began. Why were libraries burned or destroyed? Why was classic literature utterly neglected? Why did no great scholars arise, even in the Church? The new races looked in vain for benefactors. Even the souvenirs of the old Empire were lost. Nearly all the records of ancient greatness perished. The old cities were levelled to the ground. Nothing was built but monasteries, and these were as gloomy as feudal castles at a later date. The churches were heavy and mournful. Good men hid themselves, trying to escape from the miserable world, and sang monotonous chants of death and the grave. Agriculture was at the lowest state, and hunting, piracy, and robbery were resorted to as a means of precarious existence. There was no commerce. The roads were invested with vagabonds and robbers. It was the era of universal pillage and destruction. Nothing was sacred. Universal desolation filled the souls of men with despair. What state of society could be worse than that of England under the early Saxon kings? There were no dominant races and no central power. The countries of Europe relapsed into a sullen barbarism. I see no bright spot anywhere, not even in Italy, which was at this time the most overrun and the most mercilessly plundered of all the provinces of the fallen Empire. The old capital of the world was nearly depopulated. Nothing was spared of ancient art on which the barbarians could lay their hands, and nothing was valued.

This was the period of what writers call *allodial* tenure, in distinction from feudal. The allodialist owned indeed his lands, but they were subject to incessant depredations from wandering tribes of barbarians and from robbers. There was no encouragement to till the soil. There was no incentive to industry of any kind. During a reign of universal lawlessness, what man would work except for a scanty and precarious support? His cattle might be driven away, his crops seized, his house plundered. It is hard to realize that our remote ancestors were mere barbarians, who by the force of numbers overran the world. They seem to have had but one class of virtues, – – contempt of death, and the willing sacrifice of their lives in battle. The allodialist, however, was not a barbaric warrior or chieftain, but the despoiled owner of lands that his ancestors had once cultivated in peace and prosperity. He was the degenerate descendant of Celtic and Roman citizens, the victim of barbaric spoliations. His lands may have passed into the hands of the Gothic conquerors; but the Gothic or Burgundian or Frankish possessor of innumerable acres, once tilled by peaceful citizens, remained an allodial proprietor. Even he had no protection and no safety; for any new excursion of less fortunate barbarians would desolate his possessions and decimate his laborers. The small proprietor was especially subject to pillage and murder.

In the universal despair from this reign of anarchy and lawlessness, when there was no security to property and no redress of evils, the allodialist parted with his lands to some powerful chieftain, and obtained promise of protection. He even resigned the privilege of freedom to save his wretched life. He became a serf, – a semi-bondman, chained to the soil, but protected from outrage. Nothing but inconceivable miseries, which have not been painted by historians, can account for the almost simultaneous change in the ownership of land in all European countries. We can conceive of nothing but blank despair among the people who attempted to cultivate land. And there must have been the grossest ignorance and the lowest degradation when men were willing to submit to the curtailment of personal freedom and the loss of their lands, in order to find protectors.

Thus Feudalism arose in the ninth and tenth centuries from the absolute wreck of property and hopes. It was virtually the surrender of land for the promise of protection. It was the great necessity of that anarchical age. Like all institutions, it grew out of the needs of the times. Yet its universal acceptance seems to prove that the change was beneficial. Feudalism, especially in its early ages, is not to be judged by the institutions of our times, any more than is the enormous growth of spiritual power which took place when this social and political revolution was going on. Wars and devastations and untold calamities and brutal forces were the natural sequence of barbaric invasions, and of the progressive fall of the old civilization, continued from generation to generation for a period of two or three hundred years, with scarcely any interruption. You get no relief from such a dispensation of Divine Providence, unless you can solve the question why the Roman Empire was permitted to be swept away. If it must be destroyed, from the prevalence of the same vices which have uniformly undermined all empires, – utter and unspeakable rottenness and depravity, – in spite of Christianity, whether nominal or real; if eternal justice must bear sway on this earth, bringing its fearful retributions for the abuse of privileges and general wickedness, – then we accept the natural effects of that violence which consummated the ruin. The natural consequences of two hundred years of pillage and warfare and destruction of ancient institutions were, and could have been nothing other than, miseries, misrule, sufferings, poverty, insecurity, and despair. A universal conflagration must destroy everything that past ages had valued. As a relief from what was felt to be intolerable, and by men who were brutal, ignorant, superstitious, and degraded, all from the effect of the necessary evils which war creates, a sort of semi-slavery was felt to be preferable, as the price of dependence and protection.

Dependence and protection are the elemental principles of Feudalism. These were the hard necessities which the age demanded. And for three hundred years, it cannot be doubted, the relation between master and serf was beneficial. It resulted in a more peaceful state of society, – not free from great evils, but still a healthful change from the disorders of the preceding epoch. The peasant could cultivate his land comparatively free from molestation. He was still poor. Sometimes he was exposed to heavy exactions. He was bound to give a portion of the profits of his land to his lordly proprietor; and he was bound to render services in war. But, as he was not bound to serve over forty days, he was not led on distant expeditions; he was not carried far from home. He was not exposed to the ambition of military leaders. His warlike services seem to be confined to the protection of his master's castle and family, or to the assault of some neighboring castle. He was simply made to participate in baronial quarrels; and as these quarrels were frequent, his life was not altogether peaceful.

But war on a large scale was impossible in the feudal age. The military glory of the Roman conquerors was unknown, and also that of modern European monarchs. The peasant was bound to serve under the banner of a military chieftain only for a short time: then he returned to his farm. His great military weapon was the bow, – the weapon of semi-barbarians. The spear, the sword, the battle-axe were the weapons of the baronial family, – the weapons of knights, who fought on horseback, cased in defensive armor. The peasant fought on foot; and as the tactics of ancient warfare were inapplicable, and those of modern warfare unknown, the strength of armies was in cavalry and not in the infantry, as in modern times. But armies were not large from the ninth to the twelfth century, – not until the Crusades arose. Nor were they subject to a rigid discipline. They were simply an armed rabble. They were more like militia than regular forces; they fostered military virtues, without the demoralization of standing armies. In the feudal age there were no standing armies. Even at so late a period as the time of Queen Elizabeth that sovereign had to depend on the militia for the defence of the realm against the Spaniards. Standing armies are the invention of great military monarchs or a great military State. The bow and arrow were used equally to shoot men and shoot deer; but they rarely penetrated the armor of knights, or their force was broken by the heavy shield: they took effect only on the undefended bodies of the peasantry. Hence there was a great disproportion of the slain in battle between peasants and their mounted masters. War, even when confined to a small sphere, has its terrors. The sufferers were the common people, whose lives were not held of much account. History largely confines itself to battles. Hence we are apt to lose sight of the uneventful life of the people in quiet times.

But the barons were not always fighting. In the intervals of war the peasant enjoyed the rude pleasures of his home. He grew up with strong attachments, having no desire to migrate or travel. Gradually the sentiment of loyalty was born, – loyalty to his master and to his country. His life was rough, but earnest. He had great simplicity of character. He became honest, industrious, and frugal. He was contented with but few pleasures, – rural fêtes and village holidays. He had no luxuries and no craving for them. Measured by our modern scale of pleasures he led a very inglorious, unambitious, and rude life.

Contentment is one of the mysteries of existence. We should naturally think that excitement and pleasure and knowledge would make people happy, since they stimulate the intellectual powers; but on the contrary they seem to produce unrest and cravings which are never satisfied. And we should naturally think that a life of isolation, especially with no mental resources, – a hard rural existence, with but few comforts and no luxuries, – would make people discontented. Yet it does not seem to be so in fact, as illustrated by the apparent contentment of people doomed to hard labor in the most retired and dreary retreats. We wonder at their placitude, as we travel in remote and obscure sections of the country. A poor farmer, whose house is scarcely better than a hovel, surrounded with chickens and pigs, and with only a small garden, – unadorned and lonely and repulsive, – has no cravings which make the life of the favored rich sometimes unendurable. The poorer he is, and therefore the more miserable as we should think, the more contented he seems to be; while a fashionable woman or *ennuied* man, both accustomed to the luxuries and follies of city life, with all its refinements and gratification of intellectual and social pleasures, will sometimes pine in a suburban home, with all the gilded glories of rich furniture, books, beautiful gardens, greenhouses, luxurious living, horses, carriages, and everything that wealth can furnish.

So that civilization would seem often a bitter mockery, showing that intellectual life only stimulates the cravings of the soul, but does not satisfy them. And when people are poor but cultivated, the unhappiness seems to be still greater; demonstrating that cultivated intellect alone opens to the mind the existence of evils which are intensified by the difficulty of their removal, and on which the mind dwells with feelings kindred to despair. I have sometimes doubted whether an obscure farmer's daughter is any happier with her piano, and her piles of cheaply illustrated literature and translations of French novels, and her smatterings of science learned in normal schools, since she has learned too often to despise her father and mother and brother, and her uneducated rural beau, and all her surroundings, with poverty and unrest and aspiration for society eating out her soul. The happiness produced merely by intellectual pleasures and social frivolities is very small at the best, compared with that produced by the virtues of the heart and the affections kindled by deeds of devotion, or the duties which take the mind from itself. Intellectual pleasures give only a brief satisfaction, unless directed to a practical end, like the earnest imparting of knowledge in educational pursuits, or the pursuit of art for itself alone, – to create, and not to devour, as the epicure eats his dinner. Where is the happiness of devouring books with no attempt to profit by them, except in the temporary pleasure of satisfying an appetite? So even the highest means of happiness may become a savor of death unto death when perverted or unimproved. Never should we stimulate the intellect merely to feed upon itself. Unless intellectual culture is directed to what is useful, especially to the necessities or improvement of others, it is a delusion and a snare. Better far to be ignorant, but industrious and useful in any calling however humble, than to cram the mind with knowledge that leads to no good practical result. The buxom maiden of rural life, in former days absorbed in the duties of home, with no knowledge except that gained in a district school in the winter, with all her genial humanities in the society of equals no more aspiring than herself, is to me a far more interesting person than the pale-faced, languid, discontented, envious girl who has just returned from a school beyond her father's means, even if she can play upon an instrument, and has worn herself thin in exhausting studies under the stimulus of ambitious competition, or the harangues of a pedant who thinks what he calls "education" to be the end of life, – an education which reveals her own insignificance, or leads her to strive for an unattainable position.

 I am forced to make these remarks to show that the Mediaeval peasant was not necessarily miserable because he was ignorant, or isolated, or poor.

In so doing I may excite the wrath of some who think a little knowledge is *not* a dangerous thing, and may appear to be throwing cold water on one of the noblest endeavors of modern times. But I do not sneer at education. I only seek to show that it will not make people happy, unless it is directed into useful channels; and that even ignorance may be bliss when it is folly to be wise. A benevolent Providence tempers all conditions to the necessities of the times. The peasantry of Europe became earnest and stalwart warriors and farmers, even under the grinding despotism of feudal masters. With their beer and brown bread, and a fowl in the pot on a Sunday, they grew up to be hardy, bold, strong, healthy, and industrious. They furnished a material on which Christianity and a future civilization could work. They became patriotic, religious, and kind-hearted. They learned to bear their evils in patience. They were more cheerful than the laboring classes of our day, with their partial education, – although we may console ourselves with the reflection that these are passing through the fermenting processes of a transition from a lower to a higher grade of living. Look at the picture of them which art has handed down: their faces are ruddy, genial, sympathetic, although coarse and vulgar and boorish. And they learned to accept the inequalities of life without repining insolence. They were humble, and felt that there were actually some people in the world superior to themselves. I do not paint their condition as desirable or interesting by our standard, but as endurable. They were doubtless very ignorant; but would knowledge have made them any happier? Knowledge is for those who can climb by it to positions of honor and usefulness, not for those who cannot rise above the condition in which they were born, – not for those who will be snubbed and humiliated and put down by arrogant wealth and birth. Better be unconscious of suffering, than conscious of wrongs which cannot be redressed.

Let no one here misunderstand and pervert me. I am not exalting the ignorance and brutality of the feudal ages. I am not decrying the superior advantages of our modern times. I only state that ignorance and brutality were the necessary sequences of the wars and disorders of a preceding epoch, but that this very ignorance and brutality were accompanied by virtues which partially ameliorated the evils of the day; that in the despair of slavery were the hopes of future happiness; that religion took a deep hold of the human mind, even though blended with puerile and degrading superstitions; that Christianity, taking hold of the hearts of a suffering people, taught lessons which enabled them to bear their hardships with resignation; that cheerfulness was not extinguished; and that so many virtues were generated by the combined influence of suffering and Christianity, that even with ignorance human nature shone with greater lustre than among those by whom knowledge is perverted. It was not until the evil and injustice of Feudalism were exposed by political writers, and were meditated upon by the people who had arisen by education and knowledge, that they became unendurable; and then the people shook off the yoke. But how impossible would have been a French Revolution in the thirteenth century! What readers would a Rousseau have found among the people in the time of Louis VII? If knowledge breaks fetters when the people are strong enough to shake them off, ignorance enables them to bear those fetters when emancipation is impossible.

The great empire of Charlemagne was divided at his death (in A.D. 814) among his three sons, – one of whom had France, another Italy, and the third Germany. In forty-five years afterwards we find seven kingdoms, instead of three, – France, Navarre, Provence, Burgundy, Lorraine, Germany, and Italy. In a few years more there were twenty-nine hereditary fiefs. And as early as the tenth century France itself was split up into fifty-five independent sovereignties; and these small sovereignties were again divided into dukedoms and baronies. All these dukes and barons, however, acknowledged the King of France as their liege lord; yet he was not richer or more powerful than some of the dukes who swore fealty to him. The Duke of Burgundy at one time had larger territories and more power than the King of France himself. So that the central authority of kings was merely nominal; their power extended scarcely beyond the lands they individually controlled. And all the countries of Europe were equally ruled by petty kings. The kings of England seem to have centralized around their thrones more power than other European monarchs until the time of the Crusades, when they were checked, not so much by nobles as by Act of Parliament.

Now all Europe was virtually divided among these petty sovereigns, called dukes, earls, counts, and barons. Each one was virtually independent.

He coined money, administered justice, and preserved order. He ruled by hereditary right, and his estate descended to his oldest son. His revenues were derived by the extorted contributions of those who cultivated his lands, and by certain perquisites, among which were the privilege of wardship, and the profits of an estate during the minority of its possessor, and reliefs, or fines paid on the alienation of a vassal's feud; and the lord could bestow a female ward in marriage on whomever he pleased, and on her refusal take possession of her estate.

Figure 9. The Accolade. *After the painting by Sir E. Blair Leighton.*

The Feudal System

These lordly proprietors of great estates, – or nobles, – so powerful and independent, lived in castles. These strongholds were necessary in such turbulent times. They were large or small, according to the wealth or rank of the nobles who occupied them, but of no architectural beauty. They were fortresses, generally built on hills, or cragged rocks, or in inaccessible marshes, or on islands in rivers, – anywhere where defence was easiest. The nobles did not think of beautiful situations, or fruitful meadows, so much as of the safety and independence of the feudal family. They therefore lived in great isolation, travelling but little, and only at short distances (it was the higher clergy only who travelled). Though born to rank and power, they were yet rude, rough, unpolished. They were warriors. They fought on horseback, covered with defensive armor. They were greedy and quarrelsome, and hence were engaged in perpetual strife, – in the assault on castles and devastation of lands. These castles were generally gloomy, heavy, and uncomfortable, yet were very numerous in the eleventh and twelfth centuries. They were occupied by the feudal family, perhaps the chaplain, strangers of rank, bards, minstrels, and servants, who lived on the best the country afforded, but without the luxuries of our times. They lived better than the monks, as they had no vows to restrain them. But in their dreary castles the rooms were necessarily small, dark, and damp, except the banqueting hall. They were poorly lighted, there being no glass in the narrow windows, nor chimneys, nor carpets, nor mirrors, nor luxurious furniture, nor crockery, nor glassware, nor stoves, nor the refinements of cookery. The few roads of the country were travelled only by horsemen, or people on foot. There were no carriages, only a few heavy lumbering wagons. Tea and coffee were unknown, as also tropical fruits and some of our best vegetables. But game of all kinds was plenty and cheap; so also were wine and beer, and beef and mutton, and pork and poultry. The feudal family was illiterate, and read but few books. The chief pleasures were those of the chase, – hunting and hawking, – and intemperate feasts. What we call "society" was impossible, although the barons may have exchanged visits with each other. They rarely visited cities, which at that time were small and uninteresting. The lordly proprietor of ten thousand acres may have been jolly, frank, and convivial, but he was still rough, and had little to say on matters of great interests. Circumscribed he was of necessity, ignorant and prejudiced. Conscious of power, however, he was proud and insolent to inferiors. He was merely a physical man, – ruddy, healthy, strong indeed, but without refinement, or knowledge, or social graces. His castle was a fort and not a palace; and here he lived with boisterous or sullen companions, as rough and ignorant as himself. His wife and daughters were more interesting, but without those attainments which grace and adorn society. They made tapestries and embroideries, and rode horseback, and danced well, and were virtuous; but were primitive, uneducated, and supercilious. Their beauty was of the ruddy sort, – physical, but genial. They were very fond of ornaments and gay dresses; and so were their lords on festive occasions, for semi-barbarism delights in what is showy and glittering, – purple, and feathers, and trinkets.

Feudalism was intensely aristocratic. A line was drawn between the noble and ignoble classes almost as broad as that which separates liberty from slavery. It was next to impossible for a peasant, or artisan, or even a merchant to pass that line. The exclusiveness of the noble class was intolerable. It held in scorn any profession but arms; neither riches nor learning was of any account. It gloried in the pride of birth, and nourished a haughty scorn of plebeian prosperity.

It was not until cities and arts and commerce arose that the arrogance of the baron was rebuked, or his iron power broken. Haughty though ignorant, he had no pity or compassion for the poor and miserable. His peasantry were doomed to perpetual insults. Their cornfields were trodden down by the baronial hunters; they were compelled even to grind their corn in the landlord's mill, and bake their bread in his oven. They had no redress of injuries, and were scorned as well as insulted. What knight would arm himself for them; what gentle lady wept at their sorrows? The feeling of personal consequence was entirely confined to the feudal family. The poorest knight took precedence over the richest merchant. Pride of birth was carried to romantic extravagance, so that marriages seldom took place between different classes. A beautiful peasant girl could never rise above her drudgeries; and she never dreamed of rising, for the members of the baronial family were looked up to as superior beings. A caste grew up as rigid and exclusive as that of India. The noble and ignoble classes were not connected by any ties; there was nothing in common between them. Even the glory of successful warfare shed no radiance on a peasant's hut. He fought for his master, and not for himself, and scarcely for his country. He belonged to his master as completely as if he could be bought and sold. Christianity teaches the idea of a universal brotherhood; Feudalism suppressed or extinguished it. Peasants had no rights, only duties, – and duties to hard and unsympathetic masters. Can we wonder that a relation so unequal should have been detested by the people when they began to think? Can we wonder it should have created French Revolutions? When we remember how the people toiled for a mail-clad warrior, how they fought for his interests, how they died for his renown, how they were curtailed in their few pleasures, how they were not permitted even to shoot a pheasant or hare in their own grounds, we are amazed that such signal injustice should ever have been endured. It is impossible that this injustice should not have been felt; and no man ever became reconciled to injustice, unless reduced to the condition of a brute. Religious tyranny may be borne, for the priest invokes a supreme authority which all feel to be universally binding. But all tyranny over the body – the utter extinction of liberty – is hateful even to the most degraded Hottentot.

Why, then, was such an unjust and unequal relation permitted to exist so long? What good did it accomplish? What were its extenuating features? Why was it commended by historians as a good institution for the times?

It created a hardy agricultural class, inured them to the dangers and the toils of war, bound them by local attachments, and fostered a patriotic spirit. It developed the virtues of obedience, and submission to evils. It created a love of home and household duties. It was favorable to female virtue. It created the stout yeomanry who could be relied upon in danger. It made law and order possible. It defended the people from robbers. It laid a foundation for warlike prowess. It was favorable to growth of population, for war did not sweep off the people so much as those dire plagues and pestilences which were common in the Middle Ages. It was preferable to the disorders and conflagrations and depredations of preceding times. The poor man was oppressed, but he was safe so long as his lord could protect him. It was a hard discipline, but a discipline which was healthy; it preserved the seed if it did not bear the fruits of civilization. The peasantry became honest, earnest, sincere. They were made susceptible of religious impressions. They became attached to all the institutions of the Church; the parish church was their retreat, their consolation, and their joy. The priest tyrannized over the soul and the knight over the body, but the flame of piety burned steadily and warmly.

When the need of such an institution as Feudalism no longer existed, then it was broken up. Its blessings were not commensurate with its evils; but the evils were less than those which previously existed. This is, I grant, but faint praise. But the progress of society could not be rapid amid such universal ignorance: it is slow in the best of times. I do not call that state of society progressive where moral and spiritual truths are forgotten or disregarded in the triumphs of a brilliant material life. There was no progress of society from the Antonines to Theodosius, but a steady decline. But there was a progress, however slow, from Charlemagne to Philip Augustus. But for Feudalism and ecclesiastical institutions the European races might not have emerged from anarchy, or might have been subjected to a new and withering imperialism. Say what we will of the grinding despotism of Feudalism, – and we cannot be too severe on any form of despotism, – yet the rude barbarian became a citizen in process of time, with education and political rights.

Society made the same sort of advance, in the gloomy epoch we are reviewing, that the slaves in our Southern States made from the time they were imported from Africa, with their degrading fetichism and unexampled ignorance, to the time of their emancipation. How marked the progress of the Southern slaves during the two hundred years of their bondage! No degraded race ever made so marked a progress as they did in the same period, even under all the withering influences of slavery. Probably their moral and spiritual progress was greater than it will be in the next two hundred years, exposed to all the dangers of modern materialism, which saps the life of nations in the midst of the most brilliant triumphs of art. We are now on the road to a marvellous intellectual enlightenment, unprecedented and full of encouragement. But with this we face dangers also, such as undermined the old Roman world and all the ancient civilizations. If I could fix my eye on a single State or Nation in the whole history of our humanity that has escaped these dangers, that has not retrograded in those virtues on which the strength of man is based, after a certain point has been reached in civilization, I would not hazard this remark. Society escaped these evils in that agricultural period which saw the rise and fall of Feudalism, and made a slow but notable advance. That is a fact which cannot be gainsaid, and this is impressive. It shows that society, in a moral point of view, thrives better under hard restraints than when exposed to the dangers of an irreligious, material civilization.

Nor is Feudalism to be condemned as being altogether dark and uninteresting. It had redeeming features in the life of the baronial family. Under its influence arose the institution of chivalry; and though the virtues of chivalry may be poetic, and exaggerated, there can be no doubt that it was a civilizing institution, and partially redeemed the Middle Ages. It gave rise to beautiful sentiments; it blazed in new virtues, rarely seen in the old civilizations. They were peculiar to the age and to Europe, were fostered by the Church, and took a coloring from Christianity itself. Chivalry bound together the martial barons of Europe by the ties of a fraternity of knights. Those armed and mailed warriors fought on horseback, and chivalry takes its name from the French *cheval*, meaning a horse. The knights learned gradually to treat each other with peculiar courtesy. They became generous in battle or in misfortune, for they all alike belonged to the noble class, and felt a common bond in the pride of birth. It was not the memory of illustrious ancestors which created this aristocratic distinction, as among Roman patricians, but the fact that the knights were a superior order. Yet among themselves distinctions vanished. There was no higher distinction than that of a gentleman. The poorest knight was welcome at any castle or at any festivity, at the tournament or in the chase. Generally, gallantry and unblemished reputation were the conditions of social rank among the knights themselves. They were expected to excel in courage, in courtesy, in generosity, in truthfulness, in loyalty. The great patrimony of the knight was his horse, his armor, and his valor. He was bound to succor the defenceless. He was required to abstain from all mean pursuits. If his trade were war, he would divest war of its cruelties. His word was seldom broken, and his promises were held sacred. If pride of rank was generated in this fraternity of gentlemen, so also was scorn of lies and baseness. If there was no brotherhood of man, there was the brotherhood of equals. The most beautiful friendships arose from common dangers and common duties. A stranger knight was treated with the greatest kindness and hospitality. If chivalry condemned anything, it was selfishness and treachery and hypocrisy. All the old romances and chronicles record the frankness and magnanimity of knights. More was thought of moral than of intellectual excellence. Nobody was ashamed to be thought religious. The mailed warrior said his orisons every day and never neglected Mass. Even in war, prisoners were released on their parole of honor, and their ransom was rarely exorbitant. The institution tended to soften manners as well as to develop the virtues of the heart. Under its influence the rude baron was transformed into a courteous gentleman.

But the distinguishing glory of chivalry was devotion to the female sex. Respect for woman was born in the German forests before the Roman Empire fell. It was the best trait of the Germanic barbarians; but under the institution of chivalry this natural respect was ripened into admiration and gallantry. "Love of God and the ladies" was enjoined as a single duty. The knight ever came to the rescue of a woman in danger or distress, provided she was a lady. Nothing is better attested than the chivalric devotion to woman in a feudal castle. The name of a mistress of the heart was never mentioned but in profound respect. Even pages were required to choose objects of devotion, to whom they were to be loyal unto death. Woman presided in the feudal castle, where she exercised a proper restraint. She bestowed the prize of valor at tournaments and tilts. To insult a lady was a lasting disgrace, – or to reveal her secrets. For the first time in history, woman became the equal partner of her husband. She was his companion often in the chase, gaily mounted on her steed. She always dined with him, and was the presiding genius of the castle. She was made regent of kingdoms, heir of crowns, and joint manager of great estates. She had the supreme management of her household, and was consulted in every matter of importance. What an insignificant position woman filled at Athens compared with that in the feudal castle! How different the estimate of woman among the Pagan poets from that held by the Provençal poets! What a contrast to Juvenal is Sordello! The lady of a baronial hall deemed it an insult to be addressed in the language of gallantry, except in that vague and poetic sense in which every knight selected some lady as the object of his dutiful devotion. She disdained the attentions of the most potent prince if his addresses were not honorable. Nor would she bestow her love on one of whom she was not proud. She would not marry a coward or a braggart, even if he were the owner of ten thousand acres. The knight was encouraged to pay his address to any lady if he was personally worthy of her love, for chivalry created a high estimate of individual merit. The feudal lady ignored all degrees of wealth within her own rank. She was as tender and compassionate as she was heroic. She was treated as a superior, rather than as an equal. There was a poetical admiration among the whole circle of knights. A knight without an object of devotion was as "a ship without a rudder, a horse without a bridle, a sword without a hilt, a sky without a star." Even a Don Quixote must have his Dulcinea, as well as horse and armor and squire. Dante impersonates the spirit of the Middle Ages in his adoration of Beatrice. The ancient poets coupled the praises of women with the praises of wine. Woman, under the influence of chivalry, became the star of worship, an object of idolatry. We read of few divorces in the Middle Ages, or of separations, or desertions, or even alienations; these things are a modern improvement, borrowed from the customs of the Romans. The awe and devotion with which the lover regarded his bride became regard and affection in the husband. The matron maintained the rank which had been assigned to her as a maiden. The gallant warriors blended even the adoration of our Lord with adoration of our Lady, – the deification of Christ with the deification of woman. Chivalry, encouraged by the Church and always strongly allied with religious sentiments, accepted for eternal veneration the transcendent loveliness of the mother of our Lord; so that chivalric veneration for the sex culminated in the reverence which belongs to the Queen of Heaven, – *virgo fidelis; regina angelorum.* Woman assumed among kings and barons the importance which she was supposed to have in the celestial hierarchy. And besides the religious influence, the poetic imagination of the time seized upon this pure and lovely element, which passed into the songs, the tales, the talk, the thought, and the aspirations of all the knightly order.

Whence, now, this veneration for woman which arose in the Middle Ages, – a veneration, which all historians attest, such as never existed in the ancient civilization?

It was undoubtedly based on the noble qualities and domestic virtues which feudal life engendered. Women were heroines. Queen Philippa in the absence of her husband stationed herself in the Castle of Bamborough and defied the whole power of Douglas. The first military dispatch ever written in the Middle Ages was addressed to her; she even took David of Scotland a prisoner, when he invaded England. These women of chivalry were ready to undergo any fatigues to promote their husbands' interests. They were equal to any personal sacrifices. Nothing could daunt their courage. They could defend themselves in danger, showing an extraordinary fertility of resources. They earned the devotion they called out. What more calculated to win the admiration of feudal warriors than this devotion and bravery on the part of wives and daughters! They were helpmates in every sense. They superintended the details of castles. They were always employed, and generally in what were imperative duties. If they embroidered dresses or worked tapestries, they also wove the cloth for their husband's coats, and made his shirts and knit his stockings. If they trained hawks and falcons, they fed the poultry and cultivated the flowers. They understood the cares of the kitchen, and managed the servants.

But it was their moral virtues which excited the greatest esteem. They gloried in their unsullied names; their characters were above suspicion. Any violation of the marriage vow was almost unknown; an unfaithful wife was infamous. The ordinary life of a castle was that of isolation, which made women discreet, self-relying, and free from entangling excitements. They had no great pleasures, and but little society. They were absorbed with their duties, and contented with their husbands' love. The feudal castle, however, was not dull, although it was isolated, and afforded few novelties. It was full of strangers, and minstrels, and bards, and pedlars, and priests. Women could gratify their social wants without seductive excitements. They led a life favorable to friendships, which cannot thrive amid the distractions of cities. In cities few have time to cultivate friendships, although they may not be extinguished. In the baronial castle, however, they were necessary to existence.

And here, where she was so well known, woman's worth was recognized. Her caprices and frivolities were balanced by sterling qualities, – as a nurse in sickness, as a devotee to duties, as a friend in distress, ever sympathetic and kind. She was not exacting, and required very little to amuse her. Of course, she was not intellectual, since she read but few books and received only the rudiments of education; but she was as learned as her brothers, and quicker in her wits. She had the vivacity which a healthy life secures. Nor was she beautiful, according to our standard. She was a ruddy, cheerful, active, healthy woman, accustomed to exercise in the open air, – to field-sports and horseback journeys. Still less was she what we call fashionable, for the word was not known; nor was she a woman of society, for, as we have said, there was no society in a feudal castle. What we call society was born in cities, where women reign by force of mind and elegant courtesies and grace of manners, – where woman is an ornament as well as a power, without drudgeries and almost without cares, as at the courts of the Bourbon princes.

Yet I am not certain but that the foundation of courtly elegance and dignity was laid in the baronial home, when woman began her reign as the equal of her wedded lord, when she commanded reverence for her courtesies and friendships, and when her society was valued so highly by aristocratic knights. In the castle she became genial and kind and sympathetic, – although haughty to inferiors and hard on the peasantry. She was ever religious. Religious duties took up no small part of her time. Christianity raised her more than all other influences combined. You never read of an infidel woman when chivalry flourished, any more than of a "strong-minded" woman. The feudal woman never left her sphere, even amid the pleasures of the chase or the tilt. Her gentle and domestic virtues remained with her to the end, and were the most prized. Woman was worshipped because she was a woman, not because she resembled a man. Benevolence and compassion and simplicity were her cardinal virtues. Though her sports were masculine, her character was feminine. She yielded to man in matters of reason and intellect, but he yielded to her in the virtues of the heart and the radiance of the soul. She associated with man without seductive spectacles or demoralizing excitements, and retained her influence by securing his respect. In antiquity, there was no respect for the sex, even when Aspasia enthralled Pericles by the fascinations of blended intellect and beauty; but there was respect in the feudal ages, when women were unlettered and unpolished. And this respect was alike the basis of friendship and the key to power. It was not elegance of manners, nor intellectual culture, nor physical beauty which elevated the women of chivalry, but their courage, their fidelity, their sympathy, their devotion to duty, – qualities which no civilization ought to obscure, and for the loss of which no refinements of life can make up.

Thus Chivalry, – the most interesting institution of the Middle Ages, rejoicing in deeds of daring, guided by honor and renown, executing enterprises almost extravagant, battling injustice and wrong, binding together the souls of a great fraternity, scorning lies, revering truth, devoted to the Church, – could not help elevating the sex to which its proudest efforts were pledged, by cherishing elevated conceptions of love, by offering all the courtesies of friendship, by coming to the rescue of innocence, by stimulating admiration of all that is heroic, and by asserting the honor of the loved ones, even at the risk of life and limb. In the dark ages of European society woman takes her place, for the first time in the world, as the equal and friend of man, – not by physical beauty, not by graces of manner, not even by intellectual culture, but by the solid virtues of the heart, brought to light by danger, isolation, and practical duties, and by that influence which radiated from the Cross. Divest chivalry of the religious element, and you take away its glory and its fascination. The knight would be only a hardhearted warrior, oppressing the poor and miserable, and only interesting from his deeds of valor. But Christianity softened him and made him human, while it dignified the partner of his toils, and gave birth to virtues which commanded reverence. The soul of chivalry, closely examined, in its influence over men or over women, after all, was that power which is and will be through all the ages the hope and glory of our world.

Thus, with all the miseries, cruelties, injustices, and hardships of feudal life, there were some bright spots; showing that Providence never deserts the world, and that though progress may be slow in the infancy of races, yet with the light of Christianity, even if it be darkened, this progress is certain, and will be more and more rapid as Christianity achieves its victories.

AUTHORITIES

Hallam's *Middle Ages*
Sismondi's *Histoire des Français*
Guizot's *History of Civilization* (translated)
Michelet's *History of France* (translated)
Bell's *Historical Studies of Feudalism*
Lacroix's *Manners and Customs of the Middle Ages*
Mills's *History of Chivalry*
Sir Walter Scott's article in *Encyclopaedia Britannica*
Perrot's *Collection Historique des Ordres de Chivalrie*
St. Palaye's *Memoires de l'Ancienne Chivalrie*
Buckle's *History of Civilization*
Palgrave's *English Commonwealth*
Martin's *History of France*
Freeman's *Norman Conquest*
M. Fauriel's *History of Provençal Poetry*
Froissart's *Chronicles*; also the general English histories of the reign of Edward III. Don Quixote should he read in this connection. And Tennyson in his "Idylls of the King" has incorporated the spirit of ancient chivalry.

Chapter 9

THE CRUSADES

A.D. 1095-1272

The great external event of the Middle Ages was the Crusades, – indeed, they were the only common enterprise in which Europe ever engaged. Such an event ought to be very interesting, since it has reference to conflicting passions and interests. Unfortunately, in a literary point of view, there is no central figure in the great drama which the princes of Europe played for two hundred years, and hence the Crusades have but little dramatic interest. No one man represents that mighty movement. It was a great wave of inundation, flooding Asia with the unemployed forces of Europe, animated by passions which excite our admiration, our pity, and our reprobation. They are chiefly interesting for their results, and results which were unforeseen. A philosopher sees in them the hand of Providence, – the overruling of mortal wrath to the praise of Him who governs the universe. I know of no great movement of blind forces so pregnant with mighty consequences.

The Crusades were a semi-religious and a semi-military movement. They represent the passions and ideas of Europe in the twelfth and thirteenth centuries, – its chivalry, its hatred of Mohammedanism, and its desire to possess the spots consecrated by the sufferings of our Lord. Their long continuance shows the intensity of the sentiments which animated them.

They were aggressive wars, alike fierce and unfortunate, absorbing to the nations that embarked in them, but of no interest to us apart from the moral lessons to be drawn from them. Perhaps one reason why history is so dull to most people is that the greater part of it is a record of battles and sieges, of military heroes and conquerors. This is pre-eminently true of Greece, of Rome, of the Middle Ages, and of our modern times down to the nineteenth century. But such chronicles of everlasting battles and sieges do not satisfy this generation. Hence our more recent historians, wishing to avoid the monotony of ordinary history, have attempted to explore the common life of the people, and to bring out their manners and habits: they would succeed in making history more interesting if the materials, at present, were not so scanty and unsatisfactory.

The only way to make the history of wars interesting is to go back to the ideas, passions, and interests which they represent. Then we penetrate to the heart of history, and feel its life. For all the great wars of the world, we shall see, are exponents of its great moving spiritual forces. The wars of Cyrus and Alexander represent the passion of military glory; those of Marius, Sylla, Pompey, and Caesar, the desire of political aggrandizement; those of Constantine and Theodosius, the desire for political unity and the necessity of self-defence. The sweeping and desolating inundations of the barbarians, from the third to the sixth century, represent the poverty of those rude nations, and their desire to obtain settlements more favorable to getting a living. The conquests of Mohammed and his successors were made to swell the number of converts of a new religion. The perpetual strife of the baronial lords was to increase their domains. The wars of Charlemagne and Charles V. were to revive the imperialism of the Caesars, – to create new universal monarchies. The wars which grew out of the Reformation were to preserve or secure religious liberty; those which followed were to maintain the balance of power. Those of Napoleon were at first, at least nominally, to spread or defend the ideas of the French Revolution, until he became infatuated with the love of military glory. Our first great war was to secure national independence, and our second to preserve national unity. The contest between Prussia and France was to prevent the ascendency of either of those great States. The wars of the English in India were to find markets for English goods, employment for the sons of the higher classes, and a new field for colonization and political power. So all the great passions and interests which have moved mankind have found their vent in war, – rough barbaric spoliations, love of glory and political aggrandizement, desire to spread religious ideas, love of liberty, greediness for wealth, unity of nations, jealousy of other powers, even the desire to secure general peace and tranquility. Most wars have had in view the attainment of great ends, and it is in the ultimate results of them that we see the progress of nations.

Thus wars, contemplated in a philosophical aspect, in spite of their repulsiveness are invested with dignity, and really indicate great moral and intellectual movements, as well as the personal ambition or vanity of conquerors. They are the ultimate solutions of great questions, not to be solved in any other way, – unfortunately, I grant, – on account of human wickedness. And I know of no great wars, much as I loathe and detest them, and severely and justly as they may be reprobated, which have not been overruled for the ultimate welfare of society. The wars of Alexander led to the introduction of Grecian civilization into Asia and Egypt; those of the Romans, to the pacification of the world and the reign of law and order; those of barbarians, to the colonization of the worn-out provinces of the Roman Empire by hardier and more energetic nations; those of Charlemagne, to the ultimate suppression of barbaric invasions; those of the Saracens, to the acknowledgment of One God; those of Charles V., to the recognized necessity of a balance of power; those which grew out of the Reformation, to religious liberty. The Huguenots' contest undermined the ascendency of Roman priests in France; the Seven Years' War developed the naval power of England, and gave to her a prominent place among the nations, and exposed the weakness of Austria, so long the terror of Europe; the wars of Louis XIV sowed the seeds of the French Revolution; those of Napoleon vindicated its great ideas; those of England in India introduced the civilization of a Christian nation; those of the Americans secured liberty and the unity of their vast nation. The majesty of the Governor of the universe is seen in nothing more impressively than in the direction which the wrath of man is made to take.

Now these remarks apply to the Crusades. They represent prevailing ideas. Their origin was a universal hatred of Mohammedans. Like all the institutions of the Middle Ages, they were a great contradiction, – debasement in glory, and glory in debasement. With all the fierceness and superstition and intolerance of feudal barons, we see in the Crusades the exercise of gallantry, personal heroism, tenderness, Christian courtesy, – the virtues of chivalry, unselfishness, and magnanimity; but they ended in giving a new impulse to civilization, which will be more minutely pointed out before I close my lecture.

Thus the Crusades are really worthy to be chronicled by historians above anything else which took place in the Middle Ages, since they gave birth to mighty agencies, which still are vital forces in society, – even as everything in American history pales before that awful war which arrayed, in our times, the North against the South in desperate and deadly contest; the history of which remains to be written, but cannot be written till the animosities which provoked it have passed away. What a small matter to future historians is rapid colonization and development of material resources, in comparison with the sentiments which provoked that war! What will future philosophers care how many bushels of wheat are raised in Minnesota, or car-loads of corn brought from Illinois, or hogs slaughtered in Chicago, or yards of cloth woven in Lowell, or cases of goods packed in New York, or bales of carpets manufactured in Philadelphia, or pounds of cotton exported from New Orleans, or meetings of railway presidents at Cincinnati to pool the profits of their monopolies, or women's-rights conventions held in Boston, or schemes of speculators ventilated in the lobbies of Washington, or stock-jobbing and gambling operations take place in every large city of the country, – compared with the mighty marshalling of forces on the banks of the Potomac, at the call of patriotism, to preserve the life of the republic? You cannot divest war of dignity and interest when the grandest results, which affect the permanent welfare of nations, are made to appear.

The Crusades, as they were historically developed, are mixed up with the religious ideas of the Middle Ages, with the domination of popes, with the feudal system, with chivalry, with monastic life, with the central power of kings, with the birth of mercantile States, with the fears and interests of

England, France, Germany, and Italy, for two hundred years, – yea, with the architecture, commerce, geographical science, and all the arts then known. All these principalities and powers and institutions and enterprises were affected by them, so that at their termination a new era in civilization began. Grasp the Crusades, and you comprehend one of the forces which undermined the institutions of the Middle Ages.

It is not a little remarkable that the earliest cause of the Crusades, so far as I am able to trace, was the adoption by the European nations of some of the principles of Eastern theogonies which pertained to self-expiation. An Asiatic theological idea prepared the way for the war between Europe and Asia. The European pietist embraced the religious tenets of the Asiatic monk, which centred in the propitiation of the Deity by works of penance. One of the approved and popular forms of penance was a pilgrimage to sacred places, – seen equally among degenerate Christian sects in Asia Minor, and among the Mohammedans of Arabia. What place so sacred as Jerusalem, the scene of the passion and resurrection of our Lord? Ever since the Empress Helena had built a church at Jerusalem, it had been thronged with pious pilgrims. A pilgrimage to old Jerusalem would open the doors of the New Jerusalem, whose streets were of gold, and whose palaces were of pearls.

At the close of the tenth century there was great suffering in Europe, bordering on despair. The calamities of ordinary life were so great that the end of the world seemed to be at hand. Universal fear of impending divine wrath seized the minds of men. A great religious awakening took place, especially in England, France, and Germany. In accordance with the sentiments of the age, there was every form of penance to avert the anger of God and escape the flames of hell. The most popular form of penance was the pilgrimage to Jerusalem, long and painful as it was. Could the pilgrim but reach that consecrated spot, he was willing to die. The village pastor delivered the staff into his hands, girded him with a scarf, and attached to it a leathern scrip. Friends and neighbors accompanied him a little way on his toilsome journey, which lay across the Alps, through the plains of Lombardy, over Illyria and Pannonia, along the banks of the Danube, by Moesia and Dacia, to Belgrade and Constantinople, and then across the

Bosphorus, through Bithynia, Cilicia, and Syria, until the towers and walls of Tyre, Ptolemais, and Caesarea proclaimed that he was at length in the Holy Land. Barons and common people swell the number of these pilgrims. The haughty knight, who has committed unpunished murders, and the pensive saint, wrapt in religious ecstasies, rival each other in humility and zeal. Those who have no money sell their lands. Those who have no lands to sell throw themselves on Providence, and beg their way for fifteen hundred miles among strangers. The roads are filled with these travelers, – on foot, in rags, fainting from hunger and fatigue. What sufferings, to purchase the favor of God, or to realize the attainment of pious curiosity! The heart almost bleeds to think that our ancestors could ever have been so visionary and misguided; that such a gloomy view of divine forgiveness should have permeated the Middle Ages.

But the sorrows of the pious pilgrims did not end when they reached the Holy Land. Jerusalem was then in the hands of the Turks and Saracens (or Orientals, a general name given to the Arabian Mohammedans), who exacted two pieces of gold from every pilgrim as the price of entering Jerusalem, and moreover reviled and maltreated him. The Holy Sepulchre could be approached only on the condition of defiling it.

The reports of these atrocities and cruelties at last reached the Europeans, filling them with sympathy for the sufferers and indignation for the persecutors. An intense hatred of Mohammedans was generated and became universal, – a desire for vengeance, unparalleled in history. Popes and bishops weep; barons and princes swear. Every convent and every castle in Europe is animated with deadly resentment. Rage, indignation, and vengeance are the passions of the hour, – all concentrated on "the infidels," which term was the bitterest reproach that each party could inflict on the other. An infidel was accursed of God, and was consigned to human wrath. And the Mohammedans had the same hatred of Christians that Christians had of Mohammedans. In the eyes of each their enemies were infidels; and they were enemies because they were regarded as infidels.

Such a state of feeling in both Europe and Asia could not but produce an outbreak, – a spark only was needed to kindle a conflagration. That spark was kindled when Peter of Amiens, a returned hermit, aroused the martial nations to a bloody war on these enemies of God and man. He was a mean-looking man, with neglected beard and disordered dress. He had no genius, nor learning, nor political position. He was a mere fanatic, fierce, furious with ungovernable rage. But he impersonated the leading idea of the age, – hatred of "the infidels," as the Mohammedans were called. And therefore his voice was heard. The Pope used him as a tool. Two centuries later he could not have made himself a passing wonder. But he is the means of stirring up the indignation of Europe into a blazing flame. He itinerates France and Italy, exposing the wrongs of the Christians and the cruelties of the Saracens, – the obstruction placed in the way of salvation. At length a council is assembled at Clermont, and the Pope – Urban II – presides, and urges on the sacred war. In the year 1095 the Pope, in his sacred robes, and in the presence of four hundred bishops and abbots, ascends the pulpit erected in the market-place, and tells the immense multitude how their faith is trodden in the dust; how the sacred relics are desecrated; and appeals alike to chivalry and religion. More than this, he does just what Mohammed did when he urged his followers to take the sword: he announces, in fiery language, the fullest indulgence to all who take part in the expedition, – that all their sins shall be forgiven, and that heaven shall be opened to them. "It is the voice of God," they cry; "we will hasten to the deliverance of the sacred city!" Every man stimulates the passions of his neighbor. All vie in their contributions. The knights especially are enthusiastic, for they can continue their accustomed life without penance, and yet obtain the forgiveness of their sins. Religious fears are turned at first into the channel of penance; and penance is made easy by the indulgence of the martial passions. Every recruit wore a red cross, and was called *croisé*, – cross-bearer; whence the name of the holy war.

Thus the Crusades began, at the close of the eleventh century, when William Rufus was King of England, when Henry IV was still Emperor of Germany, when Anselm was reigning at Canterbury as spiritual head of the English Church, ten years after the great Hildebrand had closed his turbulent pontificate.

I need not detail the history of this first Crusade. Of the two hundred thousand who set out with Peter the Hermit, – this fiery fanatic, with no practical abilities, – only twenty thousand succeeded in reaching even Constantinople. The rest miserably perished by the way, – a most disorderly rabble. And nothing illustrates the darkness of the age more impressively than that a mere monk should have been allowed to lead two hundred thousand armed men on an enterprise of such difficulty. How little the science of war was comprehended! And even of the five hundred thousand men under Godfrey, Tancred, Bohemond, and other great feudal princes, – men of rare personal valor and courage; men who led the flower of the European chivalry, – -only twenty-five thousand remained after the conquest of Jerusalem. The glorious array of a hundred and fifty thousand horsemen, in full armor, was a miserable failure. The lauded warriors of feudal Europe effected almost nothing. Tasso attempted to immortalize their deeds; but how insignificant they were, compared with even Homer's heroes! A modern army of twenty-five thousand men could not only have put the whole five hundred thousand to rout in an hour, but could have delivered Palestine in a few months. Even one of the standing armies of the sixteenth century, under such a general as Henry IV or the Duke of Guise, could have effected more than all the crusaders of two hundred years. The crusaders numbered many heroes, but scarcely a single general. There was no military discipline among them: they knew nothing of tactics or strategy; they fought pell-mell in groups, as in the contests of barons among themselves. Individually they were gallant and brave, and performed prodigies of valor with their swords and battle-axes; but there was no direction given to their strength by leaders.

The Second Crusade, preached half a century afterwards by Saint Bernard, and commanded by an Emperor of Germany and a King of France, proved equally unfortunate. Not a single trophy consoled Europe for the additional loss of two hundred thousand men. The army melted away in foolish sieges, for which the crusaders had no genius or proper means.

The Third Crusade, and the most famous, which began in the year 1189, of which Philip Augustus of France, Richard Coeur de Lion of England, and Frederic Barbarossa of Germany were the leaders, – the three greatest monarchs of their age, – was also signally unsuccessful. Feudal armies seem to have learned nothing in one hundred years of foreign warfare; or else they had greater difficulties to contend with, abler generals to meet, than they dreamed of, who reaped the real advantages, – like Saladin. Sir Walter Scott, in his "Ivanhoe," has not probably exaggerated the military prowess of the heroes of this war, or the valor of Templars and Hospitallers; yet the finest array of feudal forces in the Middle Ages, from which so much was expected, wasted its strength and committed innumerable mistakes. It proved how useless was a feudal army for a distant and foreign war. Philip may have been wily, and Richard lion-hearted, but neither had the generalship of Saladin. Though they triumphed at Tiberias, at Jaffa, at Caesarea; though prodigies of valor were performed; though Ptolemais (or Acre), the strongest city of the East, was taken, – yet no great military results followed. More blood was shed at this famous siege, which lasted three years, than ought to have sufficed for the subjugation of Asia. There were no decisive battles, and yet one hundred battles took place under its walls. Slaughter effected nothing. Jerusalem, which had been retaken by the Saracens, still remained in their hands, and never afterwards was conquered by the Europeans. The leaders returned dejected to their kingdoms, and the bones of their followers whitened the soil of Palestine.

The Fourth Crusade, incited by Pope Innocent III, three years after, terminated with divisions among the States of Christendom, without weakening the power of the Saracens (1202-4).

Among other expeditions was one called the "Children's Crusade" (1212), a wretched, fanatical misery, resulting in the enslavement of many and the death of thousands by shipwreck and exposure.

The Fifth Crusade, commanded by the Emperor Frederic II of Germany (1228-9), was diverted altogether from the main object, and spent its force on Constantinople. That city was taken, but the Holy Land was not delivered. The Byzantine Empire was then in the last stages of decrepitude, or its capital would not have fallen, as it did, from a naval attack made by the Venetians, and in revenge for the treacheries and injuries of the Greek emperors to former crusaders. This, instead of weakening the Mussulmans, broke down the chief obstacle to their entrance into Europe shortly afterward.

The Sixth Crusade (1248-50) only secured the capture of Damietta, on the banks of the Nile.

The Seventh and last of these miserable wars was the most unfortunate of all, A.D. 1270. The saintly monarch of France perished, with most of his forces, on the coast of Africa, and the ruins of Carthage were the only conquest which was made. Europe now fairly sickened over the losses and misfortunes and defeats of nearly two centuries, during which five millions are supposed to have lost their lives. Famine and pestilence destroyed more than the sword. Before disheartened Europe could again rally, the last strongholds of the Christians were wrested away by the Mohammedans; and their gallant but unsuccessful defenders were treated with every inhumanity, and barbarously murdered in spite of truces and treaties.

Such were the famous Crusades, only the main facts of which I allude to; for to describe them all, or even the more notable incidents, would fill volumes, – all interesting to be read in detail by those who have leisure; all marked by prodigious personal valor; all disgraceful for the want of unity of action and the absence of real generalship. They indicate the enormous waste of forces which characterizes nations in their progress. This waste of energies is one of the great facts of all history, surpassed only by the apparent waste of the forces of nature or the fruits of the earth, in the transition period between the time when men roamed in forests and the time when they cultivated the land. See what a vast destruction there has been of animals by each other; what a waste of plants and vegetables, when they could not be utilized. Why should man escape the universal waste, when reason is ignored or misdirected? Of what use or value could Palestine have been to Europeans in the Middle Ages? Of what use can any country be to conquerors, when it cannot be civilized or made to contribute to their wants? Europe then had no need of Asia, and that perhaps is the reason why Europe then could not conquer Asia. Providence interfered, and rebuked the mad passions which animated the invaders, and swept them all away. Were Palestine really needed by Europe, it could be wrested from the Turks with less effort than was made by the feeblest of the crusaders. Constantinople – the most magnificent site for a central power – was indeed wrested from the Greek emperors, and kept one hundred years; but the Europeans did not know what to do with the splendid prize, and it was given to the Turks, who made it the capital of a vital empire. All the good which resulted to Europe from the temporary possession of Constantinople was the introduction into Europe of Grecian literature and art. Its political and mercantile importance was not appreciated, nor then even scarcely needed. It will one day become again the spoil of that nation which can most be benefited by it. Such is the course events are made to take.

In this brief notice of the most unsuccessful wars in which Europe ever engaged we cannot help noticing their great mistakes. We see rashness, self-confidence, depreciation of enemies, want of foresight, ignorance of the difficulties to be surmounted. The crusaders were diverted from their main object, and wasted their forces in attacking unimportant cities, or fortresses out of their way. They invaded the islands of the Mediterranean, Egypt, Africa, and Greek possessions. They quarreled with their friends, and they quarreled with each other. The chieftains sought their individual advantage rather than the general good. Nor did they provide themselves with the necessities for such distant operations. They had no commissariat, – without which even a modern army fails. They were captivated by trifles and frivolities, rather than directing their strength to the end in view. They allowed themselves to be seduced by both Greek and infidel arts and vices. They were betrayed into the most foolish courses. They had no proper knowledge of the forces with which they were to contend. They wantonly massacred their foes when they fell into their hands, increased the animosity of the Mohammedans, and united them in a concert which they should themselves have sought. They marched by land when they should have sailed by sea, and they sailed by sea when they should have marched by land. They intrusted the command to monks and inexperienced leaders. They obeyed the mandates of apostolic vicars when they should have considered military necessities. In fact there was no unity of action, and scarcely unity of end. What would the great masters of Grecian and Roman warfare have thought of these blunders and stupidities, to say nothing of modern generals! The conduct of those wars excites our contempt, in spite of the heroism of individual knights. We despise the incapacity of leaders as much as we abhor the fanaticism which animated their labors. The Crusades have no bright side, apart from the piety and valor of some who embarked in them. Hence they are less and less interesting to modern readers. The romance about them has ceased to affect us. We only see mistakes and follies; and who cares to dwell on the infirmities of human nature? It is only what is great in man that moves and exalts us. There is nothing we dwell upon with pleasure in these aggressive, useless, unjustifiable wars, except the chivalry associated with them. The reason of modern times as sternly rebukes them as the heart of the Middle Ages sickened at them.

In one aspect they are absolutely repulsive; and this in view of their vices. The crusaders were cruel. They wantonly massacred their enemies, even when defenceless. Sixty thousand people were butchered on the fall of Jerusalem; ten thousand were slaughtered in the Mosque of Omar. The Christians themselves felt safe when they sought the retreat of churches, in dire calamities at home; but they had no respect for the religious retreats of infidels. When any city fell into their hands there was wholesale assassination. And they became licentious, as well as rapacious and cruel. They learned all the vices of the East. Even under the walls of Acre they sang to the sounds of Arabian instruments, and danced amid indecent songs. When they took Constantinople they had no respect for either churches or tombs, and desecrated even the pulpit of the Patriarch. Their original religious zeal was finally lost sight of entirely in their military license. They became more hateful to the orthodox Greeks than to the infidel Saracens. And when the crusaders returned to their homes, – what few of them lived to return, – they morally poisoned the communities and villages in which they dwelt. They became vagabonds and vagrants; they introduced demoralizing amusements, and jugglers and strolling players appeared for the first time in Europe. All war is necessarily demoralizing, even war in defence of glorious principles, and especially in these times, but much more so is unjust, fanatical, and unnecessary war.

But I turn from the record of the mistakes, follies, vices, miseries, and crimes which marked the wickedest and most uncalled-for wars of European history, to consider their ultimate results: not logical results, for these were melancholy, – the depopulation of Europe; the decimation of the nobility; the poverty which enormous drains of money from their natural channels produced; the spread of vice; the decline of even feudal virtues. These evils and others followed naturally and inevitably from those distant wars. The immediate effects of all war are evil and melancholy. Murder, pillage, profanity, drunkenness, extravagance, public distress, bitter sorrows, wasted energies, destruction of property, national debts, exaltation of military maxims, general looseness of life, distaste for regular pursuits, – these are the first-fruits of war, offensive and defensive, and as inevitable and uniform as the laws of gravity. No wars were ever more disastrous than the Crusades in their immediate effects, in any way they may be viewed. It is all one dark view of disappointment, sorrow, wretchedness, and sin. There were no bright spots; no gains, only calamities. Nothing consoled Europe for the loss of five millions of her most able-bodied men, – no increase of territory, no establishment of rights, no glory, even; nothing but disgrace and ruin, as in that maddest of all modern expeditions, the invasion of Russia by Napoleon.

But after the lapse of nearly seven hundred years we can see important results on the civilization of Europe, indirectly effected, – not intended, nor designed, nor dreamed of; which results we consider beneficent, and so beneficent that the world is probably better for those horrid wars. It was fortunate to humanity at large that they occurred, although so unfortunate to Europe at the time. In the end, Europe was a gainer by them. Wickedness was not the seed of virtue, but wickedness was overruled. Woe to them by whom offences come, but it must need be that offences come. Men in their depravity will commit crimes, and those crimes are punished; but even these are made to praise a Power superior to that of devils, as benevolent as it is omnipotent, – in which fact I see the utter hopelessness of earth without a superintending and controlling Deity.

One important result of the Crusades was the barrier they erected to the conquests of the Mohammedans in Europe. It is true that the wave of Saracenic invasion had been arrested by Charles Martel four or five hundred years before; but in the meantime a new Mohammedan power sprang up, of greater vigor, of equal ferocity, and of a more stubborn fanaticism. This was that of the Turks, who had their eye on Constantinople and all Eastern Europe. And Europe might have submitted to their domination, had they instead of the Latins taken Constantinople. The conquest of that city was averted several hundred years; and when at last it fell into Turkish hands, Christendom was strong enough to resist the Turkish armies. We must remember that the Turks were a great power, even in the times of Peter the Great, and would have taken Vienna but for John Sobieski. But when Urban II, at the Council of Clermont, urged the nations of Europe to repel the infidels on the confines of Asia, rather than wait for them in the heart of Europe, the Asiatic provinces of the Greek Empire were overrun both by Turks and Saracens. They held Syria, Armenia, Asia Minor, Africa, Spain, and the Balearic Islands. Had not Godfrey come to the assistance of a division of the Christian army, when it was surrounded by two hundred thousand Turks at the battle of Dorylaeum, the Christians would have been utterly overwhelmed, and the Turks would have pressed to the Hellespont. But they were beaten back into Syria, and, for a time, as far as the line of the Euphrates. But for that timely repulse, the battles of Belgrade and Lepanto might not have been fought in subsequent ages. It would have been an overwhelming calamity had the Turks invaded Europe in the twelfth century. The loss of five millions on the plains of Asia would have been nothing in comparison to an invasion of Europe by the Mohammedans, – whether Saracens or Turks. It may be that the chivalry of Europe would have successfully repelled an invasion, as the Saracens repelled the Christians, on their soil. It may be that Asia could not have conquered Europe any easier than Europe could conquer Asia.

I do not know how far statesmanlike views entered into the minds of the leaders of the Crusades. I believe the sentiment which animated Peter and Urban and Bernard was pure hatred of the Mohammedans (because they robbed, insulted, and oppressed the pilgrims), and not any controlling fears of their invasion of Europe. If such a fear had influenced them, they would not have permitted a mere rabble to invade Asia; there would have been a sense of danger stronger than that of hatred, – which does not seem to have existed in the self-confidence of the crusaders. They thought it an easy thing to capture Jerusalem: it was a sort of holiday march of the chivalry of Europe, under Richard and Philip Augustus. Perhaps, however, the princes of Europe were governed by political rather than religious reasons. Some few long-headed statesmen, if such there were among the best informed of bishops and abbots, may have felt the necessity of the conflict in a political sense; but I do not believe this was a general conviction. There was, doubtless, a political necessity – although men were too fanatical to see more than one side – to crush the Saracens because they were infidels, and not because they were warriors. But whether they saw it or not, or armed themselves to resist a danger as well as to exterminate heresy, the ultimate effects were all the same. The crusaders failed in their direct end. They did not recover Palestine; but they so weakened or diverted the Mohammedan armies that there was not strength enough left in them to conquer Europe, or even to invade her, until she was better prepared to resist it, – as she did at the battle of Lepanto (A.D. 1571), one of the decisive battles of the world.

I have said that the Crusades were a disastrous failure. I mean in their immediate ends, not in ultimate results. If it is probable that they arrested the conquests of the Turks in Europe, then this blind and fanatical movement effected the greatest blessing to Christendom. It almost seems that the Christians were hurled into the Crusades by an irresistible fate, to secure a great ultimate good; or, to use Christian language, were sent as blind instruments by the Almighty to avert a danger they could not see. And if this be true, the inference is logical and irresistible that God uses even the wicked passions of men to effect his purposes, – as when the envy of Haman led to the elevation of Mordecai, and to the deliverance of the Jews from one of their greatest dangers.

Another and still more noticeable result of the Crusades was the weakening of the power of those very barons who embarked in the wars. Their fanaticism recoiled upon themselves, and undermined their own system. Nothing could have happened more effectually to loosen the rigors of the feudal system. It was the baron and the knight that marched to Palestine who suffered most in the curtailment of the privileges which they had abused, – even as it was the Southern planter of Carolina who lost the most heavily in the war which he provoked to defend his slave property. In both cases the fetters of the serfs and slaves were broken by their own masters, – not intentionally, of course, but really and effectually. How blind men are in their injustices! They are made to hang on the gallows which they have erected for others. To gratify his passion of punishing the infidels, whom he so intensely hated, the baron or prince was obliged to grant great concessions to the towns and villages which he ruled with an iron hand, in order to raise money for his equipment and his journey. He was not paid by Government as are modern soldiers and officers. He had to pay his own expenses, and they were heavier than he had expected or provided for. Sometimes he was taken captive, and had his ransom to raise, – to pay for in hard cash, and not in land: as in the case of Richard of England, when, on his return from Palestine, he was imprisoned in Austria, – and it took to ransom him, as some have estimated, one third of all the gold and silver of the realm, chiefly furnished by the clergy. But where was the imprisoned baron to get the money for his ransom? Not from the Jews, for their compound interest of fifty per cent every six months would have ruined him in less than two years. But the village guilds had money laid by. Merchants and mechanics in the towns, whom he despised, had money. Monasteries had money. He therefore gave new privileges to all; he gave charters of freedom to towns; he made concessions to the peasantry.

As the result of this, when the baron came back from the wars, he found himself much poorer than when he went away, – he found his lands encumbered, his castle dilapidated, and his cattle sold. In short, he was, as we say of a proud merchant now and then, "embarrassed in his circumstances." He was obliged to economize. But the feudal family would not hear of retrenchment, and the baron himself had become more extravagant in his habits. As travel and commerce had increased he had new wants, which he could not gratify without parting with either lands or prerogatives. As the result of all this he became not quite so overbearing, though perhaps more sullen; for he saw men rising about him who were as rich as he, – men whom his ancestors had despised. The artisans, who belonged to the leading guilds, which had become enriched by the necessities of barons, or by that strange activity of trade and manufactures which war seems to stimulate as well as to destroy, – these rude and ignorant people were not so servile as formerly, but began to feel a sort of importance, especially in towns and cities, which multiplied wonderfully during the Crusades. In other words, they were no longer brutes, to be trodden down without murmur or resistance. They began to form what we call a "middle class." Feudalism, in its proud ages, did not recognize a middle class. The impoverishment of nobles by the Crusades laid the foundation of this middle class, at least in large towns.

The growth of cities and the decay of feudalism went on simultaneously; and both were equally the result of the Crusades. If the noble became impoverished, the merchant became enriched; and the merchant lived, not in the country, but in some mercantile mart. The crusaders had need of ships. These were furnished by those cities which had obtained from feudal sovereigns charters of freedom. Florence, Pisa, Venice, Genoa, Marseilles, became centres of wealth and political importance. The growth of cities and the extension of commerce went hand in hand. Whatever the Crusades did for cities they did equally for commerce; and with the needs of commerce came improvement in naval architecture. As commerce grew, the ships increased in size and convenience; and the products which the ships brought from Asia to Europe were not only introduced, but they were cultivated. New fruits and vegetables were raised by European husbandmen. Plum-trees were brought from Damascus and sugar-cane from Tripoli. Silk fabrics, formerly confined to Constantinople and the East, were woven in Italian and French villages. The Venetians obtained from Tyrians the art of making glass. The Greek fire suggested gunpowder. Architecture received an immense impulse: the churches became less sombre and heavy, and more graceful and beautiful. Even the idea of the arch, some think, came from the East. The domes and minarets of Venice were borrowed from Constantinople. The ornaments of Byzantine churches and palaces were brought to Europe. The horses of Lysippus, carried from Greece to Rome, and from Rome to Constantinople, at last surmounted the palace of the Doges. Houses became more comfortable, churches more beautiful, and palaces more splendid. Even manners improved, and intercourse became more polished. Chivalry borrowed many of its courtesies from the East. There were new refinements in the arts of cookery as well as of society. Literature itself received a new impulse, as well as science. It was from Constantinople that Europe received the philosophy of Plato and Aristotle, in the language in which it was written, instead of translations through the Arabic. Greek scholars came to Italy to introduce their unrivalled literature; and after Grecian literature came Grecian art. The study of Greek philosophy gave a new stimulus to human inquiry, and students flocked to the universities. They went to Bologna to study Roman law, as well as to Paris to study the Scholastic philosophy.

Thus the germs of a new civilization were scattered over Europe. It so happened that at the close of the Crusades civilization had increased in every country of Europe, in spite of the losses they had sustained. Delusions were dispelled, and greater liberality of mind was manifest. The world opened up towards the East, and was larger than was before supposed. "Europe and Asia had been brought together and recognized each other." Inventions and discoveries succeeded the new scope for energies which the Crusades opened. The ships which had carried the crusaders to Asia were now used to explore new coasts and harbors. Navigators learned to be bolder. A navigator of Genoa – a city made by the commerce which the Crusades necessitated – crosses the Atlantic Ocean. As the magnetic needle, which a Venetian traveller brought from Asia, gave a new direction to commerce, so the new stimulus to learning which the Grecian philosophy effected led to the necessity of an easier form of writing; and printing appeared. With the shock which feudalism received from the Crusades, central power was once more wielded by kings, and standing armies supplanted the feudal. The crusaders must have learned something from their mistakes; and military science was revived. There is scarcely an element of civilization which we value, that was not, directly or indirectly, developed by the Crusades, yet which was not sought for, or anticipated even, – the centralization of thrones, the weakening of the power of feudal barons, the rise of free cities, the growth of commerce, the impulse given to art, improvements in agriculture, the rise of a middle class, the wonderful spread of literature, greater refinements in manners and dress, increased toleration of opinions, a more cheerful view of life, the simultaneous development of energies in every field of human labor, new hopes and aspirations among the people, new glories around courts, new attractions in the churches, new comforts in the villages, new luxuries in the cities. Even spiritual power became less grim and sepulchral, since there was less fear to work upon.

I do not say that the Crusades alone produced the marvellous change in the condition of society which took place in the thirteenth century, but they gave an impulse to this change. The strong sapling which the barbarians brought from their German forests and planted in the heart of Europe, – and which had silently grown in the darkest ages of barbarism, guarded by the hand of Providence, – became a sturdy tree in the feudal ages, and bore fruit when the barons had wasted their strength in Asia. The Crusades improved this fruit, and found new uses for it, and scattered it far and wide, and made it for the healing of the nations. Enterprise of all sorts succeeded the apathy of convents and castles. The village of mud huts became a town, in which manufactures began. As new wants became apparent, new means of supplying them appeared. The Crusades stimulated these wants, and commerce and manufactures supplied them. The modern merchant was born in Lombard cities, which supplied the necessities of the crusaders. Feudalism ignored trade, but the baron found his rival in the merchant-prince. Feudalism disdained art, but increased wealth turned peasants into carpenters and masons; carpenters and masons combined and defied their old masters, and these masters left their estates for the higher civilization of cities, and built palaces instead of castles. Palaces had to be adorned, as well as churches; and the painters and handicraftsmen found employment. So one force stimulated another force, neither of which would have appeared if feudal life had remained *in statu quo*.

The only question to settle is, how far the marked progress of the twelfth and thirteenth centuries may be traced to the natural development of the Germanic races under the influence of religion, or how far this development was hastened by those vast martial expeditions, indirectly indeed, but really. Historians generally give most weight to the latter. If so, then it is clear that the most disastrous wars recorded in history were made the means – blindly, to all appearance, without concert or calculation – of ultimately elevating the European races, and of giving a check to the conquering fanaticism of the enemies with whom they contended with such bitter tears and sullen disappointments.

AUTHORITIES

Michaud's *Histoire des Croisades*
Mailly's *L'Esprit des Croisades*
Choiseul-Daillecourt's *De l'Influence des Croisades Sur l'État des Peuples en Europe*
Heeren's *Ueber den Einfluss der Kreuzzüge*
Sporschill's *Geschichte der Kreuzzüge*
Hallam's *Middle Ages*
Mill's *History of the Crusades*
James's *History of the Crusades*
Michelet's *History of France* (translated)
Gibbon's *Decline and Fall*
Milman's *Latin Christianity*
Proctor's *History of the Crusades*
Mosheim.

Chapter 10

WILLIAM OF WYKEHAM: GOTHIC ARCHITECTURE

A.D. 1324-1404 AND A.D. 1100-1400

Church Architecture is the only addition which the Middle Ages made to Art; but even this fact is remarkable when we consider the barbarism and ignorance of the Teutonic nations in those dark and gloomy times. It is difficult to conceive how it could have arisen, except from the stimulus of religious ideas and sentiments, – like the vast temples of the Egyptians. The artists who built the hoary and attractive cathedrals and abbey churches which we so much admire are unknown men to us, and yet they were great benefactors. It is probable that they were practical and working architects, like those who built the temples of Greece, who quietly sought to accomplish their ends, – not to make pictures, but to make buildings, – as economically as they could consistently with the end proposed, which end they always had in view.

In this Lecture I shall not go back to classic antiquity, nor shall I undertake to enter upon any disquisition on Art itself, but simply present the historical developments of the Church architecture of the Middle Ages. It is a technical and complicated subject, but I shall try to make myself understood. It suggests, however, great ideas and national developments, and ought to be interesting.

The Romans added nothing to the architecture of the Greeks except the arch, and the use of brick and small stones for the materials of their stupendous structures. Now Christianity and the Middle Ages seized the arch and the materials of the Roman architects, and gradually formed from these a new style of architecture. In Roman architecture there was no symbolism, no poetry, nothing to represent consecrated sentiments. It was mundane in its ideas and ends; everything was for utility. The grandest efforts of the Romans were feats of engineering skill, rather than creations inspired by the love of the beautiful. What was beautiful in their edifices was borrowed from the Greeks; what was original was intended to accommodate great multitudes, whether they sought the sports of the amphitheatre or the luxury of the bath. Their temples were small, comparatively, and were Grecian.

The first stage in the development of Church architecture was reached amid the declining glories of Roman civilization, before the fall of the Empire; but the first model of a Christian church was not built until after the imperial persecutions. The early Christians worshipped God in upper chambers, in catacombs, in retired places, where they would not be molested, where they could hide in safety. Their assemblies were small, and their meetings unimportant. They did nothing to attract attention. The worshippers were mostly simple-minded, unlettered, plebeian people, with now and then a converted philosopher, or centurion, or lady of rank. They met for prayer, exhortation, the reading of the Scriptures, the singing of sacred melodies, and mutual support in trying times. They did not want grand edifices. The plainer the place in which they assembled the better suited it was to their circumstances and necessities. They scarcely needed a rostrum, for the age of sermons had not begun; still less the age of litanies and music and pomps. For such people, in that palmy age of faith and courage, when the seeds of a new religion were planted in danger and watered with tears; when their minds were directed almost entirely to the soul's welfare and future glory; when they loved one another with true Christian disinterestedness; when they stimulated each other's enthusiasm by devotion to a common cause (one Lord, one faith, one baptism); when they were too insignificant to take any social rank, too poor to be of any political account, too ignorant to attract the attention of philosophers, – *any* place where they would be unmolested and retired was enough. In process of time, when their numbers had increased, and when and wherever they were tolerated; when money began to flow into the treasuries; and especially when some gifted leader (educated perhaps in famous schools, yet who was fervent and eloquent) desired a wider field for usefulness, – then church edifices became necessary.

This original church was modelled after the ancient Basilica, or hall of justice or of commerce: at one end was an elevated tribunal, and back of this what was called the "apsis," – a rounded space with arched roof. The whole was railed off or separated from the auditory, and was reserved for the clergy, who in the fourth century had become a class. The apsis had no window, was vaulted, and its walls were covered with figures of Christ and of the saints, or of eminent Christians who in later times were canonized by the popes. Between the apsis and the auditory, called the "nave," was the altar; for by this time the Church was borrowing names and emblems from the Jews and the old religions. From the apsis to the extremity of the other end of the building were two rows of pillars supporting an upper wall, broken by circular arches and windows, called now the "clear story." In the low walls of the side aisles were also windows. Both the nave and the aisles supported a framework of roof, lined with a ceiling adorned with painting.

For some time we see no marked departure, at this stage, from the ancient basilica. The church is simple, not much adorned, and adapted to preaching. The age in which it was built was the age of pulpit orators, when bishops preached, – like Basil, Chrysostom, Ambrose, Augustine, and Leo, – when preaching was an important part of the service, by the foolishness of which the world was to be converted. Probably there were but few what we should call fine churches, but there was one at Rome which was justly celebrated, built by Theodosius, and called St. Paul's. It is now outside the walls of the modern city. The nave is divided into five aisles, and the main one, opening into the apsis, is spanned by a lofty arch supported by two colossal columns. The apsis is eighty feet in breadth. All parts of the church – one of the largest of Rome – are decorated with mosaics. It has two small transepts at the extremity of the nave, on each side of the apsis. The four rows of magnificent columns, supporting semicircular arches, are Corinthian. In this church the Greek and Roman architecture predominates. The essential form of the church is like a Pagan basilica. We see convenience, but neither splendor nor poetry. Moreover it is cheerful. It has an altar and an apsis, but it is adapted to preaching rather than to singing. The public dangers produce oratory, not chants. The voice of the preacher penetrates the minds of the people, as did that of Savonarola at Florence announcing the invasion of Italy by the French, – days of fear and anxiety, reminding us also of Chrysostom at Antioch, when in his spacious basilican church he roused the people to penitence, to avert the ire of Theodosius.

The first transition from the basilica to the Gothic church is called the *Romanesque*, and was made after the fall of the Empire, when the barbarians had erected new kingdoms on its ruins; when literature and art were indeed crushed, yet when universal desolation was succeeded by new forms of government and new habits of life; when the clergy had become an enormous power, greatly enriched by the contributions of Christian princes. This transition retained the traditions of the fallen Empire, and yet was adapted to a semi-civilized people, nominally converted to Christianity. It arose after the fall of the Merovingians, when Charlemagne was seeking to restore the glory of the Western Empire. Paganism had been suppressed by law; even heresies were extinguished in the West. Kings and people were alike orthodox, and bowed to the domination of the Church. Abbeys and convents were founded everywhere and richly endowed. The different States and kingdoms were poor, but the wealth that existed was deposited in sacred retreats. The powers of the State were the nobles, warlike and ignorant, rapidly becoming feudal barons, acknowledging only a nominal fealty to the Crown. Kings had no glory, defied by their own subjects and unsupported by standing armies. But these haughty barons were met face to face by equally haughty bishops, armed with spiritual weapons. These bishops were surrounded and supported by priests, secular and regular, – by those who ruled the people in small parishes, and those who ruled the upper classes in their monastic cells. Learning had fled to monasteries (what little there was), and the Church became a new attraction.

The architects of the Romanesque, who were probably churchmen, retained the nave of the basilica, but made it narrower, and used but two rows of columns. They introduced the transepts, or cross-enclosures, making them to project north and south of the nave, in the space separated from the apsis; and the apsis was expanded into the choir, filled with priests and choristers. The building now assumes the form of a cross. The choir is elevated several steps above the nave, and beneath it is the crypt, where the bishops and abbots and saints are buried. At the intersection of choir, nave, and transept, – an open, square place, – rises a square tower, at each corner of which is a massive pier supporting four arches. The windows are narrow, with semicircular arches. At the western entrance, at the end opposite the apse, is a small porch, where the consecrated water is placed, in an urn or basin, and this is inclosed between two towers. The old Roman atrium, or fore-court, entirely disappears. In its place is a grander façade; and the pillars – which are all internal, like those of an Egyptian temple, not external, as in the Greek temple – have no longer Grecian capitals, but new combinations of every variety, and the pillars are even more heavy and massive than the Doric. The flat wooden ceiling of the nave disappears, on account of frequent fires, and the eye rests on arches supporting a stone roof. All the arches are semicircular, like those of the Coliseum and of the Roman aqueducts and baths. They are built of small stones united by cement. The building is low and heavy, and its external beauty is in the west front or façade, with its square towers and circular window and ornamented portal. The internal beauty is from the pillars supporting the roof, and the tower which intersects the nave, choir, and transepts. Sometimes, instead of a tower there is a dome, reminding us of Byzantine workmanship.

But this Romanesque church is also connected with monastic institutions, whose extensive buildings join the church at the north or south. The church is wedded to monasticism; one supports the other, and both make a unity exceedingly efficient in the Middle Ages. The communication between the church and the convent is effected by a cloister, – a vaulted gallery surrounding a square, open space, where the brothers walk and meditate, but do not talk, except in undertone or whisper; for all the precincts are sacred, made for contemplation and silence, – a retreat from the noisy, barbaric world. Connected with the cloisters is a court opening into the refectory, where the brothers dine on herbs and eggs and a little meat, – also in silence, and, where the rule is strict, in gloom, – an ascetic, dreary discipline. The whole range of buildings is enclosed with walls, like a fortress. You see in this architecture the gloom and desolation which overspread the world. Churches are heavy and sombre; they are places for dreary meditation on the end of the world, on the failure of civilization, on the degradation of humanity, – and yet the only places where man may be brought in contact with the Deity who presides over a fallen world, exalting human hopes to heaven, where miseries end, and worship begins.

This style of architecture prevailed till the twelfth century, and was seen in its greatest perfection in Germany under the Saxon emperors, especially in the Rhenish provinces, as in the cathedrals of Spires, Mentz, Worms, and Nuremberg. Its general effect was gloomy and heavy; a separation from the outward world, – a world disgraced by feudal wars and peasants' wrongs and general ignorance, which made men sad, morose, inhuman. It flourished in ages when the poor had no redress, and were trodden under the feet of hard feudal masters; when there was no law but of brute force; when luxuries were few and comforts rare, – an age of hardship, privation, poverty, suffering; an age of isolations and sorrows, when men were forced to look beyond the grave for peace and hope, when immortality through a Redeemer was the highest inspiration of life. Everybody was agitated by fears. The clergy made use of this universal feeling by presenting the terrors of the law, – the penalty of sin, – everlasting physical burnings, from which the tortured soul could be extricated only by penance and self-expiation, offerings to the Church, and entire subserviency to the will of the priest, who held the keys of heaven and hell. The men who lived when the Romanesque churches dotted every part in Europe looked upon society and saw nothing but grief, – heavy burdens, injustices, oppressions, cruel wrongs; and they hid their faces and wept, and said: "Let us retreat from this miserable world which discord ravages; let us hide ourselves in contemplation; let us prepare to meet God in judgment; let us bring to Him our offering; let us propitiate Him; let us build Him a house, where we may chant our mournful songs." So the church arises, – in Germany, in France, in England, – solemn, mystical, massive, a type of sorrow, in the form of a cross, with "a sepulchral crypt like the man in the tomb, before the lofty spire pointed to the man who had risen to Heaven." The church is still struggling, and is not jubilant, except in Gregorian chants, and is not therefore lofty or ornamental. It is a vault. It is more like a catacomb than a basilica, for the world is buried deep in sorrows and fears. Look to any of the Saxon churches of the period when the Romanesque prevailed, and they are low, gloomy, and damp, though massive and solemn. The church as an edifice ever represents the Church as an institution or a power, ever typifies prevailing sentiments and ideas. Perhaps the finest of the old Romanesque churches was that of Cluny, in Burgundy, destroyed during the French Revolution. It had five aisles, and was five hundred and twenty feet in length. It had a stately tower at the intersection of the transepts, and six other towers. It was early Norman, and loftier than the Saxon churches, although heavy and massive like them.

But the Romanesque church, with all its varieties, is still gloomy, dark, sepulchral, reminding us of the sorrows of the Middle Ages, and the dreary character of prevailing religious sentiments, – fervent, sincere, profound, but sad, – the sentiments of an age of ignorance and faith.

The Crusades came. A new era burst upon the world. The old ideas became modified; society became more cheerful, because more chivalric, adventurous, poetic. The world opened towards the East, and was larger than was before supposed. Liberality of mind began to dawn on the darkened ages; no longer were priests supreme. The gay Provençals began to sing; the universities began to teach and to question. The Scholastic philosophy sent forth such daring thinkers as Erigena and Abélard. Orthodoxy was still supreme before such mighty intellects as Anselm, Bernard, and Thomas Aquinas, but it was assailed. Abélard put forth his puzzling questions. The Schoolmen began to think for themselves, and the iron weight of Feudalism was less oppressive. Free cities and commerce began to enrich the people. Kings were becoming more powerful; grim spiritual despotism was less arrogant. The end of the world, it was found, had not come. A glorious future began to shed forth the beams of its coming day. It was the dawn of a new civilization.

So a lighter, more cheerful, and grander architecture, with symbolic beauties, appeared with changing ideas and sentiments. The Church, no longer a gloomy power, struggling with Saracens and barbarism, but dominant, triumphant, issues forth from darksome crypts and soars upward, – elevates her vaulted roofs. "The Oriental ogive appears.... The architects heap arcade on arcade, ogive on ogive, pyramid on pyramid, and give to all geometrical symmetry and artistic grace.... The Greek column is there, but dilated to colossal proportions, and exfoliated in a variegated capital." The old Roman arch disappears, and the pointed arch is substituted, – graceful and elevated. The old Egyptian obelisk appears in the spire reaching to heaven, full of aspiration. The window becomes larger and encroaches on the naked wall, and radiates in mystic roses. The arches widen and the piers become more lofty. Stained glass appears and diffuses religious light. Every part of the church becomes decorated and symbolical and harmonious, though infinitely variegated. The altars have pictures over them. Shrines and monuments appear in the niches. The dresses of the priests are more gorgeous. The music of the choir peals forth hallelujahs. Christ is risen from the tomb. "The purple of his blood colors the windows." The roof, like pinnacles and spires, seems to reach the skies. The pressure of the walls is downwards rather than lateral. The vertical lines of Cologne are as marked as the old horizontal lines of the Parthenon. The walls too are not so heavy, and are supported by buttresses, which give increased beauty to the exterior, – greater light and shade. "Every part of the church seems to press forward and strive for greater freedom, for outward manifestation." Even the broad and expansive window presses to the outer surface of the walls, now broken by buttresses and pinnacles. The window – the eye of the edifice – is more cheerful and intelligent. More calm is the imposing façade, with its mighty towers and lofty spires, tapering like a pyramid, with its round oriel window rich in beautiful tracery, and its wide portal with sculptured saints and martyrs. And in all the churches you see geometrical proportions. "Even the cross of the church is deduced from the figure by which Euclid constructed the equilateral triangle," The columns present the proportions of the Doric, as to diameter and height. The love of the true and beautiful meet. The natural and supernatural both appear. All parts symbolize the passion of

Christ. If the crypt speaks of death, the lofty and vaulted roof and the beautiful pointed arches, and the cheerful window, and the jubilant chants speak of life. "The old church reminds one of the Christ that lay in the tomb; the new, of the Christ who arose the third day." The old fosters meditation and silence; the new kindles the imagination, by its variety of perspective arrangement and mystic representation, – still reverential, still expressive of consecrated sentiments, yet more cheerful. The foliated shaft, the rich tracery of the window, the graceful pinnacle, the Arabian gorgeousness of the interior, – as if the crusaders had learned something from the East, – the innumerable shrines and pictures, the variegated marbles of the altar, with its vessels of silver and gold, the splendid dresses of the priests, the imposing character of the ritualism, the treasures lavished everywhere, all speak greater independence, wealth, and power. The church takes the place of all amusements. Its various attractions draw together the people from their farms and shops. They are gaily dressed, as if they were attending a festival. Their condition is so improved that they have time for holidays. And these the Church multiplies; for perpetual toil is the grave of intellect. The people must have rest, amusement, excitement. All these things the Catholic Church gives, and consecrates. Crusader, baron, knight, priest, peasant, all resort to the church for benedictions. Women too are there, and in greater numbers; and they linger for the confessional. When the time comes that women stay away from church, like busy, preoccupied, sceptical men, then let us be on the watch for some great catastrophe, since practical paganism will then be restored, and the angels of light will have left the earth.

Paris and its neighborhood was the cradle of this new development of architecture which we wrongly call the Gothic, even as Paris was the centre of the new-born intelligence of the era. The word "Gothic" suggests destructive barbarism: the English, French, and Germans descended chiefly from Normans, Saxons, and Burgundians. This form of church architecture rapidly spreads to Germany, England, and Spain. The famous Suger, the minister of a powerful king, built the abbey of St. Denis. The churches of Rheims, Paris, and Bourges arose in all their grandeur. The façade of Rheims is the most significant example of the wonderful architecture of the thirteenth century. In the church of Amiens you see the perfection of the so-called Gothic, – so graceful are its details, so dazzling is its height. The central aisle is one hundred and thirty-two feet in altitude, – only surpassed by that of Beauvais, which is fourteen feet higher. It was then that the cathedral of Rouen was built, with its elegant lightness, – a marvel to modern travelers. Soon after, the cathedral of Cologne appears, more grand than either, – but left unfinished, – with its central aisle forty-four feet in width, rising one hundred and forty feet into the air, with its colossal towers, intended to support the slender openwork spires, five hundred and twenty feet in height. The whole church is five hundred and thirty-two feet in length. I confess this church made a greater impression on my mind than did any Gothic church in Europe, – more, even, than Milan, with its unnumbered pinnacles and statues and its marble roof. I could not rest while surveying its ten thousand wonders, – so much lightness combined with strength; so grand, and yet so cheerful; so exquisitely proportioned, so complicated in details, and yet a grand unity; a glorious and fit temple for the reverential worship of the Deity. Oh, how grand are those monuments which were designed to last through ages, and which are consecrated, not to traffic, not to pleasure, not to material wealth, but to the worship of that Almighty God to whom every human being is personally responsible!

I cannot enumerate the churches of Mediaeval Europe, – built possibly by the Freemasons, certainly by men familiar with all that is practical in their art, with all that is hallowed and poetical. I glance at the English cathedrals, built during this epoch, – the period of the Crusades and the revival of learning.

And here I allude to the man who furnishes me with a text to my discourse, – William of Wykeham, chancellor and prime minister of Edward III, the contemporary of Chaucer and Wyclif, – who flourished in the fourteenth century, and who built Winchester Cathedral; a great and benevolent prelate, who also founded other colleges and schools. But I merely allude to him, since my subject is the art to which he gave an impulse, rather than any single individual. No one man represents church architecture any more appropriately than any one man represents the Feudal system, or Monasticism, or the Crusades, or the French Revolution.

William of Wykeham: Gothic Architecture

Figure 10. Winchester Cathedral. *From a photograph.*

I do not think the English cathedrals are equal to those of Cologne, Rheims, Amiens, and Rouen; but they are full of interest, and they have varied excellences. That of Salisbury is the only one which is of uniform style. Its glory is in its spire, as that of Lincoln is in its west front, and that of Westminster is in its nave. Gloucester is celebrated for its choir, and York for its tower. In all are beautiful vistas of pillars and arches. But they lack the inspiration of the Catholic Church. They are indeed hoary monuments, petrified mysteries, a "passion of stone," as Michelet speaks of the marble histories which will survive his rhapsodies. They alike show the pilgrimage of humanity through gloomy centuries. If their great wooden screens were removed, which separate the choir from the nave, the cathedrals doubtless would appear to more advantage, and especially if they were filled with altars and shrines and pictures, and lighted candles on the altars, – filled also with crowds of worshippers, reverent before the gorgeously attired ministers of Divine Omnipotence, and excited by transporting chants, and the various appeals to sense and imagination. The reason must be assisted by the imagination, before the mind can revel in the glories of Gothic architecture. Imagination intensifies all our pleasures, even those of sense; and without imagination – yea, a memory stored with the pious deeds of saints and martyrs in bygone ages – a Gothic cathedral is as much a sealed book as Wordsworth is to Taine. The Protestant tourist from Michigan or Pennsylvania can "do" any cathedral in two hours, and wonder why they make such a fuss about a church not half so large as the New York Central Railroad station. The wonders of cathedrals must be studied, like the glories of a landscape, with an eye to the beautiful and the grand, cultured and practised by the contemplation of ideal excellence, when the mind summons the imagination to its aid, with all the poetry and all the history which have been learned in a life of leisure and study. How different the emotions of a Ruskin or a Tennyson, in surveying those costly piles, from those of a man fresh from a distillery or from a warehouse of cotton fabrics, or even from those of many fashionable women, whose only aesthetic accomplishment is to play languidly and mechanically on an instrument, and whose only intellectual achievement is to have devoured a dozen silly novels in the course of a summer spent in alternate sleep and dalliance! Nor does familiarity always give a zest to the pleasure which arises from the creations of art or the glories of nature. The Roman beggar passes the Coliseum or St. Peter's without notice or enjoyment, as a peasant sees unmoved the snow-capped mountains of Switzerland or the beautiful lakes of Killarney. Said sorrowfully my guide up the Rhigi, "I wish I lived in Holland, for there are men there." Yet there are those whom the ascent of Rhigi and the ruined monuments of ancient Rome would haunt for a lifetime, in whose memory they would be perpetually fresh, never to pass away, any more than the looks and the vows of early love from the mind of a sentimental woman.

The glorious old architecture whose peculiarity was the pointed arch, flourished only about three hundred years in its purity and matchless beauty. Then another change took place. The ideal became lost in meaningless ornaments. The human figure peoples the naked walls. "Man places his own image everywhere.... The tomb rises like a mausoleum in side chapels. Man is enthroned, not God." The corruption of the art keeps pace with the corruption of the Papacy and the discords of society. In the fourteenth century the Mediaeval has lost its charm and faith.

And then sets in the new era, which begins with Michael Angelo. It is marked by the revival of Greek art and Greek literature. At Florence reign the Medici. On the throne of Saint Peter sits an Alexander VI or a Julius II. Genoa is a city of merchant-palaces. Museums are collected of the excavated remains of Roman antiquity. Everybody kindles with the contemplation of the long-buried glories of a classic age; everybody reads the classic authors: Cicero is a greater oracle than Saint Augustine. Scholars flock to Italy. The popes encourage the growing taste for Pagan philosophy. Ancient art regains her long-abdicated throne, and wields her sceptre over the worshippers of the Parthenon and the admirers of Aeschylus and Thucydides. With the revived statues of Greece appear the most beautiful pictures ever produced by the hand of man; and with pictures and statues architecture receives a new development. It is the blending of the old Greek and Roman with the Gothic, and is called the Renaissance. Michael Angelo erects St. Peter's, the heathen Pantheon, on the intersection of Gothic nave and choir and transept; a glorious dome, more beautiful than any Gothic spire or tower, rising four hundred and fifty feet into the air. And in the interior are classic circular arches and pillars, so vast that one is impressed as with great feats of engineering skill. All that is variegated in marbles adorns the altars; all that is bewitching in paintings is transferred to mosaics. And this new style of Italy spreads into France and England. Sir Christopher Wren builds St. Paul's, – more Grecian than Gothic, – and fills London with new churches, not one of which is Gothic, and all different. The brain is bewildered in attempting to classify the new and ever-shifting forms of the revived Italian.

And so for three hundred years the architects mingle the Gothic with the classical, until now a mongrel architecture is the disgrace of Europe; varied but not expressive, resting on no settled principles, neither on vertical nor on horizontal lines, – blended together, sometimes Grecian porticos on Elizabethan structures, spires resting not on towers but roofs, Byzantine domes on Grecian temples, Greek columns with Lombard arches, flamboyant paneling, pendant pillars from the roof, all styles mixed up together, Corinthian pilasters acting as Gothic buttresses, and pointed arches with Doric friezes, – a heap of diverse forms, alien alike from the principles of Wykeham and Vitruvius.

And this varied mongrel style of architecture corresponds with the confused civilization of the period, – neither Greek nor Gothic, but a mixture of both; intolerant priests wrangling with pagan sceptics and infidels, – Aquaviva with Pascal, the hierarchy of the French Church with Voltaire and Rousseau, Protestant divines with the Catholic clergy; Geneva and Rome compromising at Oxford, the authority of the Fathers made antagonistic to the authority of popes, new vernacular tongues supplanting Latin in the universities; everywhere war on the Middle Ages, without full emancipation from their dogmas, ancient paganism made to uphold the Church, an unbounded activity of intellect casting off all established rules, the revival of the old Greek republics, democracy asserting its claim against absolute power; nothing settled, nothing at rest, but motion in every direction, – science combating faith, faith spurning reason, humanity arrogating divinity, the confusion of races, Babel towers of vanity and pride in the new projected enterprises, Christian nations embroiled in constant wars, gold and silver set up as idols, the rise of new powers in the shapes of new industries and new inventions, commerce filling the world with wealth, armies contending for rights as well as for the aggrandizement of monarchies: was there ever such a simmering and boiling and fermenting period of activities since the world began? In such a wild and tumultuous agitation of passions and interests and ideas, how could Art reappear either in the classic severity of Greek temples or the hoary grandeur of Mediaeval cathedrals? In this jumble we look for new creations, but no creations in art appear, only fantastic imitations. There is no creation except in a new field, that of science and mechanical inventions, – where there is the most extraordinary and astonishing development of human genius ever seen on earth, but "of the earth earthy," aiming at material good. Architecture itself is turned into great feats of engineering. It does not span the apsis of a church; it spans rivers and valleys. The church, indeed, passes out of mind, if not out of sight, in the new material age, in the multiplication of bridges and gigantic reservoirs, – old Rome brought back again in its luxuries.

And yet the exactness of science and the severity of criticism – begun fifty years ago, in the verification of principles – produce a better taste. Architects have sought to revive the purest forms of both Gothic and Grecian. If they could not create a new style, they would imitate the old: as in philosophy, they would go round in the old circles. As science revives the atoms of Democritus, so art would reproduce the ideas of Phidias and Vitruvius, and even the poetry and sanctity of the Middle Ages. Within fifty years Christendom has been covered with Gothic churches, some of which are as beautiful as those built by Freemasons. The cathedrals have been copied rigidly, even for village churches. The Parthenon reappears in the Madeleine. We no longer see, as in the eighteenth century, Gothic spires on Roman basilicas, or Grecian porticos ornamenting Norman towers. The various styles of two thousand years are not mixed up in the same building. We copy either the horizontal lines of Paganism or the vertical lines of the ages of Faith. No more harmonious Gothic edifice was ever erected than the new Catholic cathedral of New York.

The only absurdity is seen when radical Protestantism adopts the church of pomps and liturgies. When the Reformation was completed, men sought to build churches where they could hear the voice of the preacher; for the mission of Protestantism is to teach, not to sing. Protestantism glories in its sermons as much as Catholicism in its chants. If the people wish to return again to ritualism, let them have the Gothic church. If they wish to be electrified by eloquence, let them have a basilica, for the voice of the preacher is lost in high and vaulted roofs. If they wish to join in the prayers and the ceremonies of the altar, let them have the clustering pillars and the purple windows.

Everything turns upon what is meant by a church. What is it for? Is it for liturgical services, or is it for pulpit eloquence? Solve that question, and you solve the Reformation. "My house," saith the Divine Voice, "shall be called the house of prayer." It is "by the foolishness of preaching," said Paul, that men are saved.

If you will have the prayers of the Middle Ages and the sermons of the Reformation both together, then let the architects invent a new style, which shall allow the blending of prayer and pulpit eloquence. You cannot have them both in a Grecian temple, or in a Gothic church. You must combine the Parthenon with Salisbury, which is virtually a new miracle of architecture. Will that miracle be wrought? I do not know. But a modern Protestant church, with all the wonders of our modern civilization, must be something new, – some new combination which shall be worthy of the necessity of our times. This is what the architect must now aspire to accomplish; he must produce a house in which one can both hear the sermon, and be stimulated by inspiring melodies, – for the Church must have both. The psalms of David and the chants of Gregory must be blended with the fervid words of a Chrysostom and a Chalmers.

This, at least, should be borne in mind: the church edifice *must* be adapted to the end designed. The Gothic architects adapted their vaults and pillars to the ceremonies of the Catholic ritual. If it is this you want, then copy Gothic cathedrals. But if it is preaching you want, then restore the Grecian temple, – or, better still, the Roman theatre, – where the voice of the preacher is not lost either in Byzantine domes or Gothic vaults, whose height is greater than their width. The preacher must draw by the distinctness of his tones; for every preacher has not the musical voice of Chrysostom, or the electricity of St. Bernard. He can neither draw nor inspire if he cannot be heard; he speaks to stones, not to living men or women. He loses his power, and is driven to chants and music to keep his audience from deserting him. He must make his choir an orchestra; he must hide himself in priestly vestments; he must import opera singers to amuse and not instruct. He cannot instruct when he cannot be heard, and heard easily. Unless the people catch every tone of his voice his electricity will be wasted, and he will preach in vain, and be tired out by attempting to prevent echoes. The voice of Saint

Paul would be lost in some of our modern fashionable churches. Think of the absurdity of Baptists and Methodists and Presbyterians affecting to restore Gothic monuments, when the great end of sacred eloquence is lost in those devices which appeal to sense. Think of the folly of erecting a church for eight hundred people as high as Westminster Abbey. It is not the size of a church which prevents the speaker from being heard, – it is the disproportion of height with breadth and length, and the echoes produced by arcades. Spurgeon is heard easily by seven thousand people, and Talmage by six thousand, and Dr. Hall by four thousand, because the buildings in which they preach are adapted to public speaking. Those who erect theatres take care that a great crowd shall be able to catch even the whispers of actors. What would you think of the good sense and judgment of an architect who should construct a reservoir that would leak, in order to make it ornamental; or a schoolhouse without ventilation; or a theatre where actors could only be seen; or a hotel without light and convenient rooms; or a railroad bridge which would not support a heavy weight?

A Protestant church is designed, no matter what the sect may be to which it belongs, not for poetical or aesthetic purposes, not for the admiration of architectural expenditures, not even for music, but for earnest people to hear from the preacher the words of life and death, that they may be aroused by his enthusiasm, or instructed by his wisdom; where the poor are not driven to a few back seats in the gallery; where the meeting is cheerful and refreshing, where all are stimulated to duties. It must not be dark, damp, and gloomy, where it is necessary to light the gas on a foggy day, and where one must be within ten feet of the preacher to see the play of his features. Take away facilities for hearing and even for seeing the preacher, and the vitality of a Protestant service is destroyed, and the end for which the people assemble is utterly defeated. Moreover, you destroy the sacred purposes of a church if you make it so expensive that the poor cannot get sittings. Nothing is so dull, depressing, funereal, as a church occupied only by prosperous pew-holders, who come together to show their faces and prove their respectability, rather than to join in the paeans of redemption, or to learn humiliating lessons of worldly power before the altar of Omnipotence. To the poor the gospel is preached; and it is ever the common people who hear most gladly gospel truth. Ah, who are the common people? I fancy we are all common people when we are sick, or in bereavement, or in adversity, or when we come to die. But if advancing society, based on material wealth and epicurean pleasure, demands churches for the rich and churches for the poor, – if the lines of society must be drawn somewhere, – let those architects be employed who understand, at least, the first principles of their art. I do not mean those who learn to draw pictures in the back room of a studio, but conscientious men, if you cannot find sensible men. And let the pulpit itself be situated where the people can hear the speaker easily, without straining their eyes and ears. Then only will the speaker's voice ring and kindle and inspire those who come together to hear God Almighty's message; then only will he be truly eloquent and successful, since then only does his own electricity permeate the whole mass; then only can he be effective, and escape the humiliation of being only a part of a vain show, where his words are disregarded and his strength is wasted in the echoes of vaults and recesses copied from the gloomy though beautiful monuments of ages which can never, never again return, any more than can "the granite image worship of the Egyptians, the oracles of Dodona, or the bulls of the Mediaeval popes."

AUTHORITIES

Fergusson's *History of Architecture*
Durand's *Parallels*
Eastlake's *Gothic and Revival*
Ruskin, Daly, and Penrose
Britton's *Cathedrals and Architectural Antiquities*
Pugin's *Specimens and Examples of Gothic Architecture*
Rickman's *Styles of Gothic Architecture*
Street's *Gothic Architecture in Spain*
Encyclopaedia Britannica (article Architecture).

Chapter 11

JOHN WYCLIF:
DAWN OF THE REFORMATION

A.D. 1324-1384

The name of Wyclif suggests the dawn of the Protestant Reformation; and the Reformation suggests the existence of evils which made it a necessity. I do not look upon the Reformation, in its earlier stages, as a theological movement. In fact, the Catholic and Protestant theology, as expounded and systematized by great authorities, does not materially differ from that of the Fathers of the Church. The doctrines of Augustine were accepted equally by Thomas Aquinas and John Calvin. What is called systematic divinity, as taught in our theological seminaries, is a series of deductions from the writings of Paul and other apostles, elaborately and logically drawn by Athanasius, Jerome, Augustine, and other lights of the early Church, which were defended in the Middle Ages with amazing skill and dialectical acuteness by the Scholastic doctors, with the aid of the method which Aristotle, the greatest logician of antiquity, bequeathed to philosophy. Neither Luther nor Calvin departed essentially from these great deductions on such vital subjects as the existence and attributes of God, the Trinity, sin and its penalty, redemption, grace, and predestination. The creeds of modern Protestant churches are in harmony with the writings of both the Fathers and the Scholastic doctors on the fundamental principles of Christianity. There are, indeed, some ideas in reference to worship, and the sacraments, and the government of the Church, and aids to a religious life, defended by the Scholastic doctors, which Protestants do not accept, and for which there is not much authority in the writings of the Fathers. But the main difference between Protestants and Catholics is in reference to the institutions of the Church, – institutions which gradually arose with the triumph of Christianity in its contest with Paganism, and which received their full development in the Middle Ages. It was the enormous and scandalous corruptions which crept into these *institutions* which led to the cry for reform. It was the voice of Wyclif, denouncing these abuses, which made him famous and placed him in the van of reformers. These abuses were generally admitted and occasionally attacked by churchmen and laymen alike, – even by the poets. They were too flagrant to be denied.

Now what were the prominent evils in the institutions of the Church which called for reform, and in reference to which Wyclif raised up his voice? – for in his day there was only *one* Church. An enumeration of these is necessary before we can appreciate the labors and teachings of the Reformer. I can only state them; I cannot enlarge upon them. I state only what is indisputable, not in reference to theological dogmas so much as to morals and ecclesiastical abuses.

The centre and life and support of all was the Papacy, – an institution, a great government, not a religion.

I have spoken of this great power as built up by Leo I, Gregory VII, and Innocent III, and by others whom I have not mentioned. So much may be said of the necessity of a central spiritual power in the dark ages of European society that I shall not combat this power, or stigmatize it with offensive epithets. The necessities of the times probably called it into existence, like other governments, although I cannot see any argument drawn from the Scriptures, or from the history of the early Apostolic Church, to warrant its existence. Nor would I defend the long series of papal usurpations by which the Roman pontiffs got possession of the government of both Church and State. I speak not of their quarrels with princes about investitures, in which their genius and their heroism were displayed rather than by efforts in behalf of civilization.

But the popes exercised certain powers and prerogatives in England, about the time of Wyclif, which were exceedingly offensive to the secular rulers of the land. They claimed the island as a sort of property which reason and the laws did not justify, – a claim which led to heavy exactions and forced contributions on the English people that crippled the government and impoverished the nation. Boys and favorites were appointed by the popes to important posts and livings. Church preferments were almost exclusively in the hands of the Pope; and these were often bought. A yearly tribute had been forced on the nation in the time of John. Peter's pence were collected from the people. Enormous sums, under various pretences, flowed to Rome. And the clergy were taxed as well as the laity. The contributions which were derived from the sale of benefices, from investitures, from the transfer of sees, from the bestowal of rings and crosiers (badges of episcopal authority), from the confirmation of elections, and other taxes, irritated sovereigns, and called out the severest denunciation of statesmen.

Closely connected with papal exactions was the enormous increase of the Mendicant friars, especially the Dominicans and Franciscans, who had been instituted by Innocent III to uphold the papal domination. These itinerating beggars in their black-and-gray gowns infested every town and village in England. For a century after their institution, they were the ablest and perhaps the best soldiers of the Pope, and did what the Jesuits afterwards performed, and perhaps the Methodists a hundred years ago, – gained the hearts of the people and stimulated religious life; but in the fourteenth century they were a nuisance. They sold indulgences, they invented pious frauds, they were covetous under pretence of poverty, they had become luxurious in their lives, they slandered the regular clergy, they usurped the prerogatives of parish priests, they enriched their convents, they accommodated themselves to the wishes of the great, and were marked by those peculiarities of which the Jesuits were accused in the time of Pascal. As they had not in England, as in Spain and Italy, tribunals of inquisition, they were ridiculed, despised, and hated, rather than feared. One gets the truest impression of the popular estimate of these friars from the sarcasms of Chaucer. The Friar Tuck whom Sir Walter Scott has painted was a very different man from the Dominicans or the Franciscans of the thirteenth century, when they reigned in the universities, and were the confessors of monarchs and the most popular preachers of their time. In the fourteenth century they were consumed with jealousies and rivalries and animosities against each other; and all the various orders, – Dominican, Franciscan, Carmelite, – in spite of their professions of poverty, were the possessors of magnificent monasteries, and fattened on the credulity of the world. Besides these Mendicant friars, England was dotted with convents and religious houses belonging to the different orders of Benedictines, which, though enormously rich, devoured the substance of the poor. There were more than twenty thousand monks in a population of three or four millions; and most of them led idle and dissolute lives, and were subjects of perpetual reproach. Reforms of the various religious houses had been attempted, but all reforms had failed. Nor were the lives of the secular clergy much more respectable than those of the great body of monks. They are accused by all historians of avarice, venality, dissoluteness, and ignorance; and it was their incapacity, their disregard of duties, and indifference to the spiritual interests of their flocks that led to the immense popularity of the Mendicant friars, until they, in their turn, became perhaps a greater scandal than the parish priests whose functions they had usurped. Both priests and monks in the time of Bishop Grostête of Lincoln frequented taverns and gambling-houses. So enormous and scandalous was the wealth of the clergy, that as early as 1279, under Edward I, Parliament passed a statute of mortmain, forbidding religious bodies to receive bequests without the King's license.

With the increase of scandalous vices among the clergy was a corruption in the doctrines of the Church; not those which are strictly theological, but those which pertained to the sacraments, and the conditions on which absolution was given and communion administered. In the thirteenth century, as the Scholastic philosophy was reaching its fullest development, we notice the establishment of the doctrine of transubstantiation, the withholding the cup from the laity, and the necessity of confession as the condition of receiving the communion, – which corruptions increased amazingly the power of the clergy over the minds of superstitious people, and led to still more flagrant evils, like the sale of indulgences and the perversion of the doctrine of penance, originally enforced in order to aid the soul to overcome the tyranny of the body, but finally accepted as the expiation for sin; so that the door of heaven itself was opened by venal priests only to those whom they could control or rob.

Such was the state of the Church when Wyclif was born, – in 1324, near Richmond in Yorkshire, about a century after the establishment of universities, the creation of the Mendicant orders, and the memorable usurpation of Innocent III.

In the year 1340, during the reign of Edward III, we find him at the age of sixteen a student in Merton College at Oxford, – the college then most distinguished for Scholastic doctors; the college of Islip, of Bradwardine, of Occam, and perhaps of Duns Scotus. It would seem that Wyclif devoted himself with great assiduity to the study which gave the greatest intellectual position and influence in the Middle Ages, and which required a training of nineteen years in dialectics before the high degree of Doctor of Divinity was conferred by the University. We know nothing of his studious life at Oxford until he received his degree, with the title of Evangelical or Gospel Doctor, – from which we infer that he was a student of the Bible, and was more remarkable for his knowledge of the Scriptures than for his dialectical skill. But even for his knowledge of the Scholastic philosophy he was the most eminent man in the University, and he was as familiar with the writings of Saint Augustine and Jerome as with those of Aristotle. It was not then the fashion to study the text of the Scriptures so much as the commentaries upon it; and he who was skilled in the "Book of Sentences" and the "Summa Theologica" stood a better chance of preferment than he who had mastered Saint Paul.

But Wyclif, it would seem, was distinguished for his attainments in everything which commanded the admiration of his age. In 1356, when he was thirty-two, he wrote a tract on the last ages of the Church, in view of the wretchedness produced by the great plague eight years before. In 1360, at the age of thirty-six, he attacked the Mendicant orders, and his career as a reformer began, – an unsuccessful reformer, indeed, like John Huss, since the evils which he combated were not removed. He merely protested against the corruptions which good men lamented; and that is nearly all that great men can do when they are beyond their age. They are simply witnesses of truth, and fortunate are they if they do not die as martyrs; for in the early Church "witnesses" and "martyrs" were synonymous ([Greek: *martyres*]). The year following, 1361, Wyclif was presented to the rich rectory of Fillingham by Baliol College, and was promoted the same year to the wardenship of that ancient college. The learned doctor is now one of the "dons" of the university, – at that time, even more than now, a great dignitary. It would be difficult for an unlearned politician of the nineteenth century to conceive of the exalted position which a dignitary of the Church, crowned with scholastic honors, held five hundred years ago. It gave him access to the table of his sovereign, and to the halls of Parliament. It made him an oracle in all matters of the law. It created for him a hearing on all the great political as well as ecclesiastical issues of the day. What great authorities in the thirteenth century were Albertus Magnus, Thomas Aquinas, and Bonaventura! Scarcely less than they, in the next century, were Duns Scotus and John Wyclif, – far greater in influence than any of the proud feudal lords who rendered service to Edward III, broad as were their acres, and grand as were their castles. Strange as it may seem, the glory that radiated from the brow of a scholar or a saint was greatest in ages of superstition and darkness; perhaps because both scholars and saints were rare. The modern lights of learning may be better paid than in former days, but they do not stand out to the eye of admiring communities in such prominence as they did among our ancestors. Who stops and turns back to gaze reverentially on a poet or a scholar whom he passes by unconsciously, as both men and women strained their eyes to see an Abélard or a Dante? Even a Webster now would not command the homage he received fifty years ago.

It is not uninteresting to contemplate the powers that have ruled in successive ages, outside the realms of conquerors and kings. In the ninth and tenth centuries they were baronial lords in mail-clad armor; in the eleventh and twelfth centuries these powers, like those of ancient Egypt, were priests; in the thirteenth and fourteenth centuries they were the learned doctors, as in the schools of Athens when political supremacy was lost; in the sixteenth century – the era of reforms – they were controversial theologians, like those of the age of Theodosius; in the seventeenth century they were fighting nobles; in the eighteenth they were titled and hereditary courtiers and great landed proprietors; in the nineteenth they are bankers, merchants, and railway presidents, – men who control the material interests of the country. It is only at elections, though managed by politicians, that the people are a power. Socially, the magnates are the rich. It is money which in these times all classes combine to worship. If this be questioned, see the adulation which even colleges and schools of learning pay to their wealthy patrons or those from whom they seek benefits. The patrons of the schools in the Middle Ages were princes and nobles; but these princes and nobles bowed down in reverence to learned bishops and great theological doctors.

Wyclif was the representative of the schools when he attacked the abuses of the Church. It is not a little singular that the great religious movements in England have generally come from Oxford, while Cambridge has been distinguished for great movements in science. In 1365 he was appointed to the headship of Canterbury Hall, founded by Archbishop Islip, afterwards merged into Christ Church, – the most magnificent and wealthy of all the Oxford Colleges. When Islip died, in 1366, and Langham, originally a monk of Canterbury, was made archbishop, the appointment of Wyclif was pronounced void by Langham, and the revenues of the Hall of which he was warden, or president, were sequestered. Wyclif on this appealed to the Pope, who, however, ratified Langham's decree, – as it would be expected, for the Pope sustained the friars whom Wyclif had denounced. The spirit of such a progressive man was, of course, offensive to the head of the Church. In this case the Crown confirmed the decision of the Pope, 1372, since the royal license was obtained by a costly bribe. The whole transaction was so iniquitous that Wyclif could not restrain his indignation.

But before this decision of the Crown was made, the services of Wyclif had been accepted by the Parliament in its resistance to the claim which Pope Urban V had made in 1366, to the arrears of tribute due under John's vassalage. Edward III had referred this claim to Parliament, and the Parliament had rejected it without hesitation on the ground that John had no power to bind the realm without its consent. The Parliament was the mere mouthpiece of Wyclif, who was now actively engaged in political life, and probably, as Dr. Lechler thinks, had a seat in Parliament. He was, at any rate, a very prominent political character; for he was sent in 1374 to Bruges, as one of the commissioners to treat with the representatives of the French pope in reference to the appointment of foreigners to the rich benefices of the Church in England, which gave great offence to the liberal and popular party in England, – for there was such a progressive party as early as the fourteenth century, although it did not go by that name, and was not organized as parties are now. In fact, in all ages and countries there are some men who are before their contemporaries. The great grievance of which the more advanced and enlightened complained was the interference of the Pope with ecclesiastical livings in England. Wyclif led the opposition to this usurpation; and this opposition to the Pope on the part of a churchman made it necessary for him to have a protector powerful enough to shield him from papal vengeance.

This protector he found in John of Gaunt, Duke of Lancaster, who, next to the King, had the greatest authority in England. It is probable that Wyclif enjoyed at Bruges the friendship of this great man (great for his station, influence, and birth, at least), who was at the head of the opposition to the papal claims, – resisted not only by him, but by Parliament, which seems to have been composed of men in advance of their age. As early as 1371 this Parliament had petitioned the King to exclude all ecclesiastics from the great offices of State, held almost exclusively by them as the most able and learned people of the realm. From the time of Alfred this custom had not been seriously opposed by the baronial lords, who were ignorant and unenlightened; but in the fourteenth century light had broken in upon the darkness: the day had at least dawned, and the absurdity of confining the cares of State and temporal matters to men who ought to be absorbed with spiritual duties alone was seen by the more enlightened of the laity. But the King was not then prepared to part with the most efficient of his ministers because they happened to be ecclesiastics, and the custom continued for nearly two centuries longer. Bishop Williams was the last of the clergy who filled the great office of chancellor, and Archbishop Laud was the last of the clergy who became a prime minister. The reign of Elizabeth was marked, for the first time in the history of England, by the almost total exclusion of prelates from great secular offices. In the reign of Edward III it was William of Wykeham, Bishop of Winchester, who held the great seal, and the Bishop of Exeter who was lord treasurer, – probably the two men in the whole realm who were the most experienced in public affairs as men of business. Wyclif, it would appear, although he was an ecclesiastic, here took the side of Parliament against his own order. In his treatise on the "Regimen of the Church" he contends that neither doctors nor deacons should hold secular offices, or even be land stewards and clerks of account, and appeals to the authority of the Fathers and Saint Paul in confirmation of his views. At this time he was a doctor of divinity and professor of theology in the University, having been promoted to this high position in 1372, two years before he was sent as commissioner to Bruges. In 1375, he was presented to the rectory of Lutterworth in Leicestershire by the Crown, in reward for his services as an ambassador.

In 1376 Parliament renewed its assault on pontifical pretensions and exactions; and there was cause, since twenty thousand marks, or pounds, were sent annually to Rome from the Pope's collector in England, which collector was a Frenchman, – another indignity. Against these corruptions and usurpations Wyclif was unsparing in his denunciations; and the hierarchy at last were compelled, by their allegiance to Rome, to take measures to silence and punish him as a pertinacious heretic. The term "heretic" meant in those days opposition to papal authority, as much as opposition to the theological dogmas of the Church; and the brand of heresy was the greatest stigma which authority could impose. The bold denunciator of papal abuses was now in danger. He was summoned by the convocation to appear in Saint Paul's Cathedral and answer for his heresies, on which occasion were present the Archbishop of Canterbury and the arrogant Bishop of London, – the latter the son of the Earl of Devonshire, of the great family of the Courtenays. Wyclif was attended by the Duke of Lancaster and the Earl Marshal, – Henry Percy, the ancestor of the Dukes of Northumberland, – who forced themselves into the Lady's chapel, behind the high altar, where the prelates were assembled. An uproar followed from this unusual intrusion of the two most powerful men of the kingdom into the very sanctuary of prelatic authority. What could be done when the great

Oxford professor – the most learned Scholastic of the kingdom – was protected by a royal duke clothed with viceregal power, and the Earl Marshal armed with the sword of State?

The position of Wyclif was as strong as it was before he was attacked. Nor could he be silenced except by the authority of the Pope himself, – still acknowledged as the supreme lord of Christendom; and the Pope now felt that he must assert his supremacy and interpose his supreme authority, or lose his hold on England. So he hurled his weapons, not yet impotent, and fulminated his bulls, ordering the University, under penalty of excommunication, to deliver the daring heretic into the hands of the Archbishop of Canterbury or the Bishop of London; and further commanding these two prelates to warn the King against the errors of Wyclif, and to examine him as to his doctrines, and keep him in chains until the Pope's pleasure should be further known. In addition to these bulls, the Pope sent one to the King himself. It was resolved that the work should be thoroughly done this time. Yet it would appear that these various bulls threatening an interdict did not receive a welcome from any quarter. The prelates did not wish to quarrel with such an antagonist as the Duke of Lancaster, who was now the chief power in the State, the King being in his last illness. They allowed several months to pass before executing their commission, during which Wyclif was consulted by the great Council of State whether they should allow money to be carried out of the realm at the Pope's demands, and he boldly declared that they should not; thus coming in direct antagonism with hierarchal power. He also wrote at this time pamphlets vindicating himself from the charges made against him, asserting the invalidity of unjust excommunication, which, if allowed, would set the Pope above God.

At last, after seven months, the prelates took courage, and ordered the University to execute the papal bulls. To imprison Wyclif at the command of the Pope would be to allow the Pope's temporal rule in England; yet to disobey the bulls would be disregard of the papal power altogether. In this dilemma the Vice-Chancellor – himself a monk – ordered a nominal imprisonment. The result of these preliminary movements was that Wyclif appeared at Lambeth before the Archbishop, to answer his accusers. The great prelates had a different spirit from the University, which was justly proud of its most learned doctor, – a man, too, beyond his age in his progressive spirit, for the universities in those days were not so conservative as they subsequently became. At Lambeth Wyclif found unexpected support from the people of London, who broke into the archiepiscopal chapel and interrupted the proceedings, and a still more efficient aid from the Queen Dowager, – the Princess Joan, – who sent a message forbidding any sentence against Wyclif. Thus was he backed by royal authority and the popular voice, as Luther was afterwards in Saxony. The prelates were overcome with terror, and dropped the proceedings; while the Vice-Chancellor of Oxford, who had tardily and imperfectly obeyed the Pope, was cast into prison for a time and compelled to resign his office.

Wyclif had gained a great triumph, which he used by publishing a summary of his opinions in thirty-three articles, both in Latin and English. In these it would seem that he attacked the infallibility of the Pope, – liable to sin like any other person, and hence to be corrected by the voices of those who are faithful to a higher Power than his, – a blow to the exercise of excommunication from any personal grounds of malice or hatred, or when used to extort unjust or mercenary demands. He also maintained that the endowments of the clergy could be lawfully withdrawn if they were perverted or abused, – a bold assertion in his day, but which he professed he was willing to defend, even unto death. If the prelates had dared, or had possessed sufficient power, he would doubtless have suffered death from their animosity; but he was left unmolested in his retirement at his rectory, although he kept himself discreetly out of the way of danger. When the memorable schism took place in the Roman government by the election of an anti-pope, and both popes proclaimed a crusade and issued their indulgences, Wyclif, who heretofore had admitted the primacy of the Roman See, now openly proclaimed the doctrine that the Church would be better off with no pope at all. He owed his safety to the bitterness of the rival popes, who in their mutual quarrels had no time to think of him. And his opportunity was improved by writing books and homilies, in which the antichristian claims of the popes were fearlessly exposed and commented upon. In fact, he now openly denounces the Pope as Antichrist, from his pulpit at

Lutterworth, to his simple-minded parishioners, for whose good he seems to have earnestly labored, – the model of a parish priest. It is supposed that Chaucer had him in view when he wrote his celebrated description of a good parson, – "benign" and diligent, learned and pious, giving a noble example to his flock of disinterestedness and devotion to truth and duty, in contrast with the ordinary lives of the clergy of those times, who were infamous for their ignorance, sensuality, gluttony, and ostentation; frequenting taverns, and wasting their time in gambling, idleness, and disgraceful brawls.

Hitherto Wyclif had simply protested against the external evils of the Church without much effect, although protected by powerful laymen and encouraged by popular favor. The time had not come for a real and permanent reformation; but he prepared the way for it, and in no slight degree, by his translation of the Scriptures into the vernacular tongue, – the greatest service he rendered to the English people and the cause of civilization. All the great reformers, successful and unsuccessful, appealed to the Scriptures as the highest authority, even when they did not rebel against the papal power, like Savonarola in Florence, I do not get the impression that Wyclif was a great popular preacher like the Florentine reformer, or like Luther, Latimer, and Knox. He was a student, first of the Scholastic theology, and afterwards of the Bible. He lived in a quiet way, as scholars love to live, in his retired rectory near Oxford, preaching plain and simple sermons to his parishioners, but spending his time chiefly in his library, or study.

Wyclif's translation of the Bible was a great event, for it was the first which was made in English, although parts of the Bible had been translated into the Saxon tongue between the seventh and eleventh centuries. He had no predecessor in that vast work, and he labored amid innumerable obstacles. It was not a translation from the original Greek and Hebrew, for but little was known of either language in the fourteenth century: not until the fall of Constantinople into the hands of the Turks was Greek or Hebrew studied; so the translation was made from the Latin Vulgate of St. Jerome. The version of Wyclif, besides its transcendent value to the people, now able to read the Bible in their own language (before a sealed book, except to the clergy and the learned), gave form and richness to the English language. To what extent Wyclif was indebted to the labors of other men it is not easy to determine; but there is little doubt that, whatever aid he received, the whole work was under his supervision. Of course it was not printed, for printing was not then discovered; but the manuscripts of the version were very numerous, and they are to-day to be found in the great public libraries of England, and even in many private collections.

Considering that the Latin Vulgate has ever been held in supreme veneration by the Catholic Church in all ages and countries, by popes, bishops, abbots, and schoolmen; that no jealousy existed as to the reading of it by the clergy generally; that in fact it was not a sealed book to the learned classes, and was regarded universally as the highest authority in matters of faith and morals, – it seems strange that so violent an opposition should have been made to its translation into vernacular tongues, and to its circulation among the people. Wyclif's translation was regarded as an act of sacrilege, worthy of condemnation and punishment. So furious was the outcry against him, as an audacious violator who dared to touch the sacred ark with unconsecrated hands, that even a bill was brought into the House of Lords forbidding the perusal of the Bible by the laity, and it would have been passed but for John of Gaunt. At a convocation of bishops and clerical dignitaries held in St. Paul's, in 1408, it was decreed as heresy to read the Bible in English, – to be punished by excommunication. The version of Wyclif and all other translations into English were utterly prohibited under the severest penalties. Fines, imprisonment, and martyrdom were inflicted on those who were guilty of so foul a crime as the reading or possession of the Scriptures in the vernacular tongue. This is one of the gravest charges ever made against the Catholic Church. This absurd and cruel persecution alone made the Reformation a necessity, even as the translation of the Bible prepared the way for the Reformation. The translation of the Scriptures and the Reformation are indissolubly linked together. Nobody doubts that the whole influence of the Catholic hierarchy has ever been, and still continues to be, hostile to the perusal of the Scriptures by the people in the vulgar tongue; and it was this translation by Wyclif which made him more obnoxious to the Pope than all his tirades against the vices of the monks and the other evils which disgraced the Church. We cannot call this translation a reform, but it led to reforms: it arrayed the people against the usurpations of the Pope and the corruptions of the Church as an institution. Yea, more, it was the main cause of that memorable religious movement which followed the death of Wyclif: there would have been no Lollards had there been no translation of the Bible. It led also to the affirmation of that private judgment which was the foundation pillar of Protestantism, and which existed among the Lollards long before Luther delivered his message.

Figure 11. Facsimile of Page from Wyclif Bible.

And yet it is not strange that the Catholic hierarchy (I say Catholic rather than Roman, because in the fourteenth century there was but one Church, although in that Church considerable difference of opinion existed both as to matters of faith and government) should have bitterly opposed the translation of the Scriptures into vernacular tongues, since it opened the door to private judgment. If there is anything the Catholic Church has hated, it is private judgment. The very phrase is obnoxious. It means the emancipation of the people from papal domination and ecclesiastical bondage of all description; while the thing itself is subversive of all the claims which the Catholic hierarchy have ever put forth as to the authority of the Church as an institution: it has undermined and will continue to undermine spiritual despotism, – the great evil of the Middle Ages and of the Papal Church in our times. The unrestrained circulation of the Scriptures in the language the people can understand must lead to the breaking up of the false doctrines and all the instruments by which the clergy have maintained their usurpations. It necessarily opens the eyes of the people to the antichristian doctrine of penance, to the absurdity of indulgences for sin, to the unwarranted worship of the Virgin Mary, to the monstrous claim of papal infallibility, and to all other glaring usurpations by which the popes have ruled the world. There is not a false doctrine in religion, nor an antichristian form of worship, nor a usurped prerogative of the Pope and clergy, which the unrestrained perusal of the Scriptures does not expose. "*Hinc illae lacrymae.*" The dignitaries of the Roman Catholic Church are not fools. They know that the free circulation of the Scriptures in vulgar tongues does undermine their authority, and will ultimately destroy the edifice of pride and pomp and power which it took a thousand years to build. This is what they ever have consistently opposed and will continue to oppose, as a thing dangerous to them. They would have destroyed, if they could, every copy of the version which Wyclif made. And now, when they can no longer prevent the Bible from being printed, they would exclude it from the schools which they control, and from the houses of those who belong to their Church. Doubtless the well-known opposition to the circulation of the Bible in the vernacular has been exaggerated, but in the fourteenth century it was certainly bitter and furious. Wyclif might expose vices which everybody saw and lamented as a scandal, and make himself obnoxious to those who committed them; but to open the door to free inquiry and a reformed faith and hostility to the Pope, – this was a graver offence, to be visited with the severest penalties. To the storm of indignation thus raised against him Wyclif's only answer was: "The clergy cry aloud that it is heresy to speak of the Holy Scriptures in English, and so they would condemn the Holy Ghost, who gave tongues to the Apostles of Christ to speak the Word of God in all languages under heaven."

Notwithstanding the enormous cost of the Bible as translated by Wyclif, – £2, 16s. 8d., a sum probably equal to thirty pounds, or one hundred and fifty dollars of our present money, more than half the annual income of a substantial yeoman, – still it was copied and circulated with remarkable rapidity. Neither the cost of the valuable manuscript nor the opposition and vigilance of an almost omnipresent inquisition were able to suppress it.

Wyclif was now about fifty-eight years of age. He had rendered a transcendent service to the English nation, and a service that not one of his contemporaries could have performed, – to which only the foremost scholar and theologian of his day was equal. After such a work he might have reposed in his quiet parish in genial rest, conscious that he had opened a new era in the history of his country. But rest was not for him. He now appears as a doctrinal controversialist. Hitherto his attacks had been against the flagrant external evils of the Church, the enormous corruptions that had entered into the institutions which sustained the papal power. "He had been the advocate of the University in defence of her privileges, the champion of the Crown in vindication of its rights and prerogatives, the friend of the people in the preservation of their property.... He now assailed the Romish doctrine of the eucharist," but without the support of those powerful princes and nobles who had hitherto sustained him. He combats one of the prevailing ideas of the age, – a more difficult and infinitely bolder thing, – which theologians had not dared to assail, and which in after-times was a stumbling-block to Luther himself. In ascending the mysterious mount where clouds gathered around him his old friends began to desert him, for now he assailed the awful and invisible. The Church of the Middle Ages had asserted that the body of Christ was actually present in the consecrated

John Wyclif: Dawn of the Reformation   237

wafer, and few there were who doubted it. Berengar had maintained in the eleventh century that the sacred elements should be regarded as mere symbols; but he was vehemently opposed, with all the terrors of spiritual power, and compelled to abjure the heresy. In the year 1215, at a Lateran, Council, Innocent III established the doctrine of transubstantiation as one of the fundamental pillars of Catholic belief. Then metaphysics – all the weapons of Scholasticism – were called into the service of superstition to establish what is most mythical in the creed of the Church, and which implied a perpetual miracle, since at the moment of consecration the substance of the bread was taken away and the substance of Christ's body took its place. From his chair of theology at Oxford, in 1381, Wyclif attacked what Lanfranc and Anselm and the doctors of the Church had uniformly and strenuously defended. His views of the eucharist were substantially those which Archbishop Berengar had advanced three hundred years before, and of course drew down upon him the censure of the Church. In his peril he appealed, not to the Pope or the clergy, but to the King himself, – a measure of renewed audacity, for in those days no layman, however exalted, had authority in matters purely ecclesiastical. His boldness was too much even for the powerful Duke of Lancaster, his friend and patron, who forbade him to speak further on such a matter. He might attack the mendicant and itinerant friars who had forgotten their duties and their vows, but not the great mysteries of the Catholic faith. "When he questioned the priestly power of absolution and the Pope's authority in purgatory, when he struck at indulgences and special masses, he had on his side the spiritual instincts of the people;" but when he impugned the dignity of the central act of Christian worship and the highest expression of mystical devotion, it appeared to ordinary minds that he was denying all that is sacred, impressive, and authoritative in the sacrament itself, – and he gave offence to many devout minds, who had approved his attacks on the monks and the various corruptions of the Church. Even the Parliament pressed the Archbishop to make an end of such a heresy; and Courtenay, who hated Wyclif, needed not to be urged. So a council was assembled at the Dominican Convent at Blackfriars, where the "Times" office now stands, and unanimously condemned not only the opinions of Wyclif as to the eucharist, but also those in reference to the power of excommunication, and the uselessness of the religious orders. Yet he himself was allowed to escape; and the condemnation had no other effect than to drive him from Oxford to his rectory at Lutterworth, where until his death he occupied himself in literary and controversial writings. His illness soon afterwards prevented him from obeying the summons of the Pope to Rome, where he would doubtless have suffered as a martyr. In 1384 he was struck with paralysis, and died in three days after the attack, at the age of sixty, – though some say in his sixty-fourth year, – probably, in spite of ecclesiastical censure, the most revered man of his day, as well as one of the ablest and most learned. Not from the ranks of fanatics or illiterate popular orators did the Reformation come in any country, but from the greatest scholars and theologians.

This grand old man, the illustrious pioneer of reform in England, and indeed on the Continent, did not live to threescore years and ten, but, being worn out with his exhaustive labors, he died peaceably and unmolested in his retired parish. Not much is known of the details of his personal history, any more than of Shakespeare's. We know nothing of his loves and hatreds, of his habits and tastes, of his temper and person, of his friends and enemies. He stands out to the eye of posterity in solitary and mysterious loneliness. Tradition speaks of him as a successful, benignant, and charitable parish priest, giving consolation to the afflicted and to the sick. He lived in honor, – professor of theology at Oxford, holding a prebendal stall and a parochial rectory, perhaps a seat in Parliament, and was employed by the Crown as an ambassador to Bruges. He was statesman as well as theologian, and lived among the great, – more as a learned doctor than as a saint, which he was not from the Catholic standpoint. "He was the scourge of imposture, the ponderous hammer which smote the brazen idolatry of his age." He labored to expose the vices that had taken shelter in the sanctuary of the Church, – a reformer of ecclesiastical abuses rather than of the lax morals of the laity, and hence did different work from that of Savonarola, whose life was spent in a crusade against sin, wherever it was to be found. His labors were great, and his attainments remarkable for his age. He is accused of being coarse in his invectives; but that charge can also be laid to Luther and other reformers in rough and outspoken times. Considering the power of the Pope in the fourteenth century, Wyclif was as bold and courageous as Luther. The weakness of the papacy had not been exposed by the Councils of Pisa, of Constance, and of Basil; nor was popular indignation in view of the sale of indulgences as great in England as when the Dominican Tetzel peddled the papal pardons in Germany. In combating the received ideas of the age, Wyclif was even more remarkable than the Saxon reformer, who was never fully emancipated from the Mediaeval doctrine of transubstantiation; although Luther went beyond Wyclif in the completeness of his reform. Wyclif was beyond his age; Luther was the impersonation of its passions. Wyclif represented universities and learned men; Luther was the oracle of the people. The former was the Mediaeval doctor; the latter was the popular orator and preacher. The one was mild and moderate in his spirit and manners; the other was vehement, dogmatic, and often offensive, not only from his more violent and passionate nature, but for his bitter and ironical sallies. It is the manner more than the matter which offends. Had Wyclif been as satirical and boisterous as Luther was, he would not probably have ended his days in peace, and would not have accomplished so much as a preparation for reforms.

It was the peculiarity of Wyclif to recognize occasional merits in the system he denounced, even when his language was most vehement. He admitted that confession did much good to some persons, although as a universal practice, as enjoined by Innocent III, it was an evil and harmed the Church. In regard to the worship of images, while he denounced the waste of treasure on "dead stocks," he admitted that images might be used as aids to excite devotion; but if miraculous powers were attributed to them, it was an evil rather than a good. And as to the adoration of the saints, he simply maintained that since gifts can be obtained only through the mediation of Christ, it would be better to pray to him directly rather than through the mediation of saints.

In regard to the Mendicant friars, it does not appear that his vehement opposition to them was based on their vows of poverty or on the spirit which entered into monasticism in its best ages, but because they were untrue to their rule, because they were vendors of pardons, and absolved men of sins which they were ashamed to confess to their own pastors, and especially because they encouraged the belief that a benefaction to a convent would take the place of piety in the heart. It was the abuses of the system, rather than the system itself, which made him so wrathful on the "vagrant friars preaching their catchpenny sermons." And so of other abuses of the Church: he did not defy the Pope or deny his authority until it was plain that he sought to usurp the prerogatives of kings and secular rulers, and bring both the clergy and laity under his spiritual yoke. It was not as the first and chief of bishops – the head of the visible Church – that Wyclif attacked the Pope, but as a usurper and a tyrant, grasping powers which were not conferred by the early Church, and which did not culminate until Innocent III had instituted the Mendicant orders, and enforced persecution for religious opinions by the terrors of the Inquisition. The wealth of the Church was a sore evil in his eyes, since it diverted the clergy from their spiritual duties, and was the cause of innumerable scandals, and was closely connected with simony and the accumulation of benefices in the hands of a single priest.

So it was indignation in view of the corruptions of the Church and vehement attacks upon them which characterized Wyclif, rather than efforts to remove their causes, as was the case with Luther. He was not a radical reformer; he only prepared the way for radical reform, by his translation of the Scriptures into a language the people could read, more than by any attacks on the monks or papal usurpations or indulgences for sin. He was the type of a meditative scholar and theologian, thin and worn, without much charm of conversation except to men of rank, or great animal vivacity such as delights the people. Nor was he a religious genius, like Thomas à Kempis, Anselm, and Pascal. He had no remarkable insight into spiritual things; his intellectual and moral nature preponderated over the emotional, so that he was charged with intellectual pride and desire for distinction. Yet no one disputed the blamelessness of his life and the elevation of his character.

If Wyclif escaped the wrath and vengeance of Rome because of his high rank as a theological doctor, his connection with the University of Oxford, opposed to itinerating beggars with great pretensions and greedy ends, and his friendship and intercourse with the rulers of the land, his followers did not. They became very numerous, and were variously called Lollards, Wyclifites, and Biblemen. They kept alive evangelical religion until the time of Cranmer and Latimer, their distinguishing doctrine being that the Scriptures are the only rule of faith. There was no persecution of them of any account during the reign of Richard II, – although he was a hateful tyrant, – probably owing to the influence of his wife, a Bohemian princess, who read Wyclif's Bible; but under Henry IV evil days fell upon them, and persecution was intensified under Henry V (1413-1422) because of their supposed rebellion. The Lollards under Archbishop Chicheley, as early as 1416, were hunted down and burned as heretics. The severest inquisition was instituted to hunt up those who were even suspected of heresy, and every parish was the scene of cruelties. I need not here enumerate the victims of persecution, continued with remorseless severity during the whole reign of Henry VII. But it was impossible to suppress the opinions of the reformers, or to prevent the circulation of the Scriptures. The blood of martyrs was the seed of the Church. Persecution in this instance was not successful, since there was a noble material in England, as in Germany, for Christianity to work upon. It was in humble homes, among the yeomanry and the artisans, that evangelical truth took the deepest hold, as in primitive times, and produced the fervent Christians of succeeding centuries, such as no other country has produced. In no country was the Reformation, as established by Edward VI and Elizabeth, so complete and so permanent, unless Scotland and Switzerland be excepted. The glory of this radical reform must be ascribed to the humble and persecuted followers of Wyclif, – who proved themselves martyrs and witnesses, faithful unto death, – more than to any of the great lights which adorned the most brilliant period of English history.

AUTHORITIES

The Works of Wyclif, as edited by F.D. Matthew
T*he Life and Sufferings of Wicklif*, by I. Lewis (Oxford, 1820)
Life of Wiclif, by Charles Wehle Le Bas (1846)
John de Wycliffe, a Monograph, by Robert Vaughan, D.D. (London, 1853)

Turner's *History of England* should be compared with Lingard.
    Mosheim's *Ecclesiastical History*
Neander's *Church History*
Wordsworth's *Ecclesiastical Biography*
Gieseler, Milner, and general historians of the Church
Geikie's *English Reformation. A German Life* of Wyclif, by Dr. Lechler, is often quoted by Matthew, and has been fortunately translated into English. There is also a slight notice of Wyclif by Fisher, in his *History of the Reformation.*

The name of the English reformer is spelled differently by different historians, – as Wiclif, Wyclif, Wycliffe, Wyckliffe; but I have selected the latest authority upon the subject, F.D. Matthew.

INDEX

A

Albertus Magnus, ix, 87, 93, 122, 127, 128, 131, 226
allodial tenure, 163
Anselm, v, 53, 55, 82, 91, 92, 93, 95, 96, 97, 98, 99, 100, 101, 102, 103, 104, 105, 106, 107, 111, 112, 113, 115, 117, 118, 119, 124, 143, 144, 159, 189, 209, 237, 240
Anselm as a theologian, 106
archbishop of Canterbury, 91, 92, 94, 95, 96, 139, 140, 143, 145, 150, 152, 154, 229, 230
aristocratic, 88, 119, 129, 172, 175, 179
Aristotle, 34, 81, 87, 107, 108, 110, 111, 119, 120, 121, 123, 124, 127, 129, 131, 132, 133, 199, 221, 225
art, 6, 9, 10, 18, 19, 25, 27, 43, 62, 81, 124, 161, 162, 167, 168, 174, 193, 199, 200, 201, 203, 206, 212, 214, 215, 216, 217, 220
authorities, 15, 21, 44, 66, 89, 115, 119, 136, 159, 181, 202, 220, 221, 226, 241

B

baronial home, 179
Benedictines, 53, 78, 79, 80, 82, 86, 87, 132, 224
Book of Sentences, 120, 122, 129, 225

C

Cadijeh, 4, 5, 8
Charlemagne, v, ix, 23, 24, 25, 27, 28, 29, 30, 31, 32, 33, 34, 37, 38, 39, 42, 44, 50, 52, 60, 121, 162, 169, 174, 184, 185, 206
chivalry, 24, 26, 32, 34, 37, 61, 175, 176, 178, 179, 180, 181, 183, 186, 189, 190, 194, 196, 199
church architecture, 86, 203, 204, 211, 212
churches, 16, 32, 41, 46, 48, 54, 62, 77, 79, 82, 103, 125, 141, 162, 194, 199, 200, 201, 203, 205, 208, 210, 211, 212, 215, 217, 219, 220, 222
conquest of Persia, 17
constitutions of Clarendon, 148, 150, 151, 153, 157
council of Clermont, 196
creeds, 46, 222

crusades, v, 23, 79, 86, 94, 100, 124, 125, 165, 169, 183, 186, 187, 189, 192, 193, 195, 196, 197, 198, 199, 200, 202, 209, 212

D

Dawn of the Reformation, v, 221
defenders, 192
devotion to woman, 176
doctrines, 1, 2, 6, 9, 10, 12, 18, 47, 86, 107, 108, 110, 112, 113, 115, 118, 120, 145, 147, 221, 224, 230, 235
doctrines of the Magians, 2
Dominicans, 86, 87, 110, 126, 127, 223
Duke of Lancaster, 228, 229, 230, 237

E

Egypt, 4, 6, 17, 69, 70, 71, 108, 131, 185, 193, 226
Europe, 16, 17, 23, 24, 25, 27, 28, 29, 31, 32, 33, 34, 36, 37, 42, 45, 47, 49, 52, 56, 57, 59, 60, 64, 71, 76, 77, 78, 79, 82, 83, 86, 87, 91, 92, 94, 98, 101, 106, 107, 110, 116, 118, 119, 121, 131, 133, 135, 141, 142, 152, 159, 162, 168, 169, 175, 183, 185, 187, 188, 190, 191, 192, 193, 194, 195, 196, 197, 199, 200, 201, 202, 208, 212, 216

F

feudal barons, 77, 79, 186, 200, 206
Feudalism, 161, 162, 164, 169, 172, 173, 174, 175, 181, 198, 201, 209
foes, 84, 193
France, 24, 25, 26, 33, 34, 36, 37, 46, 52, 55, 56, 83, 94, 95, 97, 118, 121, 125, 126, 141, 143, 150, 151, 152, 153, 154, 155, 159, 169, 181, 184, 185, 187, 189, 190, 192, 202, 208, 215
Franciscans, 86, 87, 126, 127, 223

G

Germany, 18, 29, 32, 33, 34, 36, 37, 42, 46, 51, 52, 55, 56, 57, 60, 61, 62, 63, 64, 65, 78, 91, 94, 106, 118, 121, 125, 126, 151, 152, 154, 169, 187, 189, 190, 191, 208, 211, 239, 241
Gothic architecture, v, 32, 203, 214, 220
Gothic churches, 217
Gotschalk, 109
Gregory VII, 49, 52, 66, 94, 222

H

Hallam, 21, 40, 43, 44, 53, 66, 116, 137, 181, 202
Henry I, 60, 77, 91, 96, 103, 106, 139, 140, 141, 144, 148, 151, 160, 189, 190, 241
Henry II, 77, 139, 140, 141, 144, 148, 151, 160
Henry IV, 60, 91, 96, 189, 190, 241
high-church, 139, 144, 145, 147
higher clergy, 171
Hildebrand, v, 23, 40, 41, 45, 49, 51, 52, 54, 55, 56, 58, 59, 60, 61, 64, 65, 66, 76, 91, 92, 94, 96, 98, 103, 106, 125, 140, 143, 145, 152, 154, 189
honors, 34, 110, 141, 226

I

insoluble questions, 72

J

Jerusalem, 121, 187, 188, 190, 191, 194, 196
John of Gaunt, 228, 233

K

Koran, ix, 8, 9, 21

L

labors, 5, 11, 29, 56, 69, 76, 81, 83, 86, 94, 95, 131, 142, 193, 222, 233, 238
literature, 18, 25, 33, 35, 65, 80, 116, 130, 161, 162, 167, 193, 199, 200, 206, 215
Lombard wars, 34
Louis VII, 151, 169

M

martial fanaticism, 13
martyrdom, 96, 233
Mediaeval, v, 42, 48, 82, 87, 91, 109, 115, 130, 131, 136, 137, 167, 212, 215, 216, 220, 239
Mediaeval theology, v, 91
mendicant friars, 76, 86, 126, 129, 223, 239
Merovingian princes, 24
Middle Ages, i, iii, xi, 17, 21, 23, 31, 34, 37, 40, 42, 44, 45, 50, 53, 57, 59, 64, 66, 70, 72, 84, 86, 87, 91, 98, 101, 102, 106, 107, 108, 113, 115, 117, 118, 120, 127, 129, 130, 135, 139, 146, 153, 154, 158, 161, 173, 175, 177, 178, 180, 181, 183, 184, 186, 188, 191, 192, 194, 202, 203, 204, 207, 209, 216, 217, 218, 221, 225, 227, 235, 236
miseries, 13, 26, 28, 43, 53, 71, 73, 112, 161, 163, 164, 181, 194, 208
mistakes, 33, 191, 193, 194, 200
Mohammedanism, 2, 12, 16, 17, 18, 19, 183
monastic institutions, v, 53, 56, 69, 74, 76, 79, 82, 86, 87, 207
monasticism, 56, 72, 82, 85, 86, 87, 207, 212, 239
money-making, 12, 74
monks, 5, 26, 40, 50, 53, 54, 56, 57, 60, 70, 71, 73, 75, 76, 77, 78, 79, 80, 81, 82, 83, 84, 86, 87, 88, 92, 93, 101, 107, 108, 110, 111, 113, 125, 127, 129, 134, 155, 156, 162, 171, 193, 224, 233, 237, 240

N

Nominalism, 111, 112, 113, 131

P

Papacy, 40, 46, 50, 56, 59, 101, 215, 222
Papal Empire, v, 45
peasantry, 41, 88, 165, 168, 172, 174, 179, 198
peasants, 41, 45, 88, 107, 165, 173, 201, 208
peculiarities, 39, 223
perils, 28, 64, 129
personal history, 50, 238
Peter of Amiens, 188
philosophy, v, 6, 18, 25, 35, 71, 82, 86, 92, 106, 108, 110, 112, 115, 117, 118, 119, 122, 123, 124, 125, 128, 129, 133, 135, 136, 137, 199, 200, 209, 215, 217, 221, 224, 225
Plato, 108, 110, 111, 112, 129, 131, 132, 133, 199
political influence, 77
polygamy, 11
polytheism, 2, 3, 4, 6
Pontigny, 86, 151, 153
Pope Urban, 97, 103, 227

predestination, 108, 109, 114, 129, 221
prelatical Power, v, 139
Protestant, 12, 45, 46, 71, 102, 107, 130, 135, 214, 216, 218, 219, 221
Protestantism, 18, 217, 234

slavery, 6, 7, 26, 40, 115, 164, 168, 172, 174
struggles, 49, 139
Summa Theologica, 129, 136, 137, 225
Syria, 3, 16, 17, 69, 188, 196

R

reforms, 52, 80, 146, 224, 227, 234, 239
religious contemplation, 71
Renaissance, 215
repentance, 149
revival of Western Empire, v, 23
Roman architecture, 204, 206
Rome, 25, 26, 27, 30, 33, 36, 37, 38, 42, 51, 61, 73, 94, 97, 98, 99, 101, 103, 104, 110, 120, 126, 127, 129, 131, 142, 143, 184, 199, 205, 214, 216, 223, 229, 238, 240
royal encroachments, 103, 143, 147

S

Saint Anselm, v, 91, 115
Saint Bernard, v, 53, 69, 80, 82, 89, 92, 111, 119, 190
Saracenic conquests, v, 1, 17
Saxon conquest, 32
scholasticism, 109, 237
Second Crusade, 190
secular clergy, 53, 65, 80, 125, 224
See of Canterbury, 55, 93, 95, 96, 142, 144, 157
semi-military, 183
semi-religious, 183

T

Theobald, 140, 141, 142, 144
theology, v, 4, 46, 70, 72, 80, 84, 91, 92, 99, 107, 111, 112, 114, 115, 117, 119, 121, 122, 123, 125, 128, 129, 130, 133, 134, 136, 221, 229, 232, 237, 238
theology of the Middle Ages, 70, 72, 84, 107
Third Crusade, 190
translation of the Bible, 232, 233

U

University of Paris, 121

V

vernacular tongues, 216, 233, 235
vitality, 2, 17, 20, 35, 46, 47, 219
vow of poverty, 74, 78

W

William of Wykeham, v, 203, 212, 229

Z

zeal, 2, 87, 145, 188, 194

The Philosophy of Natural Theology

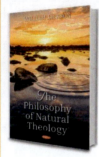

AUTHOR: William Jackson

SERIES: World Philosophy

BOOK DESCRIPTION: This book, originally published in 1876, was written in confutation of the Materialism of its time by arguments derived from Evidences of Intelligence, Design, Contrivance, and Adaptation of Means to Ends, in the Universe, and especially in Man considered in his Moral Nature, his Religious Aptitudes, and his Intellectual Powers; and in all Organic Nature.

HARDCOVER ISBN: 978-1-53613-829-0
RETAIL PRICE: $195

Philosophy of Mind

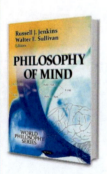

EDITORS: Russell J. Jenkins and Walter E. Sullivan

SERIES: World Philosophy

BOOK DESCRIPTION: In this book, the authors present current research in the study of the philosophy of the mind.

HARDCOVER ISBN: 978-1-62257-215-1
RETAIL PRICE: $145

THE VARIETIES OF RELIGIOUS EXPERIENCE: A STUDY IN HUMAN NATURE

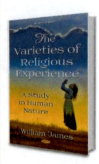

AUTHOR: William James

SERIES: Religion and Society

BOOK DESCRIPTION: In 1901, William James was appointed as Gifford Lecturer on Natural Religion at the University of Edinburgh. This book is composed of the lectures he gave during that time.

HARDCOVER ISBN: 978-1-53614-870-1
RETAIL PRICE: $250